# Great German Poems of the Romantic Era

## Berühmte Gedichte der deutschen Romantik

*A Dual-Language Book*

Edited and Translated by
**STANLEY APPELBAUM**

DOVER PUBLICATIONS, INC.
New York

Copyright © 1995 by Dover Publications, Inc.
All rights reserved under Pan American and International Copyright Conventions.

Published in Canada by General Publishing Company, Ltd., 30 Lesmill Road, Don Mills, Toronto, Ontario.
Published in the United Kingdom by Constable and Company, Ltd., 3 The Lanchesters, 162–164 Fulham Palace Road, London W6 9ER.

*Great German Poems of the Romantic Era/Berühmte Gedichte der deutschen Romantik,* first published by Dover Publications, Inc., in 1995, consists of a new selection of German poems, reprinted from standard German texts, accompanied by new English translations prepared specially for the present edition, with new introductory and back matter.

*Library of Congress Cataloging-in-Publication Data*

Great German poems of the Romantic Era = Berühmte Gedichte der deutschen Romantik : a dual-language book / edited and translated by Stanley Appelbaum.
    p.    cm.
Includes index.
ISBN 0-486-28497-2
   1. German poetry—18th century—Translations into English. 2. German poetry—19th century—Translations into English. 3. German poetry—18th century. 4. German poetry—19th century. I. Appelbaum, Stanley. II. Title: Berühmte Gedichte der deutschen Romantik.
PT1160.E5G74   1995
831'.608—dc20
    94-29812
    CIP

Manufactured in the United States of America
Dover Publications, Inc., 31 East 2nd Street, Mineola, NY 11501

# Foreword

## The Scope of the Anthology

Readers familiar with scholarly subdivisions of German literary history will observe at once that the present book places a very loose construction on the term "Romantic poetry," ranging as it does from 1770 to 1903. According to one major reference work, the 23 poets included here ought to be distributed among at least eight periods, from *"Sturm und Drang"* (Storm and Stress) through "countercurrents to Naturalism," and only Tieck, Novalis, Brentano and Eichendorff belong solidly within the Romantic period, 1798–1835 (itself duly broken down into Early, Middle and Late).

Not only would an anthology restricted to those four poets be highly specialized; it would run counter to the expectations of many, if not most, readers, who might consider Heine (for example) the very model of a Romantic but would find him assigned to "Das junge Deutschland," a liberal group with which he shared political and social views primarily. Moreover, there are quite justifiable disputes among scholars as to the chronological divisions and the placement of individual poets, not to mention the distinct possibility of a poet's being "before" or "after" his time, or subscribing to Romantic principles and views in only a portion of his work. Is Goethe in no way a Romantic even though he continued to write magnificent (and ardent) poetry decades after Novalis' death? Is Hölderlin a "Classic" merely because he used Greek mythology, even though he recreated it and *lived* it in a way that Goethe and Schiller never did?

For all these reasons, and for the satisfaction of introducing or reintroducing the reader to a pleiad of remarkable world-class poets, the present book greatly extends the notion of Romanticism, much as common parlance does in the realm of music, where "Romantic" is applied throughout the nineteenth century, even to the early works of Schoenberg.[1] As Nietzsche, the last poet included here, once remarked: "A Romantic is an artist who is made creative by his great dissatisfaction with himself—one who looks away from himself and the world around him; one who looks back." Such art is not timebound.

---

[1]Also in the realm of art, in which an important anthology of German Romantic drawings includes works dated between 1772 and 1873.

## The Arrangement and Apparatus of the Volume

Each of the 131 poems included, even those regularly abridged in anthologies, is presented here complete (although several were originally either part of a cycle or embedded in a prose work). The sequence is primarily by poets, chronologically according to birth dates. To the extent possible, each poet's group of works is also chronological, by year of composition; these years are indicated at appropriate places in the Introduction.

In order to devote as much space as possible to the poems themselves, the introductory matter has been kept almost painfully brief. After a concise summary of the period covered, in which the nature of German Romantic poetry is indicated, there are short sections on the individual poets. Here, biographical information (readily available in encyclopedias for those who wish to learn more) is kept to a minimum; in fact, included only to the extent that it clarifies the poems by which the poet is represented. Then a succinct characterization of the poet's work is followed by a statement of varying length about the poems chosen and their place in the poet's oeuvre. The footnotes sprinkled through the anthology proper are not meant to be analytical, but serve to elucidate cultural references and discuss particular difficulties of text or translation.

## The Nature of the Translation

No attempt has been made to create a literary or poetic translation that is in any way the equivalent in beauty of the originals. On the contrary, the translation, which follows the original line for line except where differences in syntax compel a slight transposition, may be found to err on the side of literalness (although avoiding unacceptable English). The intention was to offer the actual meaning (or at least one meaning) of the German text, thus providing the reader with a blueprint of the original poem as a basis for the subsequent appreciation of the other qualities that elevate it to a high literary plane.

# Contents

## Novalis (Friedrich von Hardenberg)

## Ludwig Tieck

## Clemens Brentano

## Adelbert von Chamisso

## Heinrich Heine

## Nikolaus Lenau

## Eduard Mörike

## Friedrich Hebbel

# Introduction

## The Romantic Impact on German Lyric Poetry

Lyric poetry has been one of the German lands' chief contributions to world literature from earliest times onward; but the remarkable explosion, in quantity and quality, during the nineteenth century makes that period the most noteworthy since the medieval minnesingers and *Carmina Burana* poets.

As in England, the beginnings of the turn-of-the-nineteenth-century movement are traceable to the latter eighteenth century. Influenced by the new sensitivity of such poets as Klopstock, Claudius and Hölty, and by Herder's researches into folk song and balladry, Goethe and Schiller spearheaded the Storm and Stress (*Sturm und Drang*) movement (dated roughly 1767–1785),[1] with its rejection of Enlightenment (*Aufklärung*) conventionality, its defiance of authority, its political liberalism, its greater naturalness of expression and its openness to the nonrational side of human thought and experience.

Goethe and Schiller were also the major representatives of the subsequent Classical period (*Klassik;* 1785–1832, the latter year being an artificially late one obviously used in order to include Goethe's entire life). In this period, these two poets, influenced by Greco-Roman literature and speaking as "solid" citizens now that they had matured and gained worldly position, toned down their protest and saw themselves as legislators of literary practice. This attitude gave the newer generations something to react against in their turn, partially by returning to the ideals of Storm and Stress and adapting them in a fresh, personal way.

This new era, Romanticism (*Romantik*) as strictly defined, 1798–1835, was to see the great poetic adventure of the dawning century. It gave free rein to the imagination, worshipped the Middle Ages as a national heritage, formed a bridge between true folk literature and "high" poetry, was thoroughly imbued with the idealistic philosophy of the day, was open to the influences of music and the visual arts and fresh ideas in politics and the natural sciences, was dreamy and nostalgic, idolized childhood and nature, and welcomed thoughts of night and death. These elements, in varying mixtures, would never again be

---

[1]This dating system is that used in the influential *Daten deutscher Dichtung* by Herbert A. and Elisabeth Frenzel (Cologne, 1953), but is far from being the only one possible.

completely absent from German poetry and would remain a principal keynote of the nineteenth century, although not practiced by all poets or even at every moment during a given poet's life.

Hölderlin, who has been called a Classical author, almost certainly belongs among the pioneering Romantics, along with Novalis and Tieck. Among the slightly younger Romantics, with their spiritual center at Heidelberg, were Brentano and Eichendorff; Chamisso and Uhland can be placed alongside them as minor figures.

After the spiritual uplift of the wars against Napoleon, and visions of a unified Germany freed from its autocratic princelings, came the stifling reality of the Holy Alliance, the Congress of Vienna and the Restoration. The period extending roughly from 1820 to 1850, nowadays generally known as the Biedermeier, was no longer one of idealistic confraternities of authors. The great poets of this period tended to be isolated, frustrated, world-shunning personalities, uncomfortable in bourgeois-dominated, *enrichissez-vous* Europe. The poets of this era included in the present volume, who kept the Romantic flame alive in varying ways, are Rückert, Mörike, Platen, Droste-Hülshoff and Lenau.

Heine might well be grouped with the Biedermeier poets, but, because of his infinitely greater public presence and his association with the major political and social activists of his time, he has also been placed among the "Young Germany" (*das junge Deutschland*) group (1830–1850). There is no doubt of his links to the original Romantic poets of earlier in the century: his poetry is a conscious elaboration of their form and content, and the "old legends" he cites go back no further than to Brentano and his friends.

The second half of the century brought tremendous changes: industrialization with the concomitant urbanization, organization of labor and increase in population; the successful Prussian wars against Denmark, Austria and France; and, finally, the unification of Germany as an empire. It would have been astonishing if these upheavals, and the aggressive, expansive atmosphere, had not been reflected in literature. Indeed, these years saw the development of such new trends as Realism (*Realismus*), 1850–1890, an attempt to do justice to the new conditions without the nostalgia or escapism of Romanticism, and Naturalism (*Naturalismus*, or *die Moderne*), 1880–1900, which probed beneath the surface of the new society from a "muckraking" point of view.

The poets from this half-century who are represented in the present anthology either lived off the beaten track, like the conservatives Storm and Groth, from the northern coast of Germany, or Keller and Meyer, from Switzerland; or still paid allegiance to forms and tenets of Romanticism in part of their production, like Hebbel, Fontane and Liliencron, who all wrote more "modern" works as well; or else represented a new breed of prophet denouncing current trends, like Nietzsche. By 1900 even newer poetic movements, such as Symbolism and Impressionism, had paved the way for the unprecedentedly bold experiments of the twentieth century, in some of which Romanticism played no apparent part, in others of which it remained a visible element among all the other riches bequeathed by the German past.

## Johann Wolfgang von Goethe

### (1749–1832)

A Frankfurt merchant's son, ennobled[2] in 1782, Goethe was one of the most admired men in Europe throughout the second half of his long, productive life. His lyrics, epic poems, dramas in prose and in verse, fiction, autobiography, scientific and miscellaneous writings all became models to emulate or, in his later years, brilliant irritants to younger writers dissatisfied with what they perceived as his complacent "establishment" status.

His poetry, so multifarious in style, form, mood and approach, includes a remarkable number of perfect, matchless pieces. A small selection such as the present one can only hope to represent a few of the major facets.

The first two poems were written while Goethe was a student in Strasbourg and enjoyed the favor of a country pastor's daughter. "Willkommen und Abschied" (1770, revised 1789) is considered to be the first poem into which Goethe poured the ardor of a real experience; it remains one of the great expressions of youthful love. "Heidenröslein," in folk-song form, reflects another aspect of impetuous courtship.

"Prometheus," first written in 1773 or 1774, originated as dialogue in an unfinished play. Both its form (unrhymed irregular lines, reminiscent of ancient Greek choral poetry) and its message (defiance of authority, anthropocentric self-reliance) are typical of the *Sturm und Drang* (Storm and Stress) period, of which Goethe became the most eloquent spokesman.

"Rastlose Liebe" (1776) and "An den Mond" (1777, revised 1789) are easily accessible lyric pieces of intense verbal beauty. "Der Fischer" (1778) and "Erlkönig" (1782) are brief but fine examples of narrative ballads.

---

[2]As indicated by the "von."

"Grenzen der Menschheit" (1781), though similar to "Prometheus" in form and intended as a pendant to it, differs vastly in its philosophy; placing man in a position subordinate to Heaven and even to the rest of nature, it preaches reserve and modesty. It can be seen as a portal to Goethe's Classical period, in which he was prone to pontificate as a sage and elder statesman.

" 'So laßt mich scheinen, bis ich werde' " (1796) is one of the many exquisite songs Goethe inserted into his major novel *Wilhelm Meisters Lehrjahre* (Wilhelm Meister's Years of Apprenticeship). It is sung by the girl Mignon (whose life has been tragic and who is near death) when she refuses to take off an angel's costume she has worn at a religious pageant.

The last three selections are late works, all written well within the period assigned to Romanticism by literary historians. " 'In tausend Formen magst du dich verstecken' " (1815), included in the 1819 volume *West-Östlicher Divan* (Western-Eastern Poetry Collection) inspired by medieval Persian verse, is one of the magical results of a rejuvenating love affair. "Urworte. Orphisch" (1817) is a moderately difficult philosophical or gnomic poem about human existence. The "Daimon" (inborn guardian spirit) represents a person's basic nature and character; it is in itself unchangeable, but—as the subsequent stanzas show—chance, society, love and necessity also mold our fate, even to the point of negating free will. Hope remains to us. The nature poem " 'Dämmrung senkte sich von oben' " (1827) is the eighth, and most charming, of a small cycle celebrating the seasons of the year and the times of day, *Chinesisch-Deutsche Jahres- und Tageszeiten;* the Chinese influence one might expect from the *Chinesisch-Deutsche* part of the title is very mild, if it ever existed.

## Friedrich von Schiller

### (1759–1805)

Schiller, along with Goethe, best represents the *Sturm und Drang* (Storm and Stress) and Classical periods of German literature. Not only a supreme poet, he also wrote historical works, essays on aesthetics and possibly the greatest German plays, some in prose and some (such as *Don Carlos, Maria Stuart* and *Wilhelm Tell*) in verse. A champion of liberty, Schiller literally had to escape his servitude (as a military doctor) to a German princeling (in that era before German unification) in order to write and teach. Ennobled in 1802, he had gained the respect of all Germans by the time of his premature death from a disease of the lungs.

Schiller's poetry is frequently characterized by a clearly stated or implicit moral or pedagogic message. Some of his finest poems are too long for an anthology like the present one. The eight included here, however, give a good idea of his themes, genres and forms.

"Die Größe der Welt," written in 1781 or earlier and published in 1782, combines a vivid imagination with Schiller's customary breadth of vision. "Das verschleierte Bild zu Sais," in blank verse (iambic pentameter, with variations), and "Pegasus im Joche," in rhyming lines of irregular length, were both written in 1795; the former was published in the same year, the latter a year later under the preliminary title "Pegasus in der Dienstbarkeit" (Pegasus in Bondage). Both are longish narrative poems typical of Schiller, but "Sais" is deadly serious while "Pegasus" is full of ironic humor.

"Das Mädchen aus der Fremde," written in 1796, is a particularly tender and graceful allegory of poetry. "Dithyrambe," published in 1796 under the preliminary title "Der Besuch" (The Visit), is an extremely noble and dignified example of a drinking song, a genre popular with German poets of this and later periods; it is indicative of Schiller's easy familiarity with Classical mythology.

"Hoffnung," published in 1798, is a philosophical poem. "Nänie," published in 1800, is very suitably composed in elegiac couplets, a Greco-Roman metrical scheme of alternating dactylic hexameters and dactylic pentameters, especially (though by no means exclusively) associated with epitaphs. "Sehnsucht," the most Romantic in feeling and expression of these selections, was first published in 1802, but its beautiful second stanza was not added until a year later.

## Friedrich Hölderlin

(1770–1843)

Hölderlin, often included with Goethe and Schiller as a Classical poet, was a Romantic if there ever was one. His treatment of Greek mythology and Greek poetic forms was never conventional, imitative or historicizing; he actually lived the mythology as part of his daily existence, equating poetry with priesthood and prophecy as Novalis did. The revolt of the modern Greeks against their Turkish overlords, which had broken out at about the time of Hölderlin's birth, fueled his ardor with its current-events immediacy; it provided the backdrop of what is perhaps his major work, the novel *Hyperion; oder, der Eremit in Griechenland* (Hyperion, or The Hermit in Greece; 1797–1799).

Born into a pious family, Hölderlin intended to become a pastor but had religious doubts. While trying to break into the poetic establishment by way of Schiller's magazines, he made his living by tutoring boys in various wealthy homes. Between 1796 and 1798 he was tutoring in Frankfurt, where he fell in love with the lady of the house; she appears in his poems and in his novel as Diotima, the name of a priestess who instructed Socrates in wisdom according to Plato's dialogue *The Symposium*. In 1802, returning from another tutorial position, in Bordeaux, Hölderlin had an attack of mental illness. Recovery was only partial; he was institutionalized in 1806–1807, and afterwards—completely mad until his death but occasionally still writing—he was cared for by an artisan in Tübingen.

It is difficult to anthologize Hölderlin; some of his greatest utterances, far ahead of his time, are in poems that are extremely long, or fragmentary, or extant in a bewildering number of versions. The present selection of shorter, but still important and characteristic, pieces cannot cover his whole range.

"Die Eichbäume" (1796–1797) is in a Greco-Roman meter, unrhymed dactylic hexameter, most closely associated with epic poetry. "Diotima" (1796–1797) is the third and last version of one of his poems to the woman he loved best.

"An die Parzen" (1798–1799) is written in another ancient meter, with a strictly regulated sequence of stressed and unstressed syllables: the Alcaic strophe, which was used by the Greek poet Alcaeus in the sixth century B.C. and brilliantly adapted in Latin by the Roman poet Horace in the first century B.C. "Menschenbeifall" and "Sokrates und Alkibiades" (both 1798–1799) use another ancient meter known as asclepiads. Plato's *Symposium* is also the chief source for Socrates' idealization of Alcibiades.

"Hyperions Schicksalslied" is inserted in the novel *Hyperion*, completed in 1799. " 'Da ich ein Knabe war' " probably dates from the same year. "Hälfte des Lebens" was written about 1803. " 'Die Linien des Lebens sind verschieden,' " probably the greatest four-line German poem, was written during Hölderlin's madness. It was communicated to the poet's family by his guardian in a letter of 1812.

## Novalis (Friedrich von Hardenberg)

### (1772–1801)

A truly romantic figure from the first generation of Romantic writers, as strictly defined, Novalis divided his brief life between days as a mining engineer administrating a saltworks and nights as an erotic Christian mystic. Suffering from consumption and crushed by the death of his very young fiancée in 1797, he transferred his strong emotions to a highly personal worship of Christ, in which love, night and death were equated as desirable states of being (an equation that strongly influenced Wagner's *Tristan und Isolde*). In his prose essay *Die Christenheit oder Europa* (Christianity, or Europe), Novalis—for whom poetry was also prophecy and priesthood—preached a return to the undivided Christianity that had unified medieval Europe.

Novalis' poetry is unique in German in its achievement of intense feeling and monumentality by the simplest means: brief lines with everyday vocabulary and uninvolved syntax. From the outset, it was widely acclaimed and emulated.

His collection *Hymnen an die Nacht* (Hymns to the Night), consisting of six sections, was published in 1800 with only the rhyming lines printed as verse. " 'Muß immer der Morgen wiederkommen?,' " No. 2 of the *Hymnen*, is here reprinted in the form of irregular unrhymed verse, as in the poet's manuscript. " 'Hinüber wall ich' " is the concluding, rhymed, portion of Hymn No. 5.

In 1799 Novalis composed fifteen *Geistliche Lieder* (Devotional Songs), which were not published until 1802; they were intended for practical use by congregations, although the Christology is very personal. " 'Wenn ich ihn nur habe' " and " 'Wenn alle untreu werden' " are Nos. 5 and 6, respectively, of this collection.

Another posthumous publication of 1802 was the unfinished allegorical novel (with poetical insertions) *Heinrich von Ofterdingen*. Tieck, as Novalis' literary executor, published some indications (not generally accepted as accurate) of how the novel was to continue; in these notes he preserved some poems that Novalis had intended to include in the continuation. " 'Wenn nicht mehr Zahlen und Figuren' " and " 'Lobt doch unsre stillen Feste' " (a song sung by the dead) are from this source.

## *Ludwig Tieck*

### (1773–1853)

Tieck, from Berlin but also active in Dresden and many other cities, was another of the first generation of Romantic writers, as strictly defined. One of the most influential writers of his time, a friend of numerous great contemporaries, editor of other writers' works, theater director, playwright, novelist, poet, author of short stories, Tieck left a vast literary legacy, of which a complete critical edition is still in progress. His works are characterized by an almost unbridled imagination, often displaying more vigor than polish, with a penchant for the uncanny and frightening.

Tieck's lyric poetry is essentially to be found inserted into his novels, stories and plays. The selections " 'Keinen hat es noch gereut' " and " 'Ruhe, Süßliebchen im Schatten' " are both from the story-with-songs (in the old *chantefable* tradition) *Liebesgeschichte der schönen Magelone und des Grafen Peter von Provence* (Love Story of the Beautiful Magelone and Count Peter of Provence), 1796. " 'Keinen hat es noch gereut' " is sung early in the story by a mysterious minstrel who appears at Peter's court; the second selection, particularly euphonious and meticulously crafted, is sung by Peter to Magelone as they pause for rest after he has run away with her.

"Wunder der Liebe" is concerned not only with love but also with imagination and the world of folktales. Its form, known as a "gloss," is based on Spanish literature and was introduced into German poetry by Tieck's literary circle. A four-line stanza (the "theme" of the gloss) is excerpted from a preexisting poem, and its thought is expanded (in some extreme cases, even negated) in newly composed long stanzas, each of which ends with one line of the theme. For this poem, written in 1803, Tieck excerpted the theme from his own play *Kaiser Octavianus* (first published in 1804).

## Clemens Brentano

### (1778–1842)

Son of an Italian immigrant, Brentano was orphaned before he was twenty, but was left financially independent. After years of study in different places, he established himself as a writer in Heidelberg and later in Berlin. Between 1824 and his death he was an incessant, restless traveler. Brentano was a major representative of what has been called the Younger Romantic School, formed about 1805 in Heidelberg. He has been called the most important writer of the Romantic School (as strictly defined) after Novalis and alongside Eichendorff.

With his brother-in-law Achim von Arnim, Brentano compiled the highly successful but heavily edited collection of old and new poems in folk-song style *Des Knaben Wunderhorn* (The Boy's Miraculous Horn; 1806, 1808). Besides independent poetry he wrote numerous very fanciful "literary folktales" into which many additional poems, including some of his best, were inserted. His themes, his literary techniques and his quizzical, unsatisfied spirit were of immeasurable influence on contemporaries and later writers alike.

Certain poems by Brentano, such as those commonly known as "Wiegenlied" and "Brautgesang" (these titles, like "Soldatenlied," are not Brentano's), have had great appeal for anthologists over the years, but must have been considered somewhat refractory because of their close dependence on the stories in which they occur; thus they have generally been abridged, to their impoverishment. Reprinted in their entirety here, "Wiegenlied" and "Brautgesang" may prove a happy revelation to many.

" 'O kühler Wald' " is an independent poem written probably in 1802 (possibly 1801). "Rückblick," though one might imagine it to be the jaded lament of a weary old man, was written about 1803.

"Wiegenlied" comes from one of the stories in the series *Rheinmärchen* (Folktales of the Rhine; first version written ca. 1811). "Soldatenlied" originally appeared in the festival play *Viktoria und ihre Geschwister* (Victoria and Her Siblings), written in 1813, at the time of fierce German resistance to Napoleonic France. "Brautgesang," by far the latest Brentano work included here, is part of the strange story *Gackel, Hinckel und Gackeleia* (version of 1835–1837). In the story the odd-numbered stanzas, with the recurring lamentations over the bride's loss of youthful independence, are sung by her companions (or bridesmaids), while the more melodious even-numbered stanzas, with their religious sentiments, are sung by a chorus of Lily Maidens.

## Adelbert von Chamisso

### (1781–1838)

Louis Charles Adélaïde de Chamisso was a French nobleman for whom German was an acquired language. In 1792, during the French Revolution, his family fled their home, the Château Boncourt, in the Champagne region. He worked as a painter of miniatures in Düsseldorf and served as an army officer from 1798 to 1808. He wrote a travel journal about his experiences as the official naturalist on a scientific voyage around the world between 1815 and 1818. His most famous work is his fantastic story about Peter Schlemihl, the man who sold his shadow.

Chamisso wrote a fair amount of poetry, some in a thoroughly Romantic vein and some looking forward to the bourgeois-oriented Biedermeier period. His poetic oeuvre—which includes numerous works in his beloved *terza rima* (the form Dante used in *The Divine Comedy*)—is not ranked especially high by literary historians, but a few pieces have found their place in many an anthology.

"Das Schloß Boncourt," written in 1827 (Chamisso also did a French version in 1829), is a reminiscence of his childhood home. "Die alte Waschfrau" of 1833 is a rare tribute to a nameless proletarian woman. "Der Soldat" is the only translation *into* German included in the present anthology, although the Romantic-era poets were extremely active as translators; Chamisso rendered it from the original Danish "Soldaten" (1829) by Hans Christian Andersen. Close to the Danish original, apart from a few changes necessitated by the different set of rhymes, Chamisso's version was so successful as a German poem that it became widely known and regularly figures in German anthologies.

## Ludwig Uhland

(1787–1862)

The son of a jurist, Uhland was extremely active in liberal politics as well as being a pioneer scholar of historic German language and culture. He started to write lyric poetry by 1799, eventually amassing a sizable corpus. His speciality was folklike narrative ballads. Uhland also wrote plays. Literary historians classify him under the younger school of true Romantics, some also assigning him to the Swabian school that flourished from about 1810 to about 1850, in which they also include Mörike.

Like Chamisso, Uhland is not regarded as a great poet, but the characteristic production of any era does not consist exclusively of pinnacles, and several of Uhland's poems have a secure place in the affections of readers of German.

"Der gute Kamerad," written in 1809, is located within the section "Balladen und Romanzen" in complete editions of Uhland's poems. The dialect form *nit* (for *nicht*) adds to the folk-song flavor. "Frühlingsglaube," written in 1812, is No. 2 of the cycle *Frühlingslieder* within the section "Lieder."

## Joseph von Eichendorff

(Mar. 1788–1857)

Eichendorff, another member of the younger generation of Romantics, is decidedly a major poet. A Catholic nobleman, he was born and grew up on the ancestral domain in Silesia, the sale of which in 1823 affected him deeply, fueling the "homeless" and "dispossessed" themes of his verse. After fruitful university years, he fought in the German wars of liberation in 1813 and 1815. From 1816 to 1844 he served as a bureaucrat in various German cities. He included poems in his novels and stories, as well as writing many self-standing ones.

The comparatively few themes of Eichendorff's poetry—nature, nostalgia, love, religious sentiment—had already been established by earlier Romantics, and his poetic forms are not innovative. Nevertheless, his language is highly personal; though it is crystal clear, or apparently so, in German, its extreme compactness, its use of idioms and its reliance on synaesthetic effects make it hard to render in English while still preserving any of the original flavor.

"Das zerbrochene Ringlein" was written about 1810 and inserted in the novel *Ahnung und Gegenwart* (Premonition and Presence), which Eichendorff wrote between 1810 and 1812. The poem, in folksong style, rapidly conquered the German audience and before very long was taken to be a genuinely old anonymous text. Another poem from *Ahnung und Gegenwart*, "Frische Fahrt," was first published in 1815, as part of the novel.

Eichendorff's most famous novella, which he worked on between 1817 and 1825, is "Aus dem Leben eines Taugenichts" (From the Life of a Good-for-Nothing), in which he inserted his 1817 poem "Der frohe Wandersmann."

The first stanza of "Elfe" was printed as a complete poem in 1833, the second stanza being added in an 1837 edition. "In der Fremde" was also printed in 1833, and "Sehnsucht"—with its theme of the beauties of Italy, recurring throughout the poet's work—in the following year.

"Der Einsiedler" was first printed in 1835. The exquisite "Mondnacht" was written sometime during the 1830s.


## Friedrich Rückert

(May 1788–1866)

Rückert, who wrote a vast amount of pleasant, facile verse from which very little stands out, was one of the popular but minor poets who helped give the Romantic era its flavor; he is currently classified within the Biedermeier period. His fame within his lifetime was founded on patriotic and love poems that are no longer highly regarded; his name is known to aficionados of lieder, many important composers having set his verse to music.

An editor and teacher as well as a poet, Rückert was a specialist in Persian and other Middle Eastern languages, and was an important translator. He introduced into German the medieval Persian poetic form known as the ghazel: a short poem, usually with longish lines, based on a single recurring rhyme, the rhyming syllable being set back fairly far from the line ends.

" 'Du meine Seele, du mein Herz' " occurs within the section "Erster Strauß: Erwacht" (First Bouquet: Awakened) of the 1821 volume *Liebesfrühling* (Springtime of Love), which was inspired by Rückert's engagement.

"Kehr ein bei mir!" is in the section "Östliche Rosen" (Eastern Roses) from the portion of his oeuvre called *Wanderungen* (Wanderings).

Perhaps the most famous of Rückert's poems today are the numerous *Kindertotenlieder* (Poems on the Death of His Children), which he wrote in 1833 and 1834, when two of his ten children died, but were only published posthumously in 1872. " 'In diesem Wetter, in diesem Braus' " is one of this group, from the subsection "Trost und Erhebung" (Consolation and Edification). (The reader familiar with Mahler's setting will note that the composer distorted the text extensively for musical purposes.)

"Mit vierzig Jahren" was included in the section "Erste Reihe: Eigner Herd" (First Series: His Own Hearth) of the volume *Haus- und Jahrlieder* (Songs of Home and the Year), 1832–1838.

" 'Ich bin müde, sterbensmüde,' " is a very late work (1865) that was included in the posthumous collection *Poetisches Tagebuch* (Poetic Diary). It is a slightly modified ghazel, the usually long lines appearing as two lines each. Although the ghazel form can be highly artificial in European languages, the genuine feeling and natural phrasing make this poem a particularly successful example.

## August von Platen

### (1796–1835)

Scion of an impoverished branch of a noble family, Count von Platen-Hallermünde spent much of his life in Italy after the failure of his hopes in Germany. He was tortured and embittered by his homosexuality, and his view of life is essentially a tragic one, even though some of his poems and plays are satirical. The antisemitic tinge of some of his writings elicited an unbridled personal attack in one of Heine's publicistic pieces. Platen's early death is shrouded in mystery and has been attributed to very different causes.

Platen's poems are extremely dependent on form. Besides using extremely complex ode stanzas, he favored the sonnet (producing over 80) and the ghazel, the Persian form introduced into German poetry by Rückert (Platen wrote over 150). His earliest published poems date from 1812.

"Der Pilgrim vor St. Just," written in 1819, is a fine example of his ballads on historical subjects, in which his dramatic flair is in evidence. "Wie rafft ich mich auf," written in 1820, is an extremely musical piece; critics have noted that its phrase repetitions graphically depict the rueful beating of the poet's heart (see the last line of the poem). "Tristan" (1825) with its medieval stanza form, of course refers to the legend of Tristan and Iseult, linked forever in love by the magic potion they drank together.

## Annette von Droste-Hülshoff

(Jan. 1797–1848)

The greatest nineteenth-century German woman poet was an unmarried noblewoman who spent most of her life in seclusion on family estates in her native Westphalia or on Lake Constance. In addition to verse, both secular and spiritual, she wrote novellas, the most famous of which is "Die Judenbuche" (The Jew's Beech Tree), exploring the same kind of legendary material, associated with local landscape features, that is to be found in the poem "Der Knabe im Moor." She was also to some extent a composer of music.

Droste's poetry is based on a minute observation of nature, combined with heartfelt emotion and a gift for telling a dramatic, often supernatural, story. The loneliness of her existence and the limitations placed on women by society are recurrent themes. Although she wrote nothing that could specifically be called a love poem, it seems that unhappy romances stimulated the production of her best work, which appeared in prolific spurts rather than consistently during her career. Her vocabulary is frequently difficult, highly specialized or regional. She was not widely known in her own lifetime.

All the poems selected here were written within a period of three or four years. "Der Knabe im Moor," "Am Turme" and "Im Moose" were composed sometime between October 1841 and April 1842. In her volume of poems published in 1844, she included the first-named in the section "Heidebilder" (Pictures of the Heath), which relates to her native Westphalian landscape, and the other two in the section "Fels, Wald und See" (Mountains, Forest and Lake).

"Lebt wohl" was written in the period 1843–1844, and "Im Grase" (a highly regarded poem) in the period 1844–1845, but they were not published until some time after the poet's death.

## Heinrich Heine

(Dec. 1797–1856)

It is questionable how many people still consider Heine "the greatest German poet after Goethe," as he was once famed, although he was fabulously popular in his own day and remains the nineteenth-century German poet most widely known outside of Germany, thanks to the art songs composed to his texts. He lived after the true Romantic generations, and has been classed among the *Junges Deutschland* group, but few of his familiar poems subscribe to that school of social and political agitation; on the contrary, his best-known poetry is largely a prolongation of Romantic themes and forms, reshaped for his own ends.

Heine, whose first name was Harry until his conversion in 1825, came from a family of wealthy Jewish merchants with far-flung connections. He soon gave up business for writing, however. Supported by his family and later by the French government as well, he lived mainly in Paris from 1831 on, as a correspondent and independent writer, making many trips back to his beloved Germany. In addition to a large amount of poetry, he wrote stories, essays, travel reports and much journalistic ephemera, all witty and readable. From 1848 on, Heine was chiefly bedridden with a painful ailment of the spinal cord.

The forms of Heine's poetry are refreshingly simple, as are his vocabulary and syntax; in fact, in his folk-song imitations he often just barely avoids the triviality of greeting-card verse. His characteristic method of avoiding it is by a practice that can be equally irritating: either by sarcastically inserting a word that is clichéd (like the repeated "wundersüß" in " 'Aus alten Märchen winkt es' ") or that is at a different level of diction (like the very last word in " 'Ein Wetterstrahl, beleuchtend plötzlich' "), or else by ending one poem after another with a surprise twist or punchline, usually indicating that he is not the dupe of his feelings for his sweetheart, of whose coldness or unworthiness he is fully cognizant.

" 'Aus alten Märchen winkt es' " and " 'Aus meinen großen Schmerzen' " were written about 1822 and included in the group of poems known as "Lyrisches Intermezzo," first printed in 1823, before being incorporated into the *Buch der Lieder.*

" 'Ich weiß nicht, was soll es bedeuten,' " with its Lorelei subject probably borrowed from Brentano, was written about 1824 and included in the section of the *Buch der Lieder* called "Die Heimkehr" (The Homecoming), first printed in 1826. In this case the typical Heine phrase "Ich glaube" (line 21) provides the distancing between the poet and his material, although the sonorous long "a" of "getan" does furnish a powerful, fateful conclusion. " 'Der Tod, das ist die kühle Nacht' " (written in 1826, with its reminiscences of Byron) and " 'Das ist ein schlechtes Wetter' " are also part of "Die Heimkehr." " 'Leise zieht durch mein Gemüt,' " a marvel of euphony, was first printed in a somewhat different form in 1824 and later, revised, included in the "Neuer Frühling" (New Springtime) section of *Neue Gedichte* (New Poems), 1831.

"Die schlesischen Weber," an unusually energetic and socially conscious poem, was written in response to an actual uprising of weavers in 1844. It was published in that year but never included in any volume during the poet's lifetime.

"Morphine," written between 1849 and 1851, and "Gedächtnisfeier," written in 1850 or 1851, were included in the section "Lazarus" of Book II, "Lamentationen," of the 1851 volume *Romanzero*. Both are reflections of Heine's long final illness. "Morphine" is written in a form uncharacteristic for Heine, blank iambic pentameter, suitable to its Classical imagery.

The breathtaking poem " 'Ein Wetterstrahl, beleuchtend plötzlich' " was written in 1853 or 1854, presumably after Heine received a letter from a female cousin who had visited him after many years' neglect. It was included in *Gedichte 1853 und 1854*, and later in *Letzte Gedichte* (Last Poems).

## Nikolaus Lenau

(1802–1850)

Born and raised in Hungary, Lenau was actually the nobleman Nikolaus Niembsch von Strehlenau, but wished to disguise his birth in an era dominated by the bourgeoisie. Living chiefly off a modest inheritance, he traveled very widely; one of his unsuccessful adventures was as a farmer in the American Midwest. He went mad in 1844 and died in an asylum near Vienna. Lenau, who wrote epic and dramatic poems as well as lyrics, is noted as the archetypical German poet of *Weltschmerz* (fundamental unhappiness with life), although this designation is too generalized.

A meticulous poetic craftsman, he was extremely skillful with the sonnet form. There is no critical edition dating each poem. The editions in his lifetime ranged from 1832 to 1844, the earliest volume containing pieces written between 1821 and 1831. " 'Rings ein Verstummen, ein Entfärben' " can be approximately dated since Lenau included a copy of it in a letter he wrote on January 16, 1844.

In the collected volume of Lenau's verse, "Die drei Zigeuner" is placed in section III, "Gestalten" (Figures), while "Einsamkeit" and "Frage" are in section IV, "Sonette" (Sonnets). " 'Rings ein Verstummen, ein Entfärben,' " with its numerous nominalized infinitives, is the ninth and last in a cycle of *Waldlieder* (Forest Songs) in section V.

## Eduard Mörike

(1804–1875)

Mörike, one of the most richly gifted of all German lyric poets, was largely unknown and unappreciated in his own time; only in his later years was some recognition given him, largely thanks to the efforts of Theodor Storm, who made a pilgrimage to Mörike in 1855. Much of Mörike's life, which was embittered by sickness and self-doubt, was spent as a vicar, and later pastor, in isolated rural districts. In 1856 he accepted a professorship of literature. Besides poetry, he wrote stories, the most famous of which is "Mozart auf der Reise nach Prag" (Mozart on the Journey to Prague).

A fertile imagination (creating a new mythology for his personal use), an astounding mastery of the most diverse forms, exquisite musicality, unmistakable sincerity, a range of feelings from boisterous humor to the deepest solemnity, a love of nature and a gift for observation—these are just some of the ingredients of Mörike's matchless lyrics.

"Gesang zu zweien in der Nacht," a glorification of nature, was written in 1825. "Um Mitternacht" dates from 1827, and "Fußreise," with its humanistic approach to religion, from 1828.

"An eine Äolsharfe," its Latin epigraph derived from an ode of Horace (Mörike was a great scholar of Classical languages and literature), was written in 1837; the delightful "Schön-Rohtraut," combining love and fantasy, in 1838.

"Der Feuerreiter," a gripping new vision of an old legend, was written about 1841; "Auf einer Wanderung," in 1845.

"Auf eine Lampe" (1846) is appropriately written in a very Classical meter, the so-called iambic trimeter (six iambic feet per verse), which is the meter used, among other things, for the dialogue passages of Greek drama. The turn of phrase "in ihm selbst" in the last line, where we would expect "in sich selbst," adds euphony and imparts a subtle archaic flavor.

"Denk es, o Seele!," a reflection on mortality, was written by 1852 at the latest.

## Friedrich Hebbel

### (1813–1863)

Friedrich Hebbel was one of the greatest nineteenth-century German-language playwrights after Goethe and Schiller. His great verse plays include *Herodes und Mariamne, Der Ring des Gyges* and *Die Nibelungen,* while his prose play *Maria Magdalene* provides a view of working-class life astonishing for that period of escapism in the theater.

The son of a stonemason, Hebbel had an extremely hard childhood, pulling himself up by his own bootstraps. After studying for the clergy, he attended the universities of Heidelberg and Munich in his mid-twenties. Some of his security in life was achieved by marriage to a successful actress (giving up his mistress and their children). He traveled extensively in Europe, eventually settling down in Vienna.

Hebbel wrote a large number of lyrics. Many of them are considered overly cerebral and stiff, but several emerge as particularly powerful and intense, and are anthology standards.

"Nachtlied," written in Heidelberg student days in 1836, is included in the section "Lieder" (Songs) of the collected edition of Hebbel's poetry. The other four selections in the present volume are all from the section "Vermischte Gedichte" (Miscellaneous Poems): "Sie seh'n sich nicht wieder" (written in Hamburg in 1841, remarkable for its outspoken eroticism and unsentimental realism), "Ich und Du" (written in Copenhagen in 1843), "Sommerbild" (written in Paris in the August of 1844) and "Herbstbild" (written in Vienna in the October of 1852).

## Theodor Storm

### (1817–1888)

Most famous today for his brilliant novellas and short stories, Storm prided himself above all on his poetry, which constitutes no more than a fifth of his total oeuvre; and indeed, he has been considered as the foremost traditional, or "mainstream," poet of his day, the period of Realism. A jurist, like his father, in Schleswig-Holstein, he was a regional writer who transcended the limitations often inherent in regionalism. He had begun to write poetry by the early 1840s; his major volume of poems appeared in 1852. Since no individual dates for poems have become available to the present editor, the selections are reprinted following their sequence in Storm's collected poetry. "Sommermittag" is an amusing scene from everyday rural life. "Die Stadt" is a paean to the poet's native town, Husum, on the North Sea. "Frauenhand" is characteristic of the poet's concern for, and understanding of, women.

"Von Katzen," written in blank verse (iambic pentameter), is in some ways a homage to Mörike, whom Storm particularly admired. This sort of casual, humorous—but carefully phrased and structured—narrative of household events is a trademark of the earlier poet.

"Juli" has been seen as a prefiguration of Liliencron's concise, "Impressionistic" poems.

Although Storm usually wrote in standard German (Hochdeutsch), he turned to his local Plattdeutsch for "An Klaus Groth," addressed to the great master of that dialect. The immense charm of this short piece, with its evocation of domestic felicity, made it irresistible for inclusion here. The present editor has supplied his own Hochdeutsch version in a footnote as an aid, although the dialect is not difficult, being even closer to English than standard German is.

The extremely musical "Über die Heide" is a typically Romantic lament for the past. "In Bulemanns Haus" is a striking oddity that Storm included in a subsection called "Märchen" (Folktales); it is a poem that Storm loved to recite at salon gatherings.

## Klaus Groth

### (Apr. 1819–1899)

A miller's son from Holstein, Groth became a teacher and creator of literature. He taught in his native town from 1842 to 1849, and at the University of Kiel from 1866 on. His own poetic production began by 1845, and he published some works in Hochdeutsch (standard German) in 1848. But his subsequent fame was chiefly due to the Plattdeutsch (northern dialect) poems he eventually collected in the volume *Quickborn* (Fountain of Youth); he also wrote stories in

Plattdeutsch. He traveled extensively in Germany and elsewhere in Europe, lecturing on literature and garnering many honors.

His Hochdeutsch poems, traditional in form and content but beautifully crafted, were ultimately gathered into several volumes. The three included here are all located in the collection *Hundert Blätter: Paralipomena zum Quickborn* (A Hundred Leaves: Supplement to the "Quickborn"), first published in 1854. The wistful longing for childhood bliss in "Regenlied" and " 'O wüßt ich doch den Weg zurück' " is an archetypical Romantic theme, even though Groth has been pigeonholed under the Realism period by literary historians. " 'Dein blaues Auge hält so still' " is No. 11 of a short cycle called *Klänge* (Sounds).

## Gottfried Keller

(July 1819–1890)

Keller, who was born and died in Zurich, is one of the greatest Swiss writers. Chiefly famous for his semiautobiographical novel *Der grüne Heinrich* (awkwardly known in English as *Green Henry*) and for his numerous short stories ranging from the tragedy of "Romeo und Julia auf dem Dorfe" (A Village Romeo and Juliet) to the comedy of "Kleider machen Leute" (Clothes Make the Man), he was also an accomplished if not a great poet.

A bohemian all his life, although with entrenched bourgeois values, Keller was the self-taught son of a wood turner. After an unsuccessful attempt to become a painter in Munich, he achieved fame in 1846, when his first volume of poems was published. His move to Berlin in 1850 was of great importance for his literary development, although he was always happiest back home, where for many years he was chief secretary of the local chancery.

It has been said that Keller's poems reveal his inmost feelings, his love of nature, homeland and domestic life. "An das Vaterland" was first published in 1846 in the subsection "Schweizerisches" (Things Swiss) of the section "Vermischte Gedichte" (Miscellaneous Poems) of the volume *Gedichte*. It is a fine example of a patriotic poem, a genre that was extremely popular throughout the nineteenth century. "Waldlied, I" (also known as "Im Wald") is one of two numbered Forest Songs in the section "Natur" of the 1846 *Gedichte*. The poems in that volume were written from 1843 to 1846.

"Winternacht" was first published in the section "Jahreszeiten" (Seasons) of the volume *Neuere Gedichte* (Recent Poems), with editions in 1851 and 1854. "Abendlied," with its grudging acceptance of approaching death, was included among the "Späte Gedichte" (Late Poems) in Keller's volume *Gesammelte Gedichte* (Collected Poems) of 1883.

## Theodor Fontane

(Dec. 1819–1898)

Fontane is now one of the most highly regarded of all German writers, especially for such novels as *Frau Jenny Treibel* and *Effi Briest*, with their not unfriendly dissection of Prussian society mores. Fontane, son of a pharmacist, followed the same profession in Berlin until 1849, afterwards becoming a newspaperman in various capacities, including war correspondent and theater critic. He traveled widely, being especially fond of England (he translated and adapted numerous British ballads and legends).

Fontane started writing poems by the late 1830s, and amassed a considerable poetic oeuvre (which is nevertheless only about five per cent of his vast total output). Many of his poems are in a conversational, prosy style that foreshadows certain twentieth-century trends. His great specialty was the narrative ballad (to a large extent, a continuation of the Romantic tradition). Two of his ballads, written 25 years apart, are included here.

"Gorm Grymme," written in 1864, is about the Danish king Gorm, who died about 940. His story occurs in the chronicle by Saxo Grammaticus, completed in 1208, which is also the ultimate source of Shakespeare's *Hamlet*.

"Herr von Ribbeck auf Ribbeck im Havelland," written in 1889, is based on material in a contemporary book of local Prussian legends.

## Conrad Ferdinand Meyer

(1825–1898)

A major novelist and author of short stories and novellas, Meyer is also easily the greatest Swiss poet of the nineteenth century. Born into a patrician Zurich family—his father was a statesman and historian—Meyer never felt want but suffered from melancholia and deep dissatisfaction with himself. He was briefly institutionalized in 1852, and underwent a nervous breakdown in 1891. Greatly influenced by French literature, he did a great deal of translation from French until the Franco-Prussian War of 1870 led him to favor original German material. The next two decades saw the peak of his productivity and a return of self-confidence. A writer of great refinement, he has been called the first German-language Symbolist because some of his poems are emblematic descriptions of objects for their own sake.

It has been said that Meyer's poetry owes more to technique than to inspiration. While it is true that his temperament was not fiery and he was no revolutionary innovator of forms or themes, his thought is deep and wide-ranging and the expression is choice. As for his technique, it is so remarkable that it would cover a multitude of sins, were there any to cover. The relentless revision of his work paid enormous dividends.

Many of the poems experienced decades of gestation. Hardly any other writer undertook such extensive or such fundamental recastings of already published works with an eye to perfection. The transmutations in manuscript and printed stages chronicled by the courageous editors in their apparatus to the critical edition read like an immense puzzle. In the light of this, it would be pointless in an anthology like the present one to pinpoint dates; instead, the poems are reproduced in their definitive form in the sequence in which they appear in the collected works according to the poet's wishes.

"Fülle" is the first poem in the first section, "Vorsaal" (Vestibule). It has been said that Meyer gave it this privileged position because it represented to him the abundance of creativity finally vouchsafed to him after years of little accomplishment.

The second section of Meyer's poems, entitled "Stunde" (Hour), contains the poems "Eingelegte Ruder," "Säerspruch" and "Ewig jung ist nur die Sonne."

"Auf dem Canal grande," from Section IV, "Reise" (Travel), features a brilliant use of assonance in place of pure rhyme, quite in keeping with Meyer's perception of the "shady" city of Venice.

"Stapfen," from Section V, "Liebe" (Love), is a blank-verse narrative tightly held together by repetitions of phrases and rhythms.

Finally, "In der Sistina," from Section VIII, "Genie" (Genius), is a tribute to a hero of the Italian Renaissance, the historical era that intrigued Meyer above all others.

## Detlev von Liliencron

(June 1844–1909)

Detlev, the name of an ancestor, was the Christian name adopted by the nobleman Friedrich Adolph Axel Freiherr (Baron) von Liliencron when he started publishing poetry. The family was not wealthy: the poet's father was a customs official, and the poet himself deeply in debt almost to the end of his life. Liliencron served as a Prussian officer from 1863 to 1875, fighting in the wars of 1866 and 1870 against Austria and France. Retiring because of debts, he spent the years 1875 to 1877 in the United States trying an assortment of jobs unsuccessfully. He entered the Prussian civil service in 1879. In the 1890s, to make desperately needed money, he toured as a lecturer and reciter, even appearing in cabaret in 1900. His half-dozen volumes of poetry appeared between 1883 and 1903; he also wrote plays and stories.

Modern critics argue about which "-ism" to classify Liliencron under; "Impressionism" is frequently cited. His less traditional, more rambling and talky pieces are now admired as forerunners of twentieth-century experiments, while he is also seen as a lyric predecessor of Rilke and George. In conformity with the goals of the present volume, four of the more traditional pieces in the general Romantic lineage have been chosen, although even these display Liliencron's mastery of form and his special gift of concise, direct response to sensory data.

"Wer weiß wo" and "Four in hand" both first appeared in his 1883 volume *Adjutantenritte und andere Gedichte* (Rides as an Adjutant and Other Poems). The latter poem still bore the German title "Viererzug" in early editions. "Einen Sommer lang" is from the 1892 volume *Neue Gedichte* (New Poems), and "Märztag" from the 1903 volume *Bunte Beute* (Miscellaneous Booty).

## Friedrich Nietzsche

(Oct. 1844–1900)

Nietzsche, son of a pastor, was a brilliant student despite lingering mental and physical illness that began in childhood, and became a professor of classical philology in Basel at age 25. He remained in that position for ten years, during which he started to publish the iconoclastic philological and philosophical works on which his fame rests. Beginning with a startlingly new view of ancient Greek mentality, he progressed to a point at which he renounced all traditional religion and morality, championing the special education of an elitist group of "supermen" who could guide the world in its new godless condition. His literary spokesman and alter ego was Zarathustra (the namesake of the ancient Persian prophet Zoroaster). In 1878 Nietszche began a series of nomadic travels, suffering a nervous breakdown in Turin at the beginning of 1889. He died insane.

As a writer, Nietzsche is an incomparable wielder of the German language. Although his poetic oeuvre, as strictly defined, is not extremely large, and many of the poems occur within his philosophic works, in another sense all his work is poetry, governed by a very musical sense and making use of innumerable word plays based on the sounds of German (in this he is very similar to James Joyce in English).

"Ecce homo" ("Behold the man" in Latin; a reference to the Passion of Jesus) is (in the edition of the poetical oeuvre supervised by the poet's sister) from the subdivision "Zur 'Fröhlichen Wissenschaft': Scherz, List und Rache" ([Poems] Connected with [the book] *The Joyous Science* [or, *Le Gai Savoir*]: Humor, Cunning and Revenge), written 1881–1882.

"Das trunkene Lied" appears in *Also sprach Zarathustra* (Thus Spake Zarathustra), 1883–1885.

"Parsifal-Musik" is from the subdivision "Spruchartiges aus den Werken und Aufzeichnungen der Jahre 1882–1886" (Aphoristic Poems from the Works and Sketches of the Years 1882–1886). One of the most devastating verse polemics in German, it is also an excellent example of Nietzsche's sometimes outrageous views and of his special handling of language; it is impossible not to admire and enjoy it whatever one's personal views may be.[3] Nietzsche had earlier been a fervent disciple and spokesman of Wagner for years, and had frequently enjoyed his hospitality in Lucerne and Bayreuth.

"Vereinsamt" and "Venedig" both appear in the section "Aus den Werken und Aufzeichnungen der Jahre 1882–1888" (From the Works and Sketches of the Years 1882–1888). "Vereinsamt" is actually No. 1 of a two-poem group called "Mitleid hin und her" (Compassion Back and Forth); the second poem is a brief, nasty palinode to the first, and completely unworthy of its great partner. "Venedig" is specifically dated 1888.

"Das Feuerzeichen" is one of the *Dionysos-Dithyramben*, 1884–1888. Nietzsche himself wrote as an epigraph to the series: "These are the songs of Zarathustra, which he sang to himself in order to endure his last solitude."

---

[3]The present editor is extremely fond of *Parstfal*, and neither the editor nor the publisher has the slightest wish to insult the Catholic Church by including this piece; it belongs here for its purely literary merits.

# Great German Poems of the Romantic Era

## Berühmte Gedichte der deutschen Romantik

# Johann Wolfgang von Goethe

## Willkommen und Abschied

Es schlug mein Herz, geschwind zu Pferde!
Es war getan fast eh gedacht.
Der Abend wiegte schon die Erde,
Und an den Bergen hing die Nacht;
Schon stand im Nebelkleid die Eiche,
Ein aufgetürmter Riese, da,
Wo Finsternis aus dem Gesträuche
Mit hundert schwarzen Augen sah.

Der Mond von einem Wolkenhügel
Sah kläglich aus dem Duft hervor,
Die Winde schwangen leise Flügel,
Umsausten schauerlich mein Ohr;
Die Nacht schuf tausend Ungeheuer,
Doch frisch und fröhlich war mein Mut:
In meinen Adern welches Feuer!
In meinem Herzen welche Glut!

Dich sah ich, und die milde Freude
Floß von dem süßen Blick auf mich;
Ganz war mein Herz an deiner Seite
Und jeder Atemzug für dich.
Ein rosenfarbnes Frühlingswetter
Umgab das liebliche Gesicht,
Und Zärtlichkeit für mich—ihr Götter!
Ich hofft es, ich verdient es nicht!

Doch ach, schon mit der Morgensonne
Verengt der Abschied mir das Herz:
In deinen Küssen welche Wonne!
In deinem Auge welcher Schmerz!
Ich ging, du standst und sahst zur Erden

# Johann Wolfgang von Goethe

## *Welcome and Farewell*

My heart beat: at once to horse!
The deed was nearly quicker than the thought.[1]
Evening was already cradling the earth,
And night hung upon the mountains.
The oak already stood in its garment of mist,
A towering giant, there
Where blackness peered from the bushes
With a hundred dark eyes.

From a hill of cloud the moon
Looked lamentably out of the haze,
The winds beat soft wings,
And soughed fearfully around my ears;
The night created a thousand monsters,
But my spirits were fresh and happy:
In my veins what fire!
In my heart what a blaze!

I saw you, and gentle joy
Flowed to me from your sweet glance:
My whole heart was by your side
And every breath was for you.
A rose-colored springtime atmosphere
Encircled your lovely face,
And tenderness for me—you gods!
I hoped for it, but didn't deserve it!

But alas, as soon as the morning sun rose,
Parting tightened my heart:
In your kisses what rapture!
In your eyes what pain!
I went, you stood and looked down at the ground

---

[1]Literally: "It was done almost before [it was] thought."

Und sahst mir nach mit nassem Blick:
Und doch, welch Glück, geliebt zu werden!
Und lieben, Götter, welch ein Glück!


## Heidenröslein

Sah ein Knab ein Röslein stehn,
Röslein auf der Heiden,
War so jung und morgenschön,
Lief er schnell, es nah zu sehn,
Sah's mit vielen Freuden.
Röslein, Röslein, Röslein rot,
Röslein auf der Heiden.

Knabe sprach: Ich breche dich,
Röslein auf der Heiden!
Röslein sprach: Ich steche dich,
Daß du ewig denkst an mich,
Und ich will's nicht leiden.
Röslein, Röslein, Röslein rot,
Röslein auf der Heiden.

Und der wilde Knabe brach
's Röslein auf der Heiden;
Röslein wehrte sich und stach,
Half ihm doch kein Weh und Ach,
Mußt es eben leiden.
Röslein, Röslein, Röslein rot,
Röslein auf der Heiden.


## Prometheus

Bedecke deinen Himmel, Zeus,
Mit Wolkendunst!
Und übe, dem Knaben gleich,
Der Disteln köpft,

And watched me go with moist eyes:
And yet, what happiness to be loved!
And to love, gods, what happiness!


## *Little Rose on the Heath*[2]

A boy saw a little rose standing,
Little rose on the heath;
It was so young and of such morning beauty,
He ran quickly to see it closely,
He saw it with great joy.
Little rose, rose, red rose,
Little rose on the heath.

The boy said: "I shall pluck you,
Little rose on the heath!"
The little rose said: "I shall prick you,
So that you think of me forever,
And I won't endure it."
Little rose, rose, red rose,
Little rose on the heath.

And the impetuous boy plucked
The little rose on the heath;
The little rose defended itself and pricked him,
But no "woe" or "alas" did it any good,
It just had to endure it.
Little rose, rose, red rose,
Little rose on the heath.


## *Prometheus*

Cover your sky, Zeus,
With cloudy vapor!
And, like a boy
Who beheads thistles,

---

[2]*Heiderose* = sun rose, or rockrose (*Helianthemum* spp.).

An Eichen dich und Bergeshöhn!
Mußt mir meine Erde
Doch lassen stehn,
Und meine Hütte, die du nicht gebaut,
Und meinen Herd,
Um dessen Glut
Du mich beneidest.

Ich kenne nichts Ärmers
Unter der Sonn als euch Götter!
Ihr nähret kümmerlich
Von Opfersteuern
Und Gebetshauch
Eure Majestät
Und darbtet, wären
Nicht Kinder und Bettler
Hoffnungsvolle Toren.

Da ich ein Kind war,
Nicht wußte, wo aus, wo ein,
Kehrt ich mein verirrtes Aug
Zur Sonne, als wenn drüber wär
Ein Ohr, zu hören meine Klage,
Ein Herz wie meins,
Sich des Bedrängten zu erbarmen.

Wer half mir
Wider der Titanen Übermut?
Wer rettete vom Tode mich,
Von Sklaverei?
Hast du's nicht alles selbst vollendet,
Heilig glühend Herz?
Und glühtest, jung und gut,
Betrogen, Rettungsdank
Dem Schlafenden da droben?

Ich dich ehren? Wofür?
Hast du die Schmerzen gelindert
Je des Beladenen?
Hast du die Tränen gestillet
Je des Geängsteten?

Practice on oaks and mountain heights!
You nevertheless must
Let my earth remain,
And my hut, which you did not build,
And my hearth,
For whose fire
You envy me.

I know nothing pettier
Under the sun than you gods!
You meagerly nourish
Your majesty
With imposed sacrifices
And the breath of prayers,
And you would starve if
Children and beggars
Were not fools dependent on hope.

When I was a child,
And did not know one thing from another,
I turned my bewildered eyes
Toward the sun, as if up there was
An ear to hear my lament,
A heart like mine,
To take pity on me when I was hard pressed.

Who aided me
Against the arrogance of the Titans?
Who saved me from death,
From slavery?
Did you not accomplish everything yourself,
My sacredly glowing heart?
And in your youth and goodness,
Deceived, did you not warmly give thanks for salvation
To the sleeper up above?

I honor you? What for?
Have you ever soothed my pains
When I was burdened?
Have you ever stilled my tears
When I was anguished?

Hat nicht mich zum Manne geschmiedet
Die allmächtige Zeit
Und das ewige Schicksal,
Meine Herrn und deine?

Wähntest du etwa,
Ich sollte das Leben hassen,
In Wüsten fliehn,
Weil nicht alle
Blütenträume reiften?

Heir sitz ich, forme Menschen
Nach meinem Bilde,
Ein Geschlecht, das mir gleich sei,
Zu leiden, weinen,
Genießen und zu freuen sich,
Und dein nicht zu achten,
Wie ich!


## Rastlose Liebe

Dem Schnee, dem Regen,
Dem Wind entgegen,
Im Dampf der Klüfte,
Durch Nebeldüfte,
Immer zu! Immer zu!
Ohne Rast und Ruh!

Lieber durch Leiden
Möcht ich mich schlagen,
Als so viel Freuden
Des Lebens ertragen.
Alle das Neigen
Von Herzen zu Herzen,
Ach, wie so eigen
Schaffet das Schmerzen!

Wie soll ich fliehen?
Wälderwärts ziehen?

Have I not been forged into manhood
By almighty time
And eternal destiny,
My lords and yours?

Did you perhaps imagine
That I was to hate life,
Escape into deserts,
Because not all
My budding dreams came to fruition?

Here I sit and form people
In my image,
A race that shall be like me,
To suffer, to weep,
To enjoy and to be happy—
And to pay you no mind,
Like me!

## *Restless Love*

Into the snow, the rain,
The wind,
In the vapor of the chasms,
Through misty haze,
Onward! Onward!
Without rest or repose!

I would rather force my way
Through sorrows
Than to endure so many
Joys of life.
All the inclination
Of one heart to another,
Oh, how oddly
It causes pain!

How shall I flee?
Journey toward the woods?

Alles vergebens!
Krone des Lebens,
Glück ohne Ruh,
Liebe, bist du!

## An den Mond

Füllest wieder Busch und Tal
Still mit Nebelglanz,
Lösest endlich auch einmal
Meine Seel ganz.

Breitest über mein Gefild
Lindernd deinen Blick,
Wie des Freundes Auge mild
Über mein Geschick.

Jeden Nachklang fühlt mein Herz
Froh- und trüber Zeit,
Wandle zwischen Freud und Schmerz
In der Einsamkeit.

Fließe, fließe, lieber Fluß!
Nimmer werd ich froh,
So verrauschte Scherz und Kuß,
Und die Treue so.

Ich besaß es doch einmal,
Was so köstlich ist!
Daß man doch zu seiner Qual
Nimmer es vergißt!

Rausche, Fluß, das Tal entlang,
Ohne Rast und Ruh,
Rausche, flüstre meinem Sang
Melodien zu,

Wenn du in der Winternacht
Wütend überschwillst,

All in vain!
The crown of life,
Happiness without repose:
Love, that is what you are!

## To the Moon

Again you fill bush and valley
Silently with a misty glow,
And also you finally release
My soul entirely.

You spread your gaze
Soothingly over my fields,
Like a friend's eyes gently
Looking upon my fate.

My heart feels every after-echo
Of happy and dreary times,
I walk between joy and pain
In the solitude.

Flow, flow, dear river!
I will never become happy:
Thus merriment and kisses hastened by,
And thus did faithfulness.

But I once possessed
That which is so precious!
To think that nevertheless, to one's torment,
One never forgets it!

Murmur, river, along the valley,
Without rest or repose,
Murmur, whisper melodies
To my song,

When, in the winter night, you
Furiously overflow,

Oder um die Frühlingspracht
Junger Knospen quillst.

Selig, wer sich vor der Welt
Ohne Haß verschließt,
Einen Freund am Busen hält
Und mit dem genießt,

Was, von Menschen nicht gewußt
Oder nicht bedacht,
Durch das Labyrinth der Brust
Wandelt in der Nacht.

## Der Fischer

Das Wasser rauscht', das Wasser schwoll,
Ein Fischer saß daran,
Sah nach der Angel ruhevoll,
Kühl bis ans Herz hinan.
Und wie er sitzt und wie er lauscht,
Teilt sich die Flut empor:
Aus dem bewegten Wasser rauscht
Ein feuchtes Weib hervor.

Sie sang zu ihm, sie sprach zu ihm:
„Was lockst du meine Brut
Mit Menschenwitz und Menschenlist
Hinauf in Todesglut?
Ach, wüßtest du, wie's Fischlein ist
So wohlig auf dem Grund,
Du stiegst herunter, wie du bist,
Und würdest erst gesund.

Labt sich die liebe Sonne nicht,
Der Mond sich nicht im Meer?
Kehrt wellenatmend ihr Gesicht

Or purl around the springtime splendor
Of young buds.

Blessed is he who shuts himself off
From the world without hatred,
Clasps a friend to his breast
And, together with him, enjoys

That which, not known to people
Or not considered,
Walks through the labyrinth of the heart
In the night.

## The Fisherman

The water rushed, the water rose,
A fisherman sat by it,
Looked peacefully at his rod,
Cool to the depths of his heart.
And as he sits and as he listens,
The waves separate upward:
From the agitated water there swiftly emerges
A woman of the deeps.[3]

She sang to him, she spoke to him:
"Why do you lure my brood
With human cunning and human guile
Up into the heat of death?
Ah, if you knew how comfortable
The little fishes are down at the bottom,
You would descend just as you are,
And would become hale for the first time.

"Does not the dear sun,
Does not the moon refresh itself in the sea?
Does not their face, breathing the waves,

---

[3]Very literally, "a wet woman."

Nicht doppelt schöner her?
Lockt dich der tiefe Himmel nicht,
Das feuchtverklärte Blau?
Lockt dich dein eigen Angesicht
Nicht her in ewgen Tau?"

Das Wasser rauscht', das Wasser schwoll,
Netzt' ihm den nackten Fuß;
Sein Herz wuchs ihm so sehnsuchtsvoll,
Wie bei der Liebsten Gruß.
Sie sprach zu ihm, sie sang zu ihm,
Da wars um ihn geschehn:
Halb zog sie ihn, halb sank er hin,
Und ward nicht mehr gesehn.

## Grenzen der Menschheit

Wenn der uralte
Heilige Vater
Mit gelassener Hand
Aus rollenden Wolken
Segnende Blitze
Über die Erde sät,
Küß ich den letzten
Saum seines Kleides,
Kindliche Schauer
Treu in der Brust.

Denn mit Göttern
Soll sich nicht messen
Irgendein Mensch.
Hebt er sich aufwärts
Und berührt
Mit dem Scheitel die Sterne,
Nirgends haften dann
Die unsichern Sohlen,
Und mit ihm spielen
Wolken und Winde.

Return from here doubly beautiful?
Does not the heaven of the depths lure you,
The blueness transfigured by the fluid?
Does not your own countenance lure you
Down here to the eternal dew?"

The water rushed, the water rose,
Wetted his naked foot;
His heart expanded as longingly
As if his sweetheart had greeted him.
She spoke to him, she sang to him,
Then his doom was sealed:
Partly she drew him in, partly he let himself sink,
And was never seen again.

## Limitations of Humanity

When the ancient
Holy Father
With calm hand
Sows beneficent lightnings
From rolling clouds
Onto the earth,
I kiss the nethermost
Hem of His garment,
With childlike thrills
Loyally in my heart.

For no man
Should measure himself
Against gods.
If he raises himself upward
And touches
The stars with the crown of his head,
Then nowhere
Do his unstable feet find a hold,
And clouds and winds
Make him their plaything.

Steht er mit festen,
Markigen Knochen
Auf der wohlgegründeten
Dauernden Erde,
Reicht er nicht auf,
Nur mit der Eiche
Oder der Rebe
Sich zu vergleichen.

Was unterscheidet
Götter von Menschen?
Daß viele Wellen
Vor jenen wandeln,
Ein ewiger Strom;
Uns hebt die Welle,
Verschlingt die Welle,
Und wir versinken.

Ein kleiner Ring
Begrenzt unser Leben,
Und viele Geschlechter
Reihen sich dauernd
An ihres Daseins
Unendliche Kette.


## Erlkönig

Wer reitet so spät durch Nacht und Wind?
Es ist der Vater mit seinem Kind.
Er hat den Knaben wohl in dem Arm,
Er faßt ihn sicher, er hält ihn warm.

„Mein Sohn, was birgst du so bang dein Gesicht?"
„Siehst, Vater, du den Erlkönig nicht,
Den Erlenkönig mit Kron' und Schweif?"
„Mein Sohn, es ist ein Nebelstreif."

If he stands with firm,
Vigorous bones
Upon the securely established,
Enduring earth,
He is unable
To compare himself
With even the oak
Or the grapevine.

What distinguishes
Gods from men?
It is that many waves
Move past the former,
An endless current:
We are tossed by the wave,
Swallowed up by the wave,
And we sink.

A small circle
Bounds our life,
And many generations
Are continually strung out
On the infinite chain
Of their existence.


## Elf King[4]

Who is riding so late through night and wind?
It is the father with his child.
He has the boy firmly in his arms,
He grasps him securely, he keeps him warm.

"My son, why are you hiding your face in such terror?"
"Father, don't you see the elf king?
The elf king with his crown and train?"
"My son, it is a patch of fog."

---

[4]*Erlkönig* literally is "alder king," but the *Erl-* is based on a mistaken eighteenth-century translation from a Danish source.

„Du liebes Kind, komm, geh mit mir!
Gar schöne Spiele spiel ich mit dir;
Manch bunte Blumen sind an dem Strand,
Meine Mutter hat manch gülden Gewand."

„Mein Vater, mein Vater, und hörest du nicht,
Was Erlenkönig mir leise verspricht?"
„Sei ruhig, bleibe ruhig, mein Kind;
In dürren Blättern säuselt der Wind."

„Willst, feiner Knabe, du mit mir gehn?
Meine Töchter sollen dich warten schön;
Meine Töchter führen den nächtlichen Reihn
Und wiegen und tanzen und singen dich ein."

„Mein Vater, mein Vater, und siehst du nicht dort
Erlkönigs Töchter am düstern Ort?"
„Mein Sohn, mein Sohn, ich seh es genau,
Es scheinen die alten Weiden so grau."

„Ich liebe dich, mich reizt deine schöne Gestalt;
Und bist du nicht willig, so brauch ich Gewalt."
„Mein Vater, mein Vater, jetzt faßt er mich an!
Erlkönig hat mir ein Leids getan!"

Dem Vater grausets, er reitet geschwind,
Er hält in Armen das ächzende Kind,
Erreicht den Hof mit Mühe und Not—
In seinen Armen das Kind war tot.

## "So laßt mich scheinen, bis ich werde"

So laßt mich scheinen, bis ich werde;
Zieht mir das weiße Kleid nicht aus!
Ich eile von der schönen Erde
Hinab in jenes feste Haus.

Dort ruh ich eine kleine Stille,
Dann öffnet sich der frische Blick,

"You dear child, come along with me!
I will play really beautiful games with you;
Many colorful flowers grow by the banks,
My mother has many a golden garment."

"My father, my father, and don't you hear
What the elf king is quietly promising me?"
"Be calm, stay calm, my child:
The wind is whistling in the dry leaves."

"My fine boy, do you want to come with me?
My daughters shall attend you beautifully;
My daughters lead the round dance at night,
And will rock and dance and sing you to sleep."

"My father, my father, and don't you see there
The elf king's daughters in that gloomy place?"
"My son, my son, I see it clearly:
The old willows have that gray appearance."

"I love you, your beautiful form arouses me;
And if you are not willing, I will use force."
"My father, my father, now he is seizing me!
The elf king has hurt me!"

The father is frightened, he rides swiftly,
He holds in his arms the groaning child;
He reaches his yard with effort and distress—
In his arms the child was dead.

## "Let me appear this way until I become real"

Let me appear this way until I become real;
Do not take off my white robe!
I hasten from the beautiful earth
Down to that secure abode.

There I shall rest for a brief quiet time,
Then my eyes, refreshed, will open;

Ich lasse dann die reine Hülle,
Den Gürtel und den Kranz zurück.

Und jene himmlischen Gestalten,
Sie fragen nicht nach Mann und Weib,
Und keine Kleider, keine Falten
Umgeben den verklärten Leib.

Zwar lebt ich ohne Sorg und Mühe,
Doch fühlt ich tiefen Schmerz genung.
Vor Kummer altert ich zu frühe—
Macht mich auf ewig wieder jung!

## "In tausend Formen magst du dich verstecken"

In tausend Formen magst du dich verstecken,
Doch, Allerliebste, gleich erkenn ich dich;
Du magst mit Zauberschleiern dich bedecken,
Allgegenwärt'ge, gleich erkenn ich dich.

An der Zypresse reinstem, jungem Streben,
Allschöngewachsne, gleich erkenn ich dich;
In des Kanales reinem Wellenleben,
Allschmeichelhafte, wohl erkenn ich dich.

Wenn steigend sich der Wasserstrahl entfaltet,
Allspielende, wie froh erkenn ich dich;
Wenn Wolke sich gestaltend umgestaltet,
Allmannigfalt'ge, dort erkenn ich dich.

An des geblümten Schleiers Wiesenteppich,
Allbuntbesternte, schön erkenn ich dich;
Und greift umher ein tausendarm'ger Eppich,
O Allumklammernde, da kenn ich dich.

Wenn am Gebirg der Morgen sich entzündet,
Gleich, Allerheiternde, begrüß ich dich,
Dann über mir der Himmel rein sich ründet,
Allherzerweiternde, dann atm' ich dich.

Then I shall leave behind this pure covering,
The belt and the garland.

And those heavenly beings,
They do not ask if you are man or woman,
And no garments, no folds of drapery
Encircle your transfigured body.

To be sure, I lived without worry or effort,
But I felt enough profound sorrow;
From grief I grew old too soon—
Make me eternally young again!

## "You may conceal yourself in a thousand forms"

You may conceal yourself in a thousand forms,
But, all-beloved one, I recognize you at once;
You my cover yourself with magic veils,
All-present one, I recognize you at once.

In the purest young striving of the cypress,
All-shapely one, I recognize you at once;
In the pure watery life of the canal,
All-flattering one, I surely recognize you.

When a jet of water rises and unfurls,
All-sportive one, how happily I recognize you;
When a cloud, forming shapes, changes shape,
All-manifold one, there I recognize you.

In the meadowy tapestry of the flowered veil,
All-motley-starred one, I recognize your beauty;
And if a thousand-armed ivy gropes about,
O all-embracing one, there I know you.

When the morning ignites itself against the mountain,
At once, all-cheering one, I greet you;
Then the sky forms a pure dome above me,
All-heart-expanding one, then I breathe you in.

Was ich mit äußerm Sinn, mit innerm kenne,
Du Allbelehrende, kenn ich durch dich;
Und wenn ich Allahs Namenhundert nenne,
Mit jedem klingt ein Name nach für dich.

## Urworte. Orphisch

### ΔΑΙΜΩΝ, DÄMON

Wie an dem Tag, der dich der Welt verliehen,
Die Sonne stand zum Gruße der Planeten,
Bist alsobald und fort und fort gediehen
Nach dem Gesetz, wonach du angetreten.
So mußt du sein, dir kannst du nicht entfliehen,
So sagten schon Sibyllen, so Propheten;
Und keine Zeit und keine Macht zerstückelt
Geprägte Form, die lebend sich entwickelt.

### ΤΥΧΗ, DAS ZUFÄLLIGE

Die strenge Grenze doch umgeht gefällig
Ein Wandelndes, das mit und um uns wandelt;
Nicht einsam bleibst du, bildest dich gesellig
Und handelst wohl so, wie ein andrer handelt:
Im Leben ist's bald hin-, bald widerfällig,
Es ist ein Tand und wird so durchgetandelt.
Schon hat sich still der Jahre Kreis geründet,
Die Lampe harrt der Flamme, die entzündet.

### ΕΡΩΣ, LIEBE

Die bleibt nicht aus! Er stürzt vom Himmel nieder,
Wohin er sich aus alter Öde schwang,
Er schwebt heran auf luftigem Gefieder
Um Stirn und Brust den Frühlingstag entlang,
Scheint jetzt zu fliehn, vom Fliehen kehrt er wieder,
Da wird ein Wohl im Weh, so süß und bang.
Gar manches Herz verschwebt im Allgemeinen,
Doch widmet sich das edelste dem Einen.

What I know with my outer, with my inner senses,
You all-instructing one, I know through you;
And when I recite Allah's hundred names,
With each one a name reechoes for you.


## Primal Words. Orphic

### ΔΑΙΜΩΝ, DAIMON

As on the day that lent you to the world
The sun stood to greet the planets,
You instantly thrived, and continued to do so
In accordance with the law by which you made your appearance.
Thus you must be, you cannot escape yourself;
Thus sibyls and prophets have already said;
And no passage of time nor any power can break into bits
A molded form that develops as it lives.

### ΤΥΧΗ, CHANCE

And yet a roving force that moves with and around us
Circumvents the strict boundary as it pleases;
You do not remain alone, you are formed in society,
And most likely act as someone else acts:
In life things fall out now this way, now that;
It is a toy and we toy our way through it.
The round of years has soon quietly come full circle:
The lamp awaits the flame that will light it.

### ΕΡΩΣ, LOVE

It does not fail to appear! He plunges down from heaven,
Up to which he arose from the ancient wasteland,
He hovers near on his airy wings
Around your brow and breast throughout the spring day,
Now seems to flee, returns from his flight;
Then one feels pleasure in pain, so sweet and frightening.
Many a heart drifts away in a generalized love,
But the noblest heart devotes itself to just one.

## ΑΝΑΓΚΗ, Nötigung

Da ist's denn wieder, wie die Sterne wollten:
Bedingung und Gesetz; und aller Wille
Ist nur ein Wollen, weil wir eben sollten,
Und vor dem Willen schweigt die Willkür stille:
Das Liebste wird vom Herzen weggescholten,
Dem harten Muß bequemt sich Will und Grille.
So sind wir scheinfrei denn nach manchen Jahren
Nur enger dran, als wir am Anfang waren.

## ΕΛΠΙΣ, Hoffnung

Doch solcher Grenze, solcher ehrnen Mauer
Höchst widerwärtge Pforte wird entriegelt,
Sie stehe nur mit alter Felsendauer!
Ein Wesen regt sich leicht und ungezügelt:
Aus Wolkendecke, Nebel, Regenschauer
Erhebt sie uns, mit ihr, durch sie beflügelt;
Ihr kennt sie wohl, sie schwärmt durch alle Zonen;
Ein Flügelschlag—und hinter uns Äonen!

## "Dämmrung senkte sich von oben"

Dämmrung senkte sich von oben,
Schon ist alle Nähe fern;
Doch zuerst emporgehoben
Holden Lichts der Abendstern!
Alles schwankt ins Ungewisse,
Nebel schleichen in die Höh;
Schwarzvertiefte Finsternisse
Widerspiegelnd ruht der See.

Nun am östlichen Bereiche
Ahn' ich Mondenglanz und -glut,
Schlanker Weiden Haargezweige
Scherzen auf der nächsten Flut.
Durch bewegter Schatten Spiele
Zittert Lunas Zauberschein,
Und durchs Auge schleicht die Kühle
Sänftigend ins Herz hinein.

## ΑΝΑΓΚΗ, NECESSITY

Then things are once again the way the stars wanted them:
Stipulation and law; and all our will
Is merely wanting to just because we ought to,
And, in face of the will, our freedom of choice falls silent:
What we love best is driven from our heart with curses,
Both will and caprice adapt themselves to the hard "must."
So, then, our freedom an illusion, after many years
We are merely more closely confined than we were at the outset.

## ΕΛΠΙΣ, HOPE

But the highly distasteful gate of such limitations,
Of such an unbreachable wall, is unbarred,
Even if it stands with the permanence of ancient cliffs!
A being stirs lightly and unbridled:
Out of the cloud cover, mist, rain shower
It raises us, along with it, endowed by it with wings;
You surely know it, it roves through every clime;
A wing beat—and eons are behind us!

## "Twilight has descended from above"

Twilight has descended from above,
Now everything near is far;
But first there has arisen
The evening star with its lovely light!
Everything reels into uncertainty,
Mists creep upward;
Reflecting the dark, with its patches of heightened blackness,
The lake is calm.

Now in the eastern quarter
I sense the moon's light and heat;
The hairlike branches of slender willows
Play upon the nearest waves.
Through the interplay of the restless shadows
Luna's[5] magical glow trembles,
And by way of the eyes the coolness creeps
Soothingly into the heart.

---

[5]The moon's.

# Friedrich von Schiller

## Die Größe der Welt

Die der schaffende Geist einst aus dem Chaos schlug,
Durch die schwebende Welt flieg ich des Windes Flug,
Bis am Strande
Ihrer Wogen ich lande,
Anker werf, wo kein Hauch mehr weht
Und der Markstein der Schöpfung steht.

Sterne sah ich bereits jugendlich auferstehn,
Tausendjährigen Gangs durchs Firmament zu gehn,
Sah sie spielen
Nach den lockenden Zielen;
Irrend suchte mein Blick umher,
Sah die Räume schon—sternenleer.

Anzufeuern den Flug weiter zum Reich des Nichts,
Steur ich mutiger fort, nehme den Flug des Lichts,
Nebligt trüber
Himmel an mir vorüber,
Weltsysteme, Fluten im Bach,
Strudeln dem Sonnenwanderer nach.

Seih, den einsamen Pfad wandelt ein Pilger mir
Rasch entgegen: „Halt an! Waller, was suchst du hier?"
Zum Gestade
Seiner Welt meine Pfade!
Segle hin, wo kein Hauch mehr weht
Und der Markstein der Schöpfung steht.

„Steh! Du segelst umsonst—vor dir Unendlichkeit!"
Steh! du segelst umsonst—Pilger, auch hinter mir!—
Senke nieder,
Adlergedank, dein Gefieder!
Kühne Seglerin, Phantasie,
Wirf ein mutloses Anker hie!

# Friedrich von Schiller

## *The Magnitude of the World*

Through the soaring world, which the creative Spirit
Once generated out of chaos, I am flying the wind's flight,
Until I land
At the shore of its waves,
And cast anchor where no puff of air any longer blows,
Where the boundary stone of Creation stands.

I have already seen stars resurrected in youthful glory
In order to make their thousand-years' journey through the firmament,
I saw them move sportingly
Toward the goals that lured them;
Bewildered, my gaze sought all around,
And already saw space—void of stars.

To stimulate my flight further to the realm of nothingness,
I steer more bravely forth, I take on the speed of light;
Mistily murky
Sky passes by me,
World systems, surges in the stream,
Whirl after the man who wanders through the suns.

See, along the lonely path a pilgrim travels
Swiftly toward me: "Halt! Traveler, what do you seek here?"
"To the shore
Of this world my path lies!
I am sailing to where no puff of air any longer blows,
Where the boundary stone of Creation stands."

"Stop! you sail in vain—before you is infinity!"
"Stop! you sail in vain—Pilgrim, it is behind me as well!"—
Eagle-thought,
Let your plumage fall!
Bold voyager, Imagination,
Cast a discouraged anchor here!

## Das verschleierte Bild zu Sais

Ein Jüngling, den des Wissens heißer Durst
Nach Sais in Ägypten trieb, der Priester
Geheime Weisheit zu erlernen, hatte
Schon manchen Grad mit schnellem Geist durcheilt;
Stets riß ihn seine Forschbegierde weiter,
Und kaum besänftigte der Hierophant
Den ungeduldig Strebenden. „Was hab ich,
Wenn ich nicht alles habe?" sprach der Jüngling.
„Gibt's etwa hier ein Weniger und Mehr?
Ist deine Wahrheit wie der Sinne Glück
Nur eine Summe, die man größer, kleiner
Besitzen kann und immer doch besitzt?
Ist sie nicht eine einzge, ungeteilte?
Nimm einen Ton aus einer Harmonie,
Nimm eine Farbe aus dem Regenbogen—
Und alles, was dir bleibt, ist nichts, solang
Das schöne All der Töne fehlt und Farben."

Indem sie einst so sprachen, standen sie
In einer einsamen Rotonde still,
Wo ein verschleiert Bild von Riesengröße
Dem Jüngling in die Augen fiel. Verwundert
Blickt er den Führer an und spricht: „Was ist's,
Das hinter diesem Schleier sich verbirgt?"
„Die Wahrheit", ist die Antwort. „Wie?" ruft jener,
„Nach Wahrheit streb ich ja allein, und diese
Gerade ist es, die man mir verhüllt?"

„Das mache mit der Gottheit aus", versetzt
Der Hierophant. „Kein Sterblicher, sagt sie,
Rückt diesen Schleier, bis ich selbst ihn hebe.
Und wer mit ungeweihter, schuld'ger Hand
Den heiligen, verbotnen früher hebt,
Der, spricht die Gottheit—" „Nun?" „Der sieht die Wahrheit."
„Ein seltsamer Orakelspruch! Du selbst,
Du hättest also niemals ihn gehoben?"
„Ich? Wahrlich nicht! Und war auch nie dazu
Versucht," „Das faß ich nicht. Wenn von der Wahrheit

## The Veiled Image in Sais

A youth, urged by the hot thirst for knowledge
To visit Sais in Egypt, in order to learn
The secred wisdom of the priests, had
Already hastily attained several levels through his quick intelligence;
His desire to investigate compelled him onward constantly,
And the hierophant was barely able to calm
The impatient striver. "What do I have
If I do not have everything?" said the youth.
"In this case, is there possibly a less and more?
Is your truth, like the pleasure of the senses,
Merely a sum that someone can possess to a greater
Or lesser extent and still possess it?
Is it not unique and indivisible?
Remove a tone from a harmony,
Remove a color from the rainbow—
And all that you have left is nothing, as long as
The beautiful totality of the tones and colors is gone."

While they were once speaking thus, they came to a halt
In a lonely rotunda
Where a veiled image of gigantic size
Caught the youth's eye. Amazed,
He looks at his guide and says: "What is it
That is concealed behind this veil?"
"The truth," is the answer. "What?" he cries,
"It is truth alone I am striving for, and it is
Precisely this that is being hidden from me?"

"Take that up with the deity," replies
The hierophant. " 'No mortal,' it says,
'Moves this veil until I myself lift it.
And whoever with unconsecrated, guilty hand
Lifts the sacred, forbidden veil sooner,
That man,' says the deity—" "Well?" " 'He will *see* the truth.' "
"A strange oracle! You yourself,
You, then, have never lifted it?"
"I? Certainly not! Nor was I ever tempted
To do so." "I cannot grasp that. If only this thin partition

Nur diese dünne Scheidewand mich trennte—"
„Und ein Gesetz", fällt ihm sein Führer ein.
„Gewichtiger, mein Sohn, als du es meinst,
Ist dieser dünne Flor—für deine Hand
Zwar leicht, doch zentnerschwer für dein Gewissen."

Der Jüngling ging gedankenvoll nach Hause.
Ihm raubt des Wissens brennende Begier
Den Schlaf, er wälzt sich glühend auf dem Lager
Und rafft sich auf um Mitternacht. Zum Tempel
Führt unfreiwillig ihn der scheue Tritt.
Leicht ward es ihm, die Mauer zu ersteigen,
Und mitten in das Innre der Rotonde
Trägt ein beherzter Sprung den Wagenden.

Hier steht er nun, und grauenvoll umfängt
Den Einsamen die lebenlose Stille,
Die nur der Tritte hohler Widerhall
In den geheimen Grüften unterbricht.
Von oben durch der Kuppel Öffnung wirft
Der Mond den bleichen, silberblauen Schein,
Und furchtbar wie ein gegenwärtger Gott
Erglänzt durch des Gewölbes Finsternisse
In ihrem langen Schleier die Gestalt.

Er tritt hinan mit ungewissem Schritt—
Schon will die freche Hand das Heilige berühren,
Da zuckt es heiß und kühl durch sein Gebein
Und stößt ihn weg mit unsichtbarem Arme.
Unglücklicher, was willst du tun? so ruft
In seinem Innern eine treue Stimme.
Versuchen den Allheiligen willst du?
Kein Sterblicher, sprach des Orakels Mund,
Rückt diesen Schleier, bis ich selbst ihn hebe.
Doch setzte nicht derselbe Mund hinzu:
Wer diesen Schleier hebt, soll Wahrheit schauen?
„Sei hinter ihm, was will! Ich heb ihn auf—"
Er ruft's mit lauter Stimm—„Ich will sie schauen."
Schauen!
Gellt ihm ein langes Echo spottend nach.

Separated me from the truth—"
"And a law," his guide interrupts him.
"More weighty than you imagine, my son,
Is this thin gauze—for your hand
Light, to be sure, but tremendously heavy for your conscience."

The youth went home lost in thought.
The burning desire for knowledge robs him
Of sleep, he tosses feverishly on his bed
And rouses himself about midnight. To the temple
His timid steps involuntarily lead him.
It became easy for him to climb the wall,
And into the interior of the rotunda
The rash man is borne by a spirited leap.

Here he now stands, and the lifeless silence
Embraces the solitary one terrifyingly,
Broken only by the hollow echo of footsteps
In the mysterious vaults.
From above, through the opening of the cupola, the moon
Casts a pale, silvery-blue glow,
And, awesome as an actually present god,
The figure in its long veil
Shines through the darkness of the dome.

He walks forward with uncertain steps—
His impudent hand is about to touch the sacred object
When he feels hot and cold flashes in his bones
And he is pushed away by an invisible arm.
"Wretch, what do you wish to do?" Thus calls
A loyal voice within him.
"Do you wish to tempt the sacrosanct one?
'No mortal,' said the lips of the oracle,
'Moves this veil until I myself lift it.' "
"But did not those same lips add:
'Whoever lifts this veil shall behold truth?'
No matter what is behind it, I will lift it—"
He cries in a loud voice—"I want to behold it."
"Behold it!"
Shrilly respons a long echo mockingly.

Er spricht's und hat den Schleier aufgedeckt.
Nun, fragt ihr, und was zeigte sich ihm hier?
Ich weiß es nicht. Besinnungslos und bleich,
So fanden ihn am andern Tag die Priester
Am Fußgestell der Isis ausgestreckt.
Was er allda gesehen und erfahren,
Hat seine Zunge nie bekannt. Auf ewig
War seines Lebens Heiterkeit dahin,
Ihn riß ein tiefer Gram zum frühen Grabe.
„Weh dem", dies war sein warnungsvolles Wort,
Wenn ungestüme Frager in ihn drangen,
„Weh dem, der zu der Wahrheit geht durch Schuld!
Sie wird ihm nimmermehr erfreulich sein."

## Pegasus im Joche

Auf einen Pferdemarkt—vielleicht zu Haymarket,
Wo andre Dinge noch in Ware sich verwandeln—
Bracht einst ein hungriger Poet
Der Musen Roß, es zu verhandeln.

Hell wieherte der Hippogryph
Und bäumte sich in prächtiger Parade,
Erstaunt blieb jeder stehn und rief:
Das edle, königliche Tier! Nur schade,
Daß seinen schlanken Wuchs ein häßlich Flügelpaar
Entstellt! Den schönsten Postzug würd es zieren.
Die Rasse, sagen sie, sei rar,
Doch wer wird durch die Luft kutschieren?
Und keiner will sein Geld verlieren.
Ein Pachter endlich faßte Mut.
Die Flügel zwar, spricht er, die schaffen keinen Nutzen;
Doch die kann man ja binden oder stutzen,
Dann ist das Pferd zum Ziehen immer gut.
Ein zwanzig Pfund, die will ich wohl dran wagen.
Der Täuscher, hochvergnügt, die Ware loszuschlagen,
Schlägt hurtig ein. Ein Mann, ein Wort!
Und Hans trabt frisch mit seiner Beute fort.

He speaks the words and has already removed the veil.
Now, you ask, and what met his gaze here?
I do not know. Senseless and pale,
Thus the priests found him the next day
Stretched out at the base of Isis' statue.
What he saw and experienced there
His tongue never confessed. Forever
The serenity of his life was gone;
A deep sorrow snatched him to an early grave.
"Woe to him," this was his cautionary word,
When impetuous questioners urged him to speak,
"Woe to him who approaches the truth through guilt!
It will never bring him joy."


## Pegasus Yoked

To a horse fair—perhaps in Haymarket,
Where other things as well are converted into merchandise—
A hungry poet once brought
The Muses' steed, in order to sell it.

Brightly the hippogriff[6] whinnied
And reared up splendidly when reined in;
Everyone was amazed and cried:
"The noble, royal animal! But it's a shame
That an ugly pair of wings disfigures
His slender shape! He would adorn the most beautiful post coach.
They say the breed is rare,
But who is going to coach through the air?"
And no one wants to lose his money.
A farmer finally worked up courage.
"To be sure, the wings," he says, "give no benefit;
But they can of course be tied or clipped,
Then the horse is always good as a draft animal.
Twenty pounds I am ready to risk on it."
The dealer, extremely contented to get rid of the merchandise,
Agrees rapidly. It's a deal!
And John trots briskly away with his booty.

---

[6]Pegasus was a winged horse, not strictly a hippogriff, which was a combination of horse and griffin.

Das edle Tier wird eingespannt.
Doch fühlt es kaum die ungewohnte Bürde,
So rennt es fort mit wilder Flugbegierde
Und wirft, von edelm Grimm entbrannt,
Den Karren um an eines Abgrunds Rand.
Schon gut, denkt Hans. Allein darf ich dem tollen Tiere
Kein Fuhrwerk mehr vertraun. Erfahrung macht schon klug.
Doch morgen fahr ich Passagiere,
Da stell ich es als Vorspann in den Zug.
Die muntre Krabbe soll zwei Pferde mir ersparen—
Der Koller gibt sich mit den Jahren.

Der Anfang ging ganz gut. Das leichtbeschwingte Pferd
Belebt der Klepper Schritt, und pfeilschnell fliegt der Wagen.
Doch was geschieht? Den Blick den Wolken zugekehrt
Und ungewohnt, den Grund mit festem Huf zu schlagen,
Verläßt es bald der Räder sichre Spur,
Und treu der stärkeren Natur
Durchrennt es Sumpf und Moor, geackert Feld und Hecken;
Der gleiche Taumel faßt das ganze Postgespann,
Kein Rufen hilft, kein Zügel hält es an,
Bis endlich, zu der Wandrer Schrecken,
Der Wagen, wohlgerüttelt und zerschellt,
Auf eines Berges steilem Gipfel hält.

Das geht nicht zu mit rechten Dingen,
Spricht Hans mit sehr bedenklichem Gesicht.
So wird es nimmermehr gelingen;
Laß sehn, ob wir den Tollwurm nicht
Durch magre Kost und Arbeit zwingen.
Die Probe wird gemacht. Bald ist das schöne Tier,
Eh noch drei Tage hingeschwunden,
Zum Schatten abgezehrt. Ich hab's, ich hab's gefunden!
Ruft Hans. Jetzt frisch, und spannt es mir
Gleich vor den Pflug mit meinem stärksten Stier!

Gesagt, getan. In lächerlichem Zuge
Erblickt man Ochs und Flügelpferd am Pfluge.
Unwillig steigt der Greif und strengt die letzte Macht
Der Sehnen an, den alten Flug zu nehmen.
Umsonst, der Nachbar schreitet mit Bedacht,

The noble animal is put between the traces.
But as soon as it feels the unaccustomed burden,
It dashes away with a wild desire to fly
And, inflamed by noble wrath, it overturns
The cart at the edge of a precipice.
"Fine," thinks John. "But I can no longer entrust
Any wagon to this crazy animal. Experience makes you smart.
But tomorrow I'm driving passengers,
Then I'll place it among the team as an extra horse.
The lively imp will spare me two other horses—
His mad fits will get better as years go by."

The beginning went quite well. The light-winged horse
Enlivens the pace of the nags, and the coach flies as swiftly as an arrow.
But what happens? His gaze turned toward the clouds,
And unused to strike the ground with a solid hoof,
He soon abandons the safe track of the wheels
And, true to his more vigorous nature,
He races through swamp and moor, plowed fields and hedges;
The same wildness seizes on the entire team of the post coach;
No shouting helps, no reins hold it back,
Until finally, to the horror of the travelers,
The coach, well shaken and wrecked,
Halts on the steep top of a mountain.

"There's something uncanny here,"
Says John with a very serious expression.
"It will never work out this way;
Let me see if we can't subdue this lunatic
By underfeeding and labor."
The test is made. Soon the beautiful animal,
Before even three days have elapsed,
Is as emaciated as a shadow. "I have it, I have found the way!"
Cries John. "Quickly now, yoke it
Right to the plow along with my strongest ox!"

No sooner said than done. As a ridiculous team
Ox and winged horse are seen pulling the plow.
Unwillingly the griffin climbs and strains the last strength
Of his sinews to take flight as of old.
In vain; his neighbor walks deliberately,

Und Phöbus' stolzes Roß muß sich dem Stier bequemen,
Bis nun, vom langen Widerstand verzehrt,
Die Kraft aus allen Gliedern schwindet,
Von Gram gebeugt das edle Götterpferd
Zu Boden stürzt und sich im Staube windet.

Verwünschtes Tier! bricht endlich Hansens Grimm
Laut scheltend aus, indem die Hiebe flogen.
So bist du denn zum Ackern selbst zu schlimm,
Mich hat ein Schelm mit dir betrogen.

Indem er noch in seines Zornes Wut
Die Peitsche schwingt, kommt flink und wohlgemut
Ein lustiger Gesell die Straße hergezogen.
Die Zither klingt in seiner leichten Hand
Und durch den blonden Schmuck der Haare
Schlingt zierlich sich ein goldnes Band.
Wohin, Freund, mit dem wunderlichen Paare?
Ruft er den Bau'r von weitem an.
Der Vogel und der Ochs an *einem* Seile,
Ich bitte dich, welch ein Gespann!
Willst du auf eine kleine Weile
Dein Pferd zur Probe mir vertraun,
Gib acht, du sollst dein Wunder schaun.

Der Hippogryph wird ausgespannt,
Und lächelnd schwingt sich ihm der Jüngling auf den Rücken.
Kaum fühlt das Tier des Meisters sichre Hand,
So knirscht es in des Zügels Band
Und steigt, und Blitze sprühn aus den beseelten Blicken.
Nicht mehr das vor'ge Wesen, königlich,
Ein Geist, ein Gott, erhebt es sich,
Entrollt mit einem Mal in Sturmes Wehen
Der Schwingen Pracht, schießt brausend himmelan—
Und eh der Blick ihm folgen kann,
Entschwebt es zu den blauen Höhen.

And Phoebus' proud steed must suit his pace to the ox's,
Until now, exhausted by his long resistance,
The strength vanishes from all his limbs;
Bowed by sorrow, the noble horse of the gods
Crashes to the ground and writhes in the dust.

"Damned animal!" John's anger finally bursts forth
In loud curses, while his blows fly.
"So you're too bad even for plowing;
A scoundrel palmed you off on me."

While, in the fury of his wrath, he is still
Swinging the whip, a cheerful fellow
Comes nimbly and merrily down the road.
A lyre resounds under his deft fingers,
And through the blonde hair that adorns him
A golden ribbon is decoratively wound.
"Where to, my friend, with that strange team?"
He calls to the farmer from a distance.
"A bird and an ox tied with one rope—
I ask you, what a combination!
If you are willing for a little while
To trust me with your horse for a trial,
Pay attention, you will be astonished."

The hippogriff is released from the yoke.
And, smiling, the youth vaults onto his back.
The moment the animal feels his master's sure hand,
He champs on the closure of the bit
And rises, and lightning flashes from his animated glances.
No longer the former creature, but royal,
A spirit, a god, he lifts himself up,
All at once like a storm wind unfurls
The splendor of his pinions, shoots heavenward thunderously—
And, before one's gaze can follow him,
He soars away into the blue heights.

## Das Mädchen aus der Fremde

In einem Tal bei armen Hirten
Erschien mit jedem jungen Jahr,
Sobald die ersten Lerchen schwirrten,
Ein Mädchen, schön und wunderbar.

Sie war nicht in dem Tal geboren,
Man wußte nicht, woher sie kam,
Und schnell war ihre Spur verloren,
Sobald das Mädchen Abschied nahm.

Beseligend war ihre Nähe,
Und alle Herzen wurden weit,
Doch eine Würde, eine Höhe
Entfernte die Vertraulichkeit.

Sie brachte Blumen mit und Früchte,
Gereift auf einer andern Flur,
In einem andern Sonnenlichte,
In einer glücklichern Natur.

Und teilte jedem eine Gabe,
Dem Früchte, jenem Blumen aus,
Der Jüngling und der Greis am Stabe,
Ein jeder ging beschenkt nach Haus.

Willkommen waren alle Gäste,
Doch nahte sich ein liebend Paar,
Dem reichte sie der Gaben beste,
Der Blumen allerschönste dar.

## Dithyrambe

Nimmer, das glaubt mir, erscheinen die Götter,
Nimmer allein!
Kaum daß ich Bacchus den lustigen habe,

## The Girl from a Strange Land

In a valley among poor shepherds
There appeared every spring,
As soon as the first larks whirred,
A girl, beautiful and strange.

She was not born in the valley,
No one knew where she came from,
And her track was quickly lost
As soon as the girl took her leave.

Her presence was exhilarating,
And everyone's heart expanded,
But her dignity, her majesty
Made familiarity impossible.

She brought along flowers and fruits,
Ripened on another soil,
Under another sunlight,
Amid a more benevolent nature.

And she distributed a gift to everyone,
Fruits to this person, flowers to that;
The youth and the old man leaning on a staff,
All went home with a present.

All guests were welcome,
But if a loving couple approached,
She would hand them the best of her gifts,
The very loveliest of her flowers.

## Dithyramb

Never, believe me, never do the gods appear
Alone!
No sooner do I have jolly Bacchus[7]

---

[7]The significant identifications for this poem are: Bacchus = wine, Amor = love, Hebe = cupbearer of the gods.

Kommt auch schon Amor, der lächelnde Knabe,
Phöbus der herrliche findet sich ein.
Sie nahen, sie kommen, die Himmlischen alle,
Mit Göttern erfüllt sich die irdische Halle.

Sagt, wie bewirt ich, der Erdegeborne,
Himmlischen Chor?
Schenket mir euer unsterbliches Leben,
Götter! Was kann euch der Sterbliche geben?
Hebet zu eurem Olymp mich empor!
Die Freude, sie wohnt nur in Jupiters Saale,
O füllet mit Nektar, o reicht mir die Schale!

Reich ihm die Schale! Schenke dem Dichter,
Hebe, nur ein!
Netz ihm die Augen mit himmlischem Taue,
Daß er den Styx, den verhaßten, nicht schaue,
Einer der Unsern sich dünke zu sein.
Sie rauschet, sie perlet, die himmlische Quelle,
Der Busen wird ruhig, das Auge wird helle.

## Hoffnung

Es reden und träumen die Menschen viel
Von bessern künftigen Tagen,
Nach einem glücklichen, goldenen Ziel
Sieht man sie rennen und jagen;
Die Welt wird alt und wird wieder jung,
Doch der Mensch hofft immer Verbesserung.

Die Hoffnung führt ihn ins Leben ein,
Sie umflattert den fröhlichen Knaben,
Den Jüngling locket ihr Zauberschein,
Sie wird mit dem Greis nicht begraben;
Denn beschließt er im Grabe den müden Lauf,
Noch am Grabe pflanzt er—die Hoffnung auf.

Than Amor, the smiling boy, already comes,
And majestic Phoebus arrives as well.
    They approach, they come, all the divinities,
    My earthly hall is filled with gods.

Tell me, how shall I, the earthling,
Entertain a heavenly choir?
Bestow on me your immortal life,
Gods! What can the mortal give you?
Raise me up to your Olympus!
    Joy dwells only in Jupiter's hall;
    Oh, fill the goblet with nectar and hand it to me!

Hand him the goblet! Pour for the poet,
Hebe!
Moisten his eyes with heavenly dew,
So that he does not behold the hated Styx,[8]
And so he imagines he is one of our company.
    It murmurs, it pearls, the heavenly fountain,
    The bosom grows calm, the eye grows bright.


## Hope

People speak and dream a great deal
About better days in the future,
You see them running and chasing
After a happy, golden goal;
The world grows old and grows young again,
But man always hopes for betterment.

Hope introduces him to life,
It hovers around the merry boy,
Its magical glow tempts the youth,
It is not buried with the old man;
For, if he ends his weary course in the grave,
Even at the grave he plants—hope.

---

[8]River of the underworld.

Es ist kein leerer schmeichelnder Wahn,
Erzeugt im Gehirne des Toren,
Im Herzen kündet es laut sich an:
Zu was Besserm sind wir geboren.
Und was die innere Stimme spricht,
Das täuscht die hoffende Seele nicht.

## Nänie

Auch das Schöne muß sterben! Das Menschen und Götter bezwinget,
  Nicht die eherne Brust rührt es des stygischen Zeus.
Einmal nur erweichte die Liebe den Schattenbeherrscher,
  Und an der Schwelle noch, streng, rief er zurück sein Geschenk.
Nicht stillt Aphrodite dem schönen Knaben die Wunde,
  Die in den zierlichen Leib grausam der Eber geritzt.
Nicht errettet den göttlichen Held die unsterbliche Mutter,
  Wann er, am skäischen Tor fallend, sein Schicksal erfüllt.
Aber sie steigt aus dem Meer mit allen Töchtern des Nereus,
  Und die Klage hebt an um den verherrlichten Sohn.
Siehe, da weinen die Götter, es weinen die Göttinnen alle,
  Daß das Schöne vergeht, daß das Vollkommene stirbt.
Auch ein Klaglied zu sein im Mund der Geliebten, ist herrlich,
  Denn das Gemeine geht klanglos zum Orkus hinab.


## Sehnsucht

Ach, aus dieses Tales Gründen,
Die der kalte Nebel drückt,
Könnt ich doch den Ausgang finden,

This is no empty, flattering delusion
Generated in a fool's brain,
It manifests itself loudly in our heart:
We were born for something better.
And what the inner voice says
Does not deceive the soul that hopes.

## Dirge

Even the beautiful must die! That which conquers men and gods
    Does not touch the brazen heart of Stygian Zeus.[9]
Only once did love soften the ruler of the shades,
    And still at the threshold, in his severity, he revoked his gift.[10]
Aphrodite cannot stanch the beautiful lad's[11] wound,
    Which the boar cruelly tore into his graceful body.
The immortal mother[12] cannot save the divine hero
    When, falling at the Scaean gate, he fulfills his destiny.
But she arises from the sea with all the daughters of Nereus
    And begins her lament for her exalted son.
See! Then the gods weep, all the goddesses weep
    Because the beautiful perishes, because perfection dies.
Even to be a song of woe on loved ones' lips is splendid,
    For what is commonplace descends to Orcus[13] in silence.

## Longing

Ah, if I could only find the way out
Of the depths of this valley,
Which is oppressed by chilly fog,

---

[9]That is, Hades or Pluto, the supreme ruler ("Zeus") of the underworld, where the river Styx flows.

[10]Eurydice was restored to Orpheus but had to return to the underworld because he looked back at her.

[11]Her lover Adonis, killed while hunting.

[12]Thetis, a sea nymph, daughter of Nereus, was the mother of Achilles, who was killed in the Trojan War.

[13]The underworld.

Ach wie fühlt ich mich beglückt!
Dort erblick ich schöne Hügel,
Ewig jung und ewig grün!
Hätt ich Schwingen, hätt ich Flügel,
Nach den Hügeln zög ich hin.

Harmonien hör ich klingen,
Töne süßer Himmelsruh,
Und die leichten Winde bringen
Mir der Düfte Balsam zu,
Goldne Früchte seh ich glühen,
Winkend zwischen dunkelm Laub,
Und die Blumen, die dort blühen,
Werden keines Winters Raub.

Ach wie schön muß sich's ergehen
Dort im ew'gen Sonnenschein,
Und die Luft auf jenen Höhen,
O wie labend muß sie sein!
Doch mir wehrt des Stromes Toben,
Der ergrimmt dazwischen braust,
Seine Wellen sind gehoben,
Daß die Seele mir ergraust.

Einen Nachen seh ich schwanken,
Aber ach! der Fährmann fehlt.
Frisch hinein und ohne Wanken!
Seine Segel sind beseelt.
Du mußt glauben, du mußt wagen,
Denn die Götter leihn kein Pfand,
Nur ein Wunder kann dich tragen
In das schöne Wunderland.

Ah, how fortunate I would feel!
Over there I can see lovely hills,
Eternally young and eternally green!
If I had pinions, if I had wings,
I would travel to those hills.

I hear harmonies sounding,
Tones of sweet, heavenly repose,
And the gentle breezes waft
Balmy fragrances toward me.
I see golden fruits gleaming,
Beckoning amid the dark foliage,
And the flowers that bloom there
Do not fall prey to any winter.

Ah, how beautiful the life must be
There in the eternal sunshine,
And the air on those heights,
Oh, how refreshing it must be!
But I am blocked by the raging of the stream
That furiously roars in between;
Its waters have risen so high
That my soul is frightened.

I see a boat tossing,
But, alas, the ferryman is gone.
Into it briskly and without hesitation!
Its sails are full of life.
You must believe, you must take chances,
For the gods make no pledge;
Only a miracle can carry you
Into the beautiful land of miracles.

# Friedrich Hölderlin

## Die Eichbäume

Aus den Gärten komm ich zu euch, ihr Söhne des Berges!
Aus den Gärten, da lebt die Natur geduldig und häuslich,
Pflegend und wieder gepflegt mit dem fleißigen Menschen zusammen.
Aber ihr, ihr Herrlichen! steht, wie ein Volk von Titanen
In der zahmeren Welt und gehört nur euch und dem Himmel,
Der euch nährt' und erzog, und der Erde, die euch geboren.
Keiner von euch ist noch in die Schule der Menschen gegangen,
Und ihr drängt euch fröhlich und frei, aus der kräftigen Wurzel,
Unter einander herauf und ergreift, wie der Adler die Beute,
Mit gewaltigem Arme den Raum, und gegen die Wolken
Ist euch heiter und groß die sonnige Krone gerichtet.
Eine Welt ist jeder von euch, wie die Sterne des Himmels
Lebt ihr, jeder ein Gott, in freiem Bunde zusammen.
Könnt ich die Knechtschaft nur erdulden, ich neidete nimmer
Diesen Wald und schmiegte mich gern ans gesellige Leben.
Fesselte nur nicht mehr ans gesellige Leben das Herz mich,
Das von Liebe nicht läßt, wie gern würd ich unter euch wohnen!

## Diotima

Leuchtest du wie vormals nieder,
Goldner Tag! und sprossen mir
Des Gesanges Blumen wieder
Lebenatmend auf zu dir?
Wie so anders ists geworden!
Manches, was ich trauernd mied,
Stimmt in freundlichen Akkorden
Nun in meiner Freude Lied,
Und mit jedem Stundenschlage
Werd ich wunderbar gemahnt
An der Kindheit stille Tage,
Seit ich Sie, die Eine, fand.

# Friedrich Hölderlin

## *The Oak Trees*

Out of the gardens I come to you, you sons of the mountain!
From the gardens where Nature lives patiently and domestically,
Nurturing and nurtured in turn, together with industrious mankind.
But you, you splendid beings, stand like a nation of Titans
In the tamer world, and belong only to yourselves and to the sky
That nourished you and raised you, and to the earth that bore you.
None of you has yet gone to a human school
And you thrust yourselves upward among one another, happy and free,
From your vigorous roots, and, as the eagle seizes its prey,
You seize space with powerful arms, and toward the clouds
Your sunny tops are pointed serenely and majestically.
Each one of you is a world; you live like the stars
In the sky, each one a god, together in a free association.
If only I could endure servitude, I would never envy
This forest and would gladly adapt myself to the life of society.
If only my heart did not chain me to the life of society any longer,
My heart that will not leave off loving, how gladly would I dwell among
    you!

## *Diotima*

Are you shining down as you used to,
Golden day? And are the flowers of my song
Again shooting
Upward toward you, breathing life?
How very different it has become!
Many a thing I once mournfully shunned
Now harmonizes in friendly chords
In the song of my joy,
And with the stroke of every hour
I am wondrously reminded
Of the quiet days of childhood,
Ever since I found *her*, the one and only.

Diotima! edles Leben!
Schwester, heilig mir verwandt!
Eh ich dir die Hand gegeben,
Hab ich ferne dich gekannt.
Damals schon, da ich in Träumen,
Mir entlockt vom heitern Tag,
Unter meines Gartens Bäumen,
Ein zufriedner Knabe, lag,
Da in leiser Lust und Schöne
Meiner Seele Mai begann:
Säuselte, wie Zephirstöne,
Göttliche! dein Geist mich an.

Ach! und da, wie eine Sage,
Jeder frohe Gott mir schwand,
Da ich vor des Himmels Tage
Darbend, wie ein Blinder, stand,
Da die Last der Zeit mich beugte,
Und mein Leben, kalt und bleich,
Sehnend schon hinab sich neigte
In der Toten stummes Reich:
Wünscht ich öfters noch, dem blinden
Wanderer, dies Eine mir,
Meines Herzens Bild zu finden
Bei den Schatten oder hier.

Nun! ich habe dich gefunden!
Schöner, als ich ahnend sah,
Hoffend in den Feierstunden,
Holde Muse! bist du da;
Von den Himmlischen dort oben,
Wo hinauf die Freude flieht,
Wo, des Alterns überhoben,
Immerheitre Schöne blüht,
Scheinst du mir herabgestiegen,
Götterbotin! weiltest du
Nun in gütigem Genügen
Bei dem Sänger immerzu.

Sommerglut und Frühlingsmilde,
Streit und Friede wechselt hier

Diotima! Noble being!
Sister, sacredly related to me!
Before I gave you my hand
I knew you from afar.
As early as the time when, in dreams
Elicited from me by the serene day,
I lay, a contented boy,
Beneath the trees in my garden,
When with quiet pleasure and beauty
The Maytime of my soul began—
Divine one! your spirit
Murmured to me like the tones of the west wind.

Ah! and then, like a legend,
All happy gods disappeared from my view,
When I stood before heaven's daylight
Living in want like a blind man;
When the burden of time bowed me down,
And my life, cold and pale,
Was already descending longingly
Into the mute realm of the dead—
I still often wished this one boon
For myself, the blind wanderer,
To find the image of my heart
Among the shades or here.

Now I have found you!
Lovelier than I foresaw
In my hopes during idle hours,
You are here, fair Muse!
From the heavenly gods in the realm above,
To which joy ascends,
Where, exempt from growing old,
Eternally serene beauty blossoms,
You seem to have come down to me,
Messenger of the gods! even though you have remained
In benevolent fulfillment
Beside your poet all the while.

Summer's heat and springtime's mildness,
Conflict and peace alternate here

Vor dem stillen Götterbilde
Wunderbar im Busen mir;
Zürnend unter Huldigungen
Hab ich oft, beschämt, besiegt,
Sie zu fassen schon gerungen,
Die mein Kühnstes überfliegt;
Unzufrieden im Gewinne,
Hab ich stolz darob geweint,
Daß zu herrlich meinem Sinne
Und zu mächtig sie erscheint.

Ach! an deine stille Schöne,
Seligholdes Angesicht!
Herz! an deine Himmelstöne
Ist gewohnt das meine nicht;
Aber deine Melodien
Heitern mählich mir den Sinn,
Daß die trüben Träume fliehen,
Und ich selbst ein andrer bin.
Bin ich dazu denn erkoren?
Ich, zu deiner hohen Ruh,
So zu Licht und Lust geboren,
Göttlich Glückliche! wie du?—

Wie dein Vater und der meine,
Der in heitrer Majestät
Über seinem Eichenhaine
Dort in lichter Höhe geht,
Wie er in die Meereswogen,
Wo die kühle Tiefe blaut,
Steigend an des Himmels Bogen,
Klar und still herunterschaut:
So will ich aus Götterhöhen,
Neugeweiht in schönrem Glück,
Froh, zu singen und zu sehen,
Nun zu Sterblichen zurück.

Wondrously in my heart
In front of the silent divine image;
Angry in the midst of homages,
Shamed, conquered, I have often
Struggled to grasp the woman
Who surpasses my boldest imaginings;
Discontented though a winner,
I have wept in my pride
Because she appeared to my mind
To be too splendid and too mighty.

Ah! To your quiet beauty,
Blissfully fair countenance;
Dear heart, to your heavenly tones
My own heart is not accustomed;
But your melodies
Gradually make my mind serene,
So that my gloomy dreams flee,
And I myself am another man.
Have I, then, been chosen for this?
Divinely fortunate one, was I born,
Like you, for your sublime repose,
For such light and pleasure?

Just as your father and mine,[14]
Who in serene majesty
Is proceeding there high up in the brightness
Over his grove of oaks;
Just as, ascending the bow of heaven,
He looks down in clarity and silence
Into the waves of the sea,
Where the cool depths run blue—
Thus will I from divine heights,
Newly consecrated in a lovelier fortune,
Happy, to sing and to see,
Now return to mortals.

---

[14]The sky and sun god.

## An die Parzen

Nur Einen Sommer gönnt, ihr Gewaltigen!
  Und Einen Herbst zu reifem Gesange mir,
    Daß williger mein Herz, vom süßen
      Spiele gesättiget, dann mir sterbe!

Die Seele, der im Leben ihr göttlich Recht
  Nicht ward, sie ruht auch drunten im Orkus nicht;
    Doch ist mir einst das Heil'ge, das am
      Herzen mir liegt, das Gedicht, gelungen,

Willkommen dann, o Stille der Schattenwelt!
  Zufrieden bin ich, wenn auch mein Saitenspiel
    Mich nicht hinabgeleitet; Einmal
      Lebt ich, wie Götter, und mehr bedarf's nicht.


## Menschenbeifall

Ist nicht heilig mein Herz, schöneren Lebens voll,
  Seit ich liebe? warum achtetet ihr mich mehr,
    Da ich stolzer und wilder,
      Wortereicher und leerer war?

Ach! der Menge gefällt, was auf den Marktplatz taugt,
  Und es ehret der Knecht nur den Gewaltsamen;
    An das Göttliche glauben
      Die allein, die es selber sind.


## Sokrates und Alkibiades

„Warum huldigest du, heiliger Sokrates,
  Diesem Jünglinge stets? Kennest du Größers nicht?
    Warum siehet mit Liebe,
      Wie auf Götter, dein Aug auf ihn?“

## To the Fates

Grant me only one summer, you mighty ones!
   And one autumn for ripened song,
     So that my heart, sated with the sweet
      Music, may then die more willingly!

The soul that in life did not receive
   Its divine due does not rest even below in Orcus;[15]
     But if I once accomplish the sacred thing that
      My heart is set on—the poem—

Welcome, then, O silence of the world of shades!
   I am satisfied even if my lyre
     Does not accompany me below; once
      I lived like gods, and no more is needed.

## People's Approval

Is my heart not holy, full of more beautiful life,
   Since I am in love? Why did you esteem me more
     When I was prouder and wilder,
      More verbose and emptier?

Alas! The crowd likes what is suitable for the marketplace,
   And the servant honors only the violent man;
     Only those believe in the divine
      Who are themselves divine.

## Socrates and Alcibiades [16]

"Why, holy Socrates, do you pay homage
   To this youth constantly? Do you not know anything greater?
     Why do your eyes look upon him
      With love, as upon gods?"

---

[15]The underworld.

[16]The Athenian philosopher and the playboy-adventurer of whom he was fond.

Wer das Tiefste gedacht, liebt das Lebendigste.
Hohe Tugend versteht, wer in die Welt geblickt,
Und es neigen die Weisen
Oft am Ende zu Schönem sich.

## Hyperions Schicksalslied

Ihr wandelt droben im Licht
Auf weichem Boden, selige Genien!
Glänzende Götterlüfte
Rühren euch leicht,
Wie die Finger der Künstlerin
Heilige Saiten.

Schicksallos, wie der schlafende
Säugling, atmen die Himmlischen;
Keusch bewahrt
In bescheidener Knospe,
Blühet ewig
Ihnen der Geist,
Und die seligen Augen
Blicken in stiller
Ewiger Klarheit.

Doch uns ist gegeben,
Auf keiner Stätte zu ruhn,
Es schwinden, es fallen
Die leidenden Menschen
Blindlings von einer
Stunde zur andern,
Wie Wasser von Klippe
Zu Klippe geworfen,
Jahrlang ins Ungewisse hinab.

He who has thought most deeply loves what is most vital;
He who has looked into the world understands lofty virtue,[17]
And wise men often incline
Toward the beautiful at the last.


## Hyperion's Song of Destiny

You walk up there in the light
Upon soft ground, blessed genii!
Gleaming divine breezes
Touch you gently,
As the fingers of the woman musician
Touch sacred strings.

Without destiny, like the sleeping
Infant, the heavenly ones breathe;
Preserved chastely
In a modest bud,
Their spirit
Blossoms eternally,
And there blessed eyes
Gaze in tranquil,
Eternal clarity.

But is it our lot
To find rest nowhere;
Suffering mankind
Wastes away, falls
Blindly from one
Hour to the next,
Like water hurled from crag
To crag,
For years and years down into uncertainty.

---

[17]Some editions read "Jugend" for "Tugend"; thus, "understands the nobility of youth."

## *"Da ich ein Knabe war"*

Da ich ein Knabe war,
    Rettet' ein Gott mich oft
    Vom Geschrei und der Rute der Menschen,
    Da spielt ich sicher und gut
    Mit den Blumen des Hains,
    Und die Lüftchen des Himmels
    Spielten mit mir.

Und wie du das Herz
Der Pflanzen erfreust,
Wenn sie entgegen dir
Die zarten Arme strecken,

So hast du mein Herz erfreut,
Vater Helios! und wie Endymion
War ich dein Liebling
Heilige Luna!

O all ihr treuen
Freundlichen Götter!
Daß ihr wüßtet,
Wie euch meine Seele geliebt!

Zwar damals rief ich noch nicht
Euch mit Namen, auch ihr
Nanntet mich nie, wie die Menschen sich nennen,
Als kennten sie sich.

Doch kannt ich euch besser,
Als ich je die Menschen gekannt,
Ich verstand die Stille des Äthers,
Der Menschen Worte verstand ich nie.

Mich erzog der Wohllaut
Des säuselnden Hains,
Und lieben lernt ich
Unter den Blumen.

Im Arme der Götter wuchs ich groß.

## "When I was a boy"

When I was a boy
A god often saved me
From the shouting and the rod of people;
Then I played safely and well
With the flowers of the grove,
And the breezes of the sky
Played with me.

And just as you delight
The heart of plants
When they stretch
Their tender arms toward you,

Thus you delighted my heart,
Father Helios![18] And like Endymion
I was your beloved,
Sacred Luna![19]

O all you faithful,
Friendly gods!
I wish you knew
How my soul loved you!

To be sure, at the time I did not yet call
You by name, you too
Never named me the way people name one another,
As if they knew one another.

But I knew you better
Than I ever knew people;
I understood the silence of the heavens,
I never understood the words of people.

I was raised by the euphony
Of the rustling grove,
And I learned to love
Amid the flowers.

In the arm of the gods I grew to manhood.

---

[18] The sun god.
[19] The moon goddess (in Greek, Selene), who loved the young shepherd Endymion.

## Hälfte des Lebens

Mit gelben Birnen hänget
Und voll mit wilden Rosen
Das Land in den See,
Ihr holden Schwäne,
Und trunken von Küssen
Tunkt ihr das Haupt
Ins heilignüchterne Wasser.

Weh mir, wo nehm ich, wenn
Es Winter ist, die Blumen, und wo
Den Sonnenschein,
Und Schatten der Erde?
Die Mauern stehn
Sprachlos und kalt, im Winde
Klirren die Fahnen.

## "Die Linien des Lebens sind verschieden"

Die Linien des Lebens sind verschieden,
Wie Wege sind und wie der Berge Grenzen.
Was hier wir sind, kann dort ein Gott ergänzen
Mit Harmonien und ewigem Lohn und Frieden.

## Halfway Through Life

With yellow pears
And full of wild roses,
The land overhangs the lake,
You lovely swans,
And, intoxicated with kisses,
You dip your heads
Into the sacred sober water.

Woe is me, when it is winter,
Where will I get the flowers, and where
The sunshine,
And the earth's shade?
The walls stand
Speechless and cold, in the wind
The weather vanes clatter.

## "The lines of life are varied" [20]

The lines of life are varied,
As roads are, and as the boundaries of the mountains.
What we are here, a god can supplement there
With harmonies and eternal reward and peace.

---

[20]In some editions, this poem bears the title "An Zimmern" (To Zimmer [his host for many of the years of his mental illness] ).

# Novalis (Friedrich von Hardenberg)

### *"Muß immer der Morgen wiederkommen?"*

Muß immer der Morgen wiederkommen?
Endet nie des Irdischen Gewalt?
Unselige Geschäftigkeit verzehrt
Den himmlischen Anflug der Nacht?
Wird nie der Liebe geheimes Opfer
Ewig brennen?
Zugemessen ward
Dem Lichte seine Zeit
Und dem Wachen—
Aber zeitlos ist der Nacht Herrschaft,
Ewig ist die Dauer des Schlafs.
Heiliger Schlaf!
Beglücke zu selten nicht
Der Nacht geweihte—
In diesem irdischen Tagwerk.
Nur die Toren verkennen dich
Und wissen von keinem Schlafe
Als dem Schatten,
Den du mitleidig auf uns wirfst
In jener Dämmrung
Der wahrhaften Nacht.
Sie fühlen dich nicht
In der golden Flut der Trauben,
In des Mandelbaums
Wunderöl
Und dem braunen Safte des Mohns.
Sie wissen nicht,
Daß du es bist,
Der des zarten Mädchens
Busen umschwebt
Und zum Himmel den Schoß macht—
Ahnden nicht,
Daß aus alten Geschichten
Du himmelöffnend entgegentrittst

# Novalis (Friedrich von Hardenberg)

## *"Must the morning always return?"*

Must the morning always return?
Will the power of the earthbound never end?
Must the accursed bustle of business consume
The heavenly approach of the night?
Will love's secret sacrifice never
Burn eternally?
Light
And wakefulness
Had their time allotted to them—
But the sovereignity of the night is timeless,
The duration of sleep is eternal.
Holy sleep!
Do not bring happiness too seldom
To those who are devoted to the night—
In this earthly daily round.
Only fools fail to recognize you
And know of no sleep
But the shadow
That you compassionately cast upon us
In that twilight
Of the genuine night.
They do not feel you
In the golden blood of grapes,
In the almond tree's
Wondrous oil
And the brown juice of the poppy.
They do not know
That it is you
Who hover around the bosom
Of the tender girl
And make her lap a heaven—
They are unaware
That out of old stories
You step forth to meet us, opening up heaven,

Und den Schlüssel trägst
Zu den Wohnungen der seligen,
Unendlicher Geheimnisse
Schweigender Bote.

## "Hinüber wall ich"

Hinüber wall ich,
Und jede Pein
Wird einst ein Stachel
Der Wollust sein.
Noch wenig Zeiten,
So bin ich los,
Und liege trunken
Der Lieb' im Schoß.
Unendliches Leben
Wogt mächtig in mir
Ich schaue von oben
Herunter nach dir.
An jenem Hügel
Verlischt dein Glanz—
Ein Schatten bringet
Den kühlenden Kranz.
O! sauge, Geliebter,
Gewaltig mich an,
Daß ich entschlummern
Und lieben kann.
Ich fühle des Todes
Verjüngende Flut,
Zu Balsam und Äther
Verwandelt mein Blut—
Ich lebe bei Tage
Voll Glauben und Mut
Und sterbe die Nächte
In heiliger Glut.

And that you carry the key
To the dwelling places of the blessed,
A silent messenger
Bearing infinite secrets.


## "*I am journeying over*"

I am journeying over,
And every pain
Will one day be a pang
Of sensual pleasure.
Just a little time longer,
And I will be free,
And will lie enraptured
In the lap of love.
Unending life
Surges powerfully within me,
From above I look
Down at you.
Against that hill
Your light is extinguished—
A shade brings
The cooling garland.
O beloved, absorb me
Forcefully,
So that I can slumber off,
So that I can love.
I feel death's
Rejuvenating tide,
Into balm and ether
My blood transformed—
I live by day
Full of faith and courage
And in the nights die
In a sacred blaze.

## "Wenn ich ihn nur habe"

Wenn ich ihn nur habe,
Wenn er mein nur ist,
Wenn mein Herz bis hin zum Grabe
Seine Treue nie vergißt:
Weiß ich nichts von Leide,
Fühle nichts als Andacht, Lieb' und Freude.

Wenn ich ihn nur habe,
Lass' ich alles gern,
Folg' an meinem Wanderstabe
Treugesinnt nur meinem Herrn;
Lasse still die Andern
Breite, lichte, volle Straßen wandern.

Wenn ich ihn nur habe,
Schlaf' ich fröhlich ein,
Ewig wird zu süßer Labe
Seines Herzens Flut mir sein,
Die mit sanftem Zwingen
Alles wird erweichen und durchdringen.

Wenn ich ihn nur habe,
Hab' ich auch die Welt;
Selig wie ein Himmelsknabe,
Der der Jungfrau Schleier hält.
Hingesenkt im Schauen
Kann mir vor dem Irdischen nicht grauen.

Wo ich ihn nur habe,
Ist mein Vaterland;
Und es fällt mir jede Gabe
Wie ein Erbteil in die Hand;
Längst vermißte Brüder
Find' ich nun in seinen Jüngern wieder.

## "If only I have Him"

If only I have Him,
If only He is mine,
If my heart all the way to the grave
Never forgets His loyalty:
I know nothing of sorrow,
Feel nothing but pity, love and joy.

If only I have Him,
I gladly leave all else;
Leaning on my traveler's staff, I follow
Only my Lord with a faithful mind;
I calmly allow the others
To travel the broad, bright, busy roads.

If only I have Him,
I fall asleep happily;
His heart's blood will forever be
A sweet refreshment to me;
With gentle compulsion
It will soften and permeate everything.

If only I have Him,
I have the world as well;
Blessed as a heavenly boy
Who holds the Virgin's veil.
Sunk in contemplation,
I cannot be afraid of anything earthly.

Wherever I have Him
Is my homeland;
And every gift falls
Into my hand like an inheritance;
Long-lost brothers
I now find again in His disciples.

## "Wenn alle untreu werden"

Wenn alle untreu werden,
So bleib' ich dir doch treu;
Daß Dankbarkeit auf Erden
Nicht ausgestorben sei.
Für mich umfing dich Leiden,
Vergingst für mich in Schmerz;
Drum geb' ich dir mit Freuden
Auf ewig dieses Herz.

Oft muß ich bitter weinen,
Daß du gestorben bist
Und mancher von den Deinen
Dich lebenslang vergißt.
Von Liebe nur durchdrungen
Hast du so viel getan,
Und doch bist du verklungen,
Und keiner denkt daran.

Du stehst voll treuer Liebe
Noch immer jedem bei,
Und wenn dir keiner bliebe,
So bleibst du dennoch treu;
Die treuste Liebe sieget,
Am Ende fühlt man sie,
Weint bitterlich und schmieget
Sich kindlich an dein Knie.

Ich habe dich empfunden,
O! lasse nicht von mir;
Laß innig mich verbunden
Auf ewig sein mit dir.
Einst schauen meine Brüder
Auch wieder himmelwärts,
Und sinken liebend nieder,
Und fallen dir ans Herz.

## "When all become unfaithful"

When all become unfaithful,
I still remain faithful to You,
So that gratitude on earth
May not be extinct.
For me sorrow embraced You,
You perished for me in pain;
Therefore with joy I give You
This heart forever.

Often I must weep bitterly
Because You are dead
And many among Your followers
Forget You all their lives.
Only because You were saturated with love
Did You do so much,
And yet You have died away,
And no one thinks about it.

You still stand by everyone,
Full of faithful love,
And even if no one were left to You,
You nevertheless would remain faithful.
The most faithful love conquers,
People finally perceive it,
Weep bitterly and cling
Like children to Your knees.

I have felt You;
Oh, do not abandon me;
Let me eternally be
Inwardly bound to You.
One day my brothers
Will also look upward again,
And will sink down lovingly
And fall upon Your breast.

## "Wenn nicht mehr Zahlen und Figuren"

Wenn nicht mehr Zahlen und Figuren
Sind Schlüssel aller Kreaturen,
Wenn die, so singen oder küssen
Mehr als die Tiefgelehrten wissen,
Wenn sich die Welt ins freie Leben
Und in die Welt wird zurückbegeben,
Wenn dann sich wieder Licht und Schatten
Zu echter Klarheit wieder gatten
Und man in Märchen und Gedichten
Erkennt die wahren Weltgeschichten,
Dann fliegt vor *einem* geheimen Wort
Das ganze verkehrte Wesen fort.

## "Lobt doch unsre stillen Feste"

Lobt doch unsre stillen Feste,
Unsre Gärten, unsre Zimmer,
Das bequeme Hausgeräte,
User Hab' und Gut.
Täglich kommen neue Gäste,
Diese früh, die andern späte,
Auf den weiten Herden immer
Lodert neue Lebens-Glut.

Tausend zierliche Gefäße
Einst betaut mit tausend Tränen,
Goldne Ringe, Sporen, Schwerter,
Sind in unserm Schatz:
Viel Kleinodien und Juwelen
Wissen wir in dunkeln Höhlen,
Keiner kann den Reichtum zählen,
Zählt' er auch ohn' Unterlaß.

Kinder der Vergangenheiten,
Helden aus den grauen Zeiten,
Der Gestirne Riesengeister,
Wunderlich gesellt,

## "When numbers and figures no longer"

When numbers and figures no longer
Are keys to everything created,
When those who sing or kiss
Know more than the learned scholars,
When the world returns to a free life
And to the world,
When then once more light and shadow
Will couple to produce genuine clarity,
And people will recognize that the true histories of the world
Lie in fairy tales and poems,
Then at a single secret word
This whole wrongheaded existence will fly away.

## "Do praise our quiet festivities"

Do praise our quiet festivities,
Our gardens, our rooms,
The convenient household equipment,
Our property and possessions.
New guests arrive daily,
Some early, some late;
On our broad hearths there always
Flares new heat of life.

A thousand decorative vessels
Once bedewed with a thousand tears,
Golden rings, spurs, swords
Are in our treasury:
Many gems and jewels
We know of in dark caves;
No one can count our riches
Even if he were to count uninterruptedly.

Children of past ages,
Heroes of gray antiquity,
The giant spirits of the heavenly bodies,
Miraculously assembled,

Holde Frauen, ernste Meister,
Kinder und verlebte Greise
Sitzen hier in Einem Kreise,
Wohnen in der alten Welt.

Keiner wird sich je beschweren,
Keiner wünschen fortzugehen,
Wer an unsern vollen Tischen
Einmal fröhlich saß.
Klagen sind nicht mehr zu hören,
Keine Wunden mehr zu sehen,
Keine Tränen abzuwischen;
Ewig läuft das Stundenglas.

Tiefgerührt von heilger Güte
Und versenkt in selges Schauen
Steht der Himmel im Gemüte,
Wolkenloses Blau;
Lange fliegende Gewande
Tragen uns durch Frühlingsauen,
Und es weht in diesem Lande
Nie ein Lüftchen kalt und rauh.

Süßer Reiz der Mitternächte,
Stiller Kreis geheimer Mächte,
Wollust rätselhafter Spiele,
Wir nur kennen euch.
Wir nur sind am hohen Ziele,
Bald in Strom uns zu ergießen
Dann in Tropfen zu zerfließen
Und zu nippen auch zugleich.

Uns ward erst die Liebe, Leben;
Innig wie die Elemente
Mischen wir des Daseins Fluten,
Brausend Herz mit Herz.
Lüstern scheiden sich die Fluten,
Denn der Kampf der Elemente
Ist der Liebe höchstes Leben,
Und des Herzens eignes Herz.

Lovely women, serious masters,
Children and worn-out aged people
Sit here in one circle,
Dwell in the old world.

No one will ever complain,
No one will wish to leave
Who has once sat joyfully
At our full tables.
Laments are no longer to be heard,
No wounds are to be seen any more,
No tears to be wiped away;
The hourglass runs eternally.

Deeply moved by holy goodness,
And immersed in blissful contemplation,
Heaven remains in our mind,
A cloudless blue;
Long, fluttering garments
Carry us through springtime meadows,
And in this land there never blows
The slightest cold and raw wind.

Sweet charm of the midnights,
Quiet circle of secret powers,
The pleasure of mysterious games,
Only we know you.
Only we have reached the supreme goal:
First to pour ourselves out in a stream,
Then to break up into small drops,
And also to sip at the same time.

Only now has love become life for us;
Inwardly, like the elements,
We mingle the currents of existence,
Roaring heart to heart.
A prey to desire, the currents separate,
For the battle of the elements
Is the highest life of love,
And the heart's own heart.

Leiser Wünsche süßes Plaudern
Hören wir allein, und schauen
Immerdar in selge Augen,
Schmecken nichts als Mund und Kuß.
Alles was wir nur berühren
Wird zu heißen Balsamfrüchten,
Wird zu weichen zarten Brüsten,
Opfern kühner Lust.

Immer wächst und blüht Verlangen
Am Geliebten festzuhangen,
Ihn im Innern zu empfangen,
Eins mit ihm zu sein,
Seinem Durste nicht zu wehren,
Sich im Wechsel zu verzehren,
Voneinander sich zu nähren,
Voneinander nur allein.

So in Lieb' und hoher Wollust
Sind wir immerdar versunken,
Seit der wilde trübe Funken
Jener Welt erlosch;
Seit der Hügel sich geschlossen,
Und der Scheiterhaufen sprühte,
Und dem schauernden Gemüte
Nun das Erdgesicht zerfloß.

Zauber der Erinnerungen,
Heilger Wehmut süße Schauer
Haben innig uns durchklungen,
Kühlen unsre Glut.
Wunden gibt's, die ewig schmerzen,
Eine göttlich tiefe Trauer
Wohnt in unser aller Herzen,
Löst uns auf in Eine Flut.

Und in dieser Flut ergießen
Wir uns auf geheime Weise
In den Ozean des Lebens
Tief in Gott hinein;
Und aus seinem Herzen fließen

We alone hear the sweet conversation
Of gentle wishes, and constantly look
Into blissful eyes,
We taste nothing but lips and kisses.
Everything that we merely touch
Turns into hot, balmy fruits,
Turns into soft, tender breasts,
Victims of bold pleasure.

Always there grows and blossoms the desire
To cling to the loved one,
To receive him inwardly,
To be one with him,
Not to restrain his thirst,
To consume one another alternately,
To feed upon one another.
And only upon one another.

Thus in love and supreme pleasure
We are constantly immersed,
Ever since the wild, gloomy spark
Of that other world went out;
Ever since the hill closed,
And the pyre scattered sparks,
And the face of the earth dissolved
In our trembling mind.

The magic of recollections
And the sweet shudder of holy melancholy
Have resounded deep within us
And cool our blazing heat.
There are wounds that ache forever,
A divinely profound mourning
Dwells in all our hearts
And dissolves us into one current.

And in this current we empty
Ourselves in a secret fashion
Into the ocean of life
Deep into God;
And from His heart we flow

Wir zurück zu unserm Kreise,
Und der Geist des höchsten Strebens
Taucht in unsre Wirbel ein.

Schüttelt eure goldnen Ketten
Mit Smaragden und Rubinen,
Und die blanken saubern Spangen,
Blitz und Klang zugleich.
Aus des feuchten Abgrunds Betten,
Aus den Gräbern und Ruinen,
Himmelsrosen auf den Wangen
Schwebt in's bunte Fabelreich.

Könnten doch die Menschen wissen,
Unsre künftigen Genossen,
Daß bei allen ihren Freuden
Wir geschäftig sind:
Jauchzend würden sie verscheiden,
Gern das bleiche Dasein missen,—
O! die Zeit ist bald verflossen,
Kommt Geliebte doch geschwind!

Helft uns nur den Erdgeist binden,
Lernt den Sinn des Todes fassen
Und das Wort des Lebens finden;
Einmal kehrt euch um.
Deine Macht muß bald verschwinden,
Dein erborgtes Licht verblassen,
Werden dich in kurzem binden,
Erdgeist, deine Zeit ist um.

Back to our own circle,
And the spirit of extreme striving
Dives into our whirlpool.

Shake your golden chains
With emeralds and rubies,
And the shiny neat brooches,
Lightning-flash and sound at the same time.
Out of the beds of the damp abyss,
Out of the graves and ruins,
With heavenly roses on your cheeks,
Soar into the colorful realm of fable.

If people, our future companions,
Could only know
That we are actively involved
In all their joys:
They would pass away in exultation,
They would gladly forgo their pallid existence—
Oh! the time elapses so soon;
Do come quickly, loved ones!

Just help us fetter the earth spirit,
Learn to grasp the meaning of death
And find the word of life;
For once, reverse yourselves.
Your power, earth spirit, must soon disappear,
Your borrowed light must grow pale,
We shall soon place you in fetters,
Your time is up.

# Ludwig Tieck

## *"Keinen hat es noch gereut"*

Keinen hat es noch gereut,
Der das Roß bestiegen,
Um in frischer Jugendzeit
Durch die Welt zu fliegen.

Berge und Auen,
Einsamer Wald,
Mädchen und Frauen
Prächtig im Kleide,
Golden Geschmeide,
Alles erfreut ihn mit schöner Gestalt.

Wunderlich fliehen
Gestalten dahin,
Schwärmerisch glühen
Wünsche in jugendlich trunkenem Sinn.

Ruhm streut ihm Rosen,
Schnell in die Bahn,
Lieben und Kosen,
Lorbeer und Rosen,
Führen ihn höher und höher hinan.

Rund um ihn Freuden,
Feinde beneiden,
Erliegend, den Held—
Dann wählt er bescheiden
Das Fräulein, das ihm nur vor allen gefällt.

Und Berge und Felder
Und einsame Wälder
Mißt er zurück.
Die Eltern in Tränen,
Ach alle ihr Sehnen—
Sie alle vereinigt das lieblichste Glück.

# Ludwig Tieck

## "No one has yet regretted it"

No one has yet regretted it
Who has mounted his steed
In order to dash through the world
In the days of his vigorous youth.

Mountains and meadows,
Lonely forest,
Girls and women
In splendid attire,
Golden jewelry,
Everything delights him with its pleasing form.

Forms flee by
Wondrously,
Wishes glow
Rapturously in his young, exuberant mind.

Fame quickly strews
Roses in his path;
Loving and caressing,
Laurels and roses,
Lead him higher and higher upward.

Round about him, joys;
Enemies envy
The hero as they succumb—
Then he modestly chooses
The young woman he likes most of all.

And through mountains and fields
And lonely forests
He makes his way back.
His parents in tears,
Ah, all their longing—
They are all united in the loveliest happiness.

Sind Jahre verschwunden,
Erzählt er dem Sohn
In traulichen Stunden
Und zeigt seine Wunden,
Der Tapferkeit Lohn.
So bleibt das Alter selbst noch jung,
Ein Lichtstrahl in der Dämmerung.

## "Ruhe, Süßliebchen im Schatten"

Ruhe, Süßliebchen im Schatten
Der grünen dämmernden Nacht,
Es säuselt das Gras auf den Matten,
Es fächelt und kühlt dich der Schatten,
Und treue Liebe wacht.
  Schlafe, schlaf ein,
  Leiser rauscht der Hain—
  Ewig bin ich dein.

Schweigt, ihr versteckten Gesänge,
Und stört nicht die süßeste Ruh!
Es lauscht der Vögel Gedränge,
Es ruhen die lauten Gesänge,
  Schließ, Liebchen, dein Auge zu.
  Schlafe, schlaf ein,
  Im dämmernden Schein—
  Ich will dein Wächter sein.

Murmelt fort ihr Melodieen,
  Rausche nur, du stiller Bach,
Schöne Liebesphantasieen
Sprechen in den Melodieen,
  Zarte Träume schwimmen nach,
    Durch den flüsternden Hain
  Schwärmen goldene Bienelein,
  Und summen zum Schlummer dich ein.

When years have elapsed,
He tells his story to his son
In intimate hours
And shows his wounds,
The reward of his bravery.
Thus old age itself still stays young,
A ray of light in the dusk.


## "Rest, sweet beloved, in the shade"

Rest, sweet beloved, in the shade
  Of the green, dusky night.
The grass in the meadows is whispering,
The shade fans and cools you,
  And faithful love keeps watch.
    Sleep, go to sleep,
  The grove is rustling more softly—
  I am yours forever.

Be silent, you hidden songs,
  And do not disturb this sweetest repose!
The throng of birds is listening,
Their loud songs are at rest;
  Loved one, close your eyes.
    Sleep, go to sleep,
  In the twilight glow—
  I will be your guardian.

Murmur on, you melodies;
  Go on babbling, you quiet brook;
Beautiful fantasies of love
Speak in the melodies,
  Gentle dreams float after them;
    Through the whispering grove
  Little golden bees swarm
  And hum you into slumber.

## *Wunder der Liebe*

Mondbeglänzte Zaubernacht,
Die den Sinn gefangen hält,
Wundervolle Märchenwelt,
Steig auf in der alten Pracht!

Liebe läßt sich suchen, finden,
Niemals lernen oder lehren;
Wer da will die Flamm entzünden,
Ohne selbst sich zu versehren,
Muß sich reinigen der Sünden.
Alles schläft, weil er noch wacht;
Wann der Stern der Liebe lacht,
Goldne Augen auf ihn blicken,
Schaut er trunken von Entzücken
Mondbeglänzte Zaubernacht.

Aber nie darf er erschrecken,
Wenn sich Wolken dunkel jagen,
Finsternis die Sterne decken,
Kaum der Mond es noch will wagen,
Einen Schimmer aufzuwecken.
Ewig steht der Liebe Zelt,
Von dem eignen Licht erhellt;
Aber Mut nur kann zerbrechen,
Was die Furcht will ewig schwächen,
Die den Sinn gefangen hält.

Keiner Liebe hat gefunden,
Dem ein trüber Ernst beschieden;
Flüchtig sind die goldnen Stunden,
Welche immer den vermieden,
Den die bleiche Sorg umwunden:
Wer die Schlange an sich hält,
Dem ist Schatten vorgestellt;
Alles, was die Dichter sangen,
Nennt der Arme, eingefangen,
Wundervolle Märchenwelt.

## Miracle of Love

Moonlit magical night
That holds the mind prisoner,
Fantastic fairy-tale world,
Rise up in your ancient glory!

Love may be sought and found,
Never learned or taught;
Whoever wishes to ignite the flame
Without injuring himself
Must purify himself of sins.
Everyone else is asleep while he is still awake;
When the star of love laughs,
And golden eyes gaze at him,
Intoxicated with rapture he beholds a
Moonlit magical night.

But he must never be afraid
When gloomy clouds pursue one another,
When darkness covers the stars,
When the moon will scarcely still dare
To arouse a glimmer.
Eternally stands the canopy of love,
Illuminated by its own light;
But only courage can smash
The weakness forever caused by the fear[21]
That holds the mind prisoner.

No one has found love
If his nature is drearily solemn;
Fleeting are the golden hours,
Which always shun the man
Who is in the coils of pale care:
Whoever clasps a serpent to himself
Is confronted with shadow;
Everything that the poets sang
The poor man, in his captivity, calls a
Fantastic fairy-tale world.

---

[21]Literally, "That which fear ever wishes to weaken."

Herz, im Glauben auferblühend,
Fühlt alsbald die goldnen Scheine,
Die es lieblich in sich ziehend
Macht zu eigen sich und seine,
In der schönsten Flamme glühend.

Ist das Opfer angefacht,
Wird's dem Himmel dargebracht;
Hat dich Liebe angenommen,
Auf dem Altar hell entglommen
Steig auf in der alten Pracht!

The heart blossoming in faith
Feels at once the golden beams,
Which it absorbs lovingly into itself
And makes its own, its possession,
Glowing in the most beautiful flame.
Once the sacrifice is set on fire,
It is offered to Heaven;
If love has accepted you,
Brightly catching fire on the altar,
Rise up in your ancient glory!

# Clemens Brentano

## *"O kühler Wald"*

O kühler Wald
Wo rauschest Du,
In dem mein Liebchen geht,
O Widerhall
Wo lauschest du,
Der gern mein Lied versteht.

O Widerhall,
O sängst Du ihr
Die süßen Träume vor,
Die Lieder all,
O bring' sie ihr,
Die ich so früh verlor.—

Im Herzen tief,
Da rauscht der Wald,
In dem mein Liebchen geht,
In Schmerzen schlief
Der Widerhall,
Die Lieder sind verweht.

Im Walde bin
Ich so allein,
O Leibchen wandre hier,
Verschallet auch
Manch Lied so rein,
Ich singe andre Dir.

## *Rückblick*

Ich wohnte unter vielen, vielen Leuten,
Und sah sie alle tot und stille stehn,
Sie sprachen viel von hohen Lebensfreuden

# Clemens Brentano

## *"O cool forest"*

O cool forest
In which my loved one walks,
Where are you rustling?
O echo
That gladly understands my song,
Where are you listening?

O echo,
Oh, if you could sing to her
My sweet dreams!
All the songs,
Oh, bring them to her,
Whom I lost so soon.—

Deep in my heart,
There the forest rustles
In which my loved one walks;
In sorrows the echo
Has fallen asleep,
The songs have wafted away.

In the forest I
Am so alone;
O loved one, come to me here;
Even if many a song
So pure dies away,
I shall sing others to you.

## *Retrospect*

I dwelt among many, many people,
And saw them all stand dead and still;
They spoke a lot about the great joys of life

Und liebten, sich im kleinsten Kreis zu drehn;
So war mein Kommen schon ein ewig Scheiden,
Und jeden hab ich einmal nur gesehn,
Denn nimmer hielt mich's; flüchtiges Geschicke
Trieb wild mich fort, sehnt ich mich gleich zurücke!

Und manchem habe ich die Hand gedrücket,
Der freundlich meinem Schritt entgegensah,
Hab in mir selbst die Kränze all gepflücket,
Denn keine Blume war, kein Frühling da,
Und hab im Flug die Unschuld mit geschmücket,
War sie verlassen meinem Wege nah;
Doch ewig, ewig trieb mich's schnell zu eilen,
Konnt niemals meines Werkes Freude teilen!

Rund um mich war die Landschaft wild und öde,
Kein Morgenrot, kein goldner Abendschein,
Kein kühler Wind durch dunkle Wipfel wehte,
Es grüßte mich kein Sänger in dem Hain.
Auch aus dem Tal schallt' keines Hirten Flöte,
Die Welt schien mir in sich erstarrt zu sein.
Ich hörte in des Stromes wildem Brausen
Nur eignen Fluges Flügelschläge sausen!

Nur in mir selbst die Tiefe zu ergründen,
Senkt ich ins Herz mit Geistesmacht den Blick;
Doch hier auch konnt es eigne Ruh nicht finden,
Kehrt friedlos stets zur Außenwelt zurück;
Es sah wie Traum das Leben unten schwinden,
Las in den Sternen ewiges Geschick,
Und rings um mich eiskalte Stimmen sprachen:
„Das Herz, es will vor Wonne schier verzagen!"

Ich sah sie nicht, die großen Süßigkeiten
Vom Überfluß der Welt; sie schien mir schal,
Ich mußt hinweg mit schnellem Fittich gleiten.
Hinabgedrückt von unerkannter Qual,
Konnt nimmer ich Frucht und Genuß erbeuten,
Und zählte stumm der Flügelschläge Zahl,
Von ewigen, unfühlbar mächt'gen Wogen
In weite, weite Ferne hingezogen!

And loved to move in the smallest possible circle;
So my arrival was already an eternal departure,
And I saw each of them only once,
For I was never tied down; a fleeting destiny
Drove me away wildly, even though I longed to be back!

And I have shaken hands with many a man
Who looked kindly on my approaching steps;
All the garlands I have culled were within myself,
For no flower, no springtime existed,
And in my flight I adorned innocence with them
When, forsaken, it came near my path;
But ever, ever I was driven to hasten away,
I could never share my joy in my accomplishment!

All around me the landscape was wild and barren,
No blush of sunrise, no golden evening glow;
No cool wind blew through dark treetops,
No songbird greeted me in the grove.
Even from the valley no shepherd's flute resounded,
The world seemed to me to be frozen in itself.
In the wild roaring of the stream I heard
Only the wing beats of my own flight whirring!

Merely to sound the depths within myself
I looked into my heart with the force of my mind;
But here, too, my heart could not find congenial repose,
It constantly returned restlessly to the world outside;
It watched life fade away below like a dream,
It read eternal destiny in the stars,
And round about me ice-cold voices said:
"Your heart is nearly about to despair from sheer bliss!"

I did not see them, the great delicacies
Of the world's abundance; it seemed insipid to me,
I had to glide away on rapid wings.
Oppressed by an unidentified sorrow,
I could never win fruition or enjoyment,
And mutely counted the number of my wing beats,
Drawn into the far, far distance
By eternal, impalpably powerful surges!

Und so noch jetzt! Wohl muß ich es gestehen,
Daß Dinge mich umscheinen, menschengleich;
Zu hören sie, ja leibhaft sie zu sehen
Kann ich nicht leugnen; doch bleibt mir dies Reich
Der Welt so fremd und hohl, daß all ihr Drehen
So viel nicht schafft, daß mir der Zweifel weich',
Ob Sein, ob Nichtsein seinen Spuk hier treibe,
Ob solcher Welt auch Seele wohn im Leibe!

## [Wiegenlied]

Singet leise, leise, leise,
Singt ein flüsternd Wiegenlied,
Von dem Monde lernt die Weise,
Der so still am Himmel zieht.

Denn es schlummern in dem Rheine
Jetzt die lieben Kinder klein,
Ameleya wacht alleine
Weinend in dem Mondenschein.

Singt ein Lied so süß gelinde,
Wie die Quellen auf den Kieseln,
Wie die Bienen um die Linde
Summen, murmeln, flüstern, rieseln.

## [Soldatenlied]

Es leben die Soldaten
So recht von Gottes Gnaden,
Der Himmel ist ihr Zelt,
Ihr Tisch das grüne Feld.

Ihr Bette ist der Rasen,
Trompeter müssen blasen:
Guten Morgen! Gute Nacht!
Daß man mit Lust erwacht.

And so it still is! I certainly must admit
That things resembling people appear around me;
That I hear them, yes, that I see them in the flesh
I cannot deny; yet this kingdom of the world
Remains so foreign and hollow to me, that all its turning
Is not sufficient to remove my doubts
Whether being or nonbeing is noisily bustling here,
Whether a world like this even has a soul in its body!

## [Lullaby]

Sing softly, softly, softly,
Sing a whispering lullaby;
Learn the melody from the moon,
Which passes so calmly in the sky.

For now the dear little children[22]
Are slumbering in the Rhine;
Ameleya alone is awake,
Weeping in the moonlight.

Sing a song as sweetly gentle
As those that the brooks over the pebbles,
As those that the bees around the lime tree
Hum, murmur, whisper, trickle.

## [Soldiers' Song]

Soldiers live
By the grace of God, really;
The sky is their tent,
Their table the green field.

Their bed is the turf;
Trumpeters have to blow
"Good morning" and "Good night,"
So that they awaken pleasurably.

---

[22]This stanza, usually tacitly omitted in anthologies, is closely related to the fanciful story
in which the poem occurs.

Ihr Wirtschild ist die Sonne,
Ihr Freund die volle Tonne,
Ihr Schlafbuhl ist der Mond,
Der in der Sternschanz wohnt.

Die Sterne haben Stunden,
Die Sterne haben Runden
Und werden abgelöst,
Drum Schildwach sei getröst'.

Wir richten mit dem Schwerte,
Der Leib gehört der Erde
Die Seel dem Himmelszelt,
Der Rock bleibt in der Welt.

Wer fällt, der bleibet liegen,
Wer steht, der kann noch siegen,
Wer übrigbleibt hat recht,
Wer fortläuft, der ist schlecht.

Zum Hassen oder Lieben
Ist alle Welt getrieben,
Es bleibet keine Wahl,
Der Teufel ist neutral.

Bedienet uns ein Bauer,
So schmeckt der Wein fast sauer,
Doch ists ein schöner Schatz,
So kriegt sie einen Schmatz.


## [Brautgesang]

Komm heraus, komm heraus, o du schöne, schöne Braut,
Deine guten Tage sind nun alle, alle aus,
Dein Schleierlein weht so feucht und tränenschwer,
O, wie weinet die schöne Braut so sehr!
Mußt die Mägdlein lassen stehn,
Mußt nun zu den Frauen gehn.

Their inn sign is the sun,
Their friend the full cask,
Their paramour is the moon,
Which lives in the earthwork of stars.

The stars have their hours of service,
The stars have sentry duty
And relieve one another;
So, sentry, be consoled.

We settle things with our sword;
Our body belongs to the earth,
Our soul to the tent of the sky,
Our uniform remains in the world.

Whoever falls in battle just lies there;
Whoever stands may still win,
Whoever survives is in the right,
Whoever runs away is bad.

Toward hatred or toward love
The whole world is driven;
No choice remains,
Only the devil is neutral.

When a farmer serves us,
The wine tastes almost sour;
But if it's a pretty darling,
She receives a kiss.


## *[Bridal Song]*

Come out, come out, you lovely, lovely bride,
Your happy days are now all, all over;
Your little veil blows so damp and heavy with tears;
Oh, how the lovely bride is weeping!
You must leave the girls behind,
You must now join the women.

Ihr klugen Jungfraun zieht hinaus,
Die Lampen sind geschmücket,
Ans Herz den reinen Blumenstrauß
Der Bräutigam nun drücket,
Ihr Lilien gebt der Braut Geleit,
Ihr tragt ein schönres Ehrenkleid,
Ein hochzeitlicheres Geschmeid,
Als Salomo in Herrlichkeit.

Lege an, lege an heut auf kurze, kurze Zeit
Dein Seidenröslein, dein reiches Brustgeschmeid,
Dein Schleierlein weht so feucht und tränenschwer,
O, wie weinet die schöne Braut so sehr!
Mußt die Zöpflein schließen ein
Unterm goldnen Häubelein.

Heb an du liebe Nachtigall
Dein kunstreich Figurieren,
Hilf uns mit deinem süßen Schall
Das Brautlied musizieren,
Das Lerchlein soll sein—„dir, dir, dir,
Dir Gott sei Lob" auch für und für
Erschwingen in dem höchsten Ton
Bis auf zu Gott im Himmelsthron.

Lache nicht, lache nicht, deine Gold- und Perlenschuh
Werden dich schon drücken, sind eng genug dazu!
Dein Schleierlein weht so feucht und tränenschwer,
O, wie weinet die schöne Braut so sehr!
Wenn die andern tanzen gehn,
Mußt du bei der Wiege stehn.

Du blauer Himmel spann' ein Zelt,
Den Bräutigam zu grüßen,
Ihr Blümlein webet übers Feld
Den Teppich ihm zu Füßen,
Ihr Lüftlein reget dann geschwind
Die Glöcklein, daß sie duftend lind

You wise virgins, come out,[23]
Your lamps are trimmed;
The bridegroom now presses
Your pure bouquet against your heart.
You lilies, accompany the bride;
You wear a lovelier robe of honor,
Adornment more befitting a wedding,
Than Solomon in his glory.

Put on, put on today for a brief, brief while
Your little silk rose, your rich corsage jewelry;
Your little veil blows so damp and heavy with tears;
Oh, how the lovely bride is weeping!
You must tuck in your braids
Beneath your little golden cap.

You dear nightingale, begin
Your artistic coloratura,
Help us with your sweet voice
To play the bridal song;
The little lark must also steadily
Raise up his "You, You, You, God, be praised"[24]
In the highest tones
All the way to God on His heavenly throne.

Do not laugh, do not laugh, your shoes of gold and pearls
Will soon be too tight for you, they are narrow enough for it!
Your little veil blows so damp and heavy with tears;
Oh, how the lovely bride is weeping!
When the others go dancing,
You must stand by the cradle.

You blue sky, spread a canopy
To greet the bridegroom;
You flowers, weave a carpet
Over the field at his feet;
You breezes, then quickly shake
The little bellflowers, so that with mild fragrance

---

[23]This entire stanza contains familiar references to the New Testament.
[24]The German imitates the song of the lark.

Tau-Perlen streuen auf der Au
Ums arme Kind von Hennegau.

Winke nur, winke nur, sind gar leichte, leichte Wink,
Bis den Finger drücket der goldne Treuering.
Dein Schleierlein weht so feucht und tränenschwer,
O, wie weinet die schöne Braut so sehr!
Ringlein sehn heut lieblich aus,
Morgen werden Fesseln draus.

Wir Lilien aus dem Lilienthal,
Wir kehren einstens wieder,
Dann in ein Bettchen eng und schmal
Sinkt müd dein Brautkleid nieder,
Dann naht der Seelenbräutigam
Das Lamm von königlichem Stamm,
Und wer ihm nicht entgegengeht,
Bleibt unerhört und unerhöht.

Springe heut, springe heut deinen letzten, letzten Tanz,
Welken erst die Rosen, stehen Dornen in dem Kranz!
Dein Schleierlein weht so feucht und tränenschwer,
O, wie weinet die schöne Braut so sehr!
Mußt die Blümlein lassen stehn,
Mußt nun auf den Acker gehn.

Führt sternenreine Engelein
Die Braut auf guter Weide,
Durch Leib und Leid, bis klar und rein
Der Geist im Lilienkleide
Sich scheidet von dem Dornental
Und mit uns singt beim Hochzeitsmahl:
O Stern und Blume, Geist und Kleid
Lieb, Leid und Zeit und Ewigkeit!

They may scatter pearls of dew on the meadow
Around the poor child of Hennegau.[25]

Wave your hand, wave your hand, they are truly light, light waves,
Until the golden wedding ring squeezes your finger.
Your little veil blows so damp and heavy with tears;
Oh, how the lovely bride is weeping!
The little rings look lovely today,
Tomorrow they will turn into fetters.

We lilies from the lily valley,
We will come back some day;
Then into a cramped and narrow little bed
Your wedding dress will wearily sink down;
Then the Bridegroom of Souls will approach,
The Lamb of royal lineage,
And whoever does not go to meet Him
Remains with prayers unheard and soul unexalted.

Leap today, leap today in your last, last dance;
When the roses wither, there will be thorns in the wreath!
Your little veil blows so damp and heavy with tears;
Oh, how the lovely bride is weeping!
You must leave the little flowers behind,
You must now go out to till the fields.

Starry-pure angels, lead
The bride to good pasture,
Through love and sorrow, until clear and pure
Her spirit in its lily garment
Departs from this valley of thorns
And sings with us at the wedding feast:
O star and flower, spirit and robe,
Love, sorrow, and time and eternity![26]

---

[25]The "poor child" is the bride.
[26]The last two lines, a motto of Brentano's, occur repeatedly in his late works.

# Adelbert von Chamisso

## *Das Schloß Boncourt*

Ich träum als Kind mich zurücke
Und schüttle mein greises Haupt;
Wie sucht ihr mich heim, ihr Bilder,
Die lang ich vergessen geglaubt?

Hoch ragt aus schatt'gen Gehegen
Ein schimmerndes Schloß hervor,
Ich kenne die Türme, die Zinnen,
Die steinerne Brücke, das Tor.

Es schauen vom Wappenschilde
Die Löwen so traulich mich an,
Ich grüße die alten Bekannten
Und eile den Burghof hinan.

Dort liegt die Sphinx am Brunnen,
Dort grünt der Feigenbaum,
Dort, hinter diesen Fenstern,
Verträumt ich den ersten Traum.

Ich tret in die Burgkapelle
Und suche des Ahnherrn Grab,
Dort ist's, dort hängt vom Pfeiler
Das alte Gewaffen herab.

Noch lesen umflort die Augen
Die Züge der Inschrift nicht,
Wie hell durch die bunten Scheiben
Das Licht darüber auch bricht.

So stehst du, o Schloß meiner Väter,
Mir treu und fest in dem Sinn
Und bist von der Erde verschwunden,
Der Pflug geht über dich hin.

# Adelbert von Chamisso

## *Boncourt Castle*

I dream myself back to childhood
And shake my hoary head;
How is it that you suddenly visit me, you images
That I believed to be long forgotten?

A glittering castle looms loftily
Out of shady enclosures;
I know the towers, the battlements,
The stone bridge, the gate.

From the coat of arms the lions
Look at me so familiarly;
I greet the old acquaintances
And hasten up the courtyard.

There lies the sphinx at the well,
There is the fig tree, all green;
There, behind these windows,
I dreamed away my first dream.

I enter the castle chapel
And seek my ancestor's grave;
There it is, there his old set of weapons
Hangs down from the pillar.

My bleary eyes cannot yet read
The words of the inscription
No matter how brightly, through the colored panes,
The light breaks in upon them.

Thus you stand, O castle of my fathers,
Faithful and firm in my mind;
And yet you have vanished from the earth,
The plow moves over you.

Sei fruchtbar, o teurer Boden,
Ich segne dich mild und gerührt,
Und segn' ihn zwiefach, wer immer
Den Pflug nun über dich führt.

Ich aber will auf mich raffen,
Mein Saitenspiel in der Hand,
Die Weiten der Erde durchschweifen
Und singen von Land zu Land.

## Die alte Waschfrau

Du siehst geschäftig bei dem Linnen
Die Alte dort in weißem Haar,
Die rüstigste der Wäscherinnen
Im sechsundsiebenzigsten Jahr.
So hat sie stets mit sauerm Schweiß
Ihr Brot in Ehr und Zucht gegessen
Und ausgefüllt mit treuem Fleiß
Den Kreis, den Gott ihr zugemessen.

Sie hat in ihren jungen Tagen
Geliebt, gehofft und sich vermählt;
Sie hat des Weibes Los getragen,
Die Sorgen haben nicht gefehlt;
Sie hat den kranken Mann gepflegt,
Sie hat drei Kinder ihm geboren;
Sie hat ihn in das Grab gelegt
Und Glaub und Hoffnung nicht verloren.

Da galts, die Kinder zu ernähren;
Sie griff es an mit heiterm Mut,
Sie zog sie auf in Zucht und Ehren,
Der Fleiß, die Ordnung sind ihr Gut.
Zu suchen ihren Unterhalt
Entließ sie segnend ihre Lieben,
So stand sie nun allein und alt,
Ihr war ihr heitrer Mut geblieben.

Be fruitful, O dear soil,
I bless you gently and emotionally
And give a double blessing to whoever
Is now guiding the plow over you.

But I wish to rouse myself,
My lyre in my hand,
To roam the far corners of the earth
And sing from land to land.

## The Old Washerwoman

You see the old white-haired woman there
Busy with the laundry,
The most vigorous of the washerwomen
Though she is seventy-six.
Thus has she always by the sweat of her brow
Eaten her bread with honor and decency,
And with loyal diligence has filled
The place that God allotted to her.

In her young days she
Loved, hoped and married;
She has suffered women's fate,
Worries were not lacking;
She nursed her sick husband,
She bore him three children;
She placed him in the grave
But did not lose her faith and hope.

Then it was necessary to feed her children;
She undertood this with serene courage;
She raised them in decency and honor;
Diligence and good order are her property.
To seek their means of support
She sent her loved ones away with a blessing;
So now she was alone and old,
But her serene courage stayed with her.

Sie hat gespart und hat gesonnen
Und Flachs gekauft und nachts gewacht,
Den Flachs zu feinem Garn gesponnen,
Das Garn dem Weber hingebracht;
Der hats gewebt zu Leinewand.
Die Schere brauchte sie, die Nadel,
Und nähte sich mit eigner Hand
Ihr Sterbehemde sonder Tadel.

Ihr Hemd, ihr Sterbehemd, sie schätzt es,
Verwahrts im Schrein am Ehrenplatz;
Es ist ihr Erstes und ihr Letztes,
Ihr Kleinod, ihr ersparter Schatz.
Sie legt es an, des Herren Wort
Am Sonntag früh sich einzuprägen;
Dann legt sie's wohlgefällig fort,
Bis sie darin zur Ruh sie legen.

Und ich, an meinem Abend, wollte,
Ich hätte, diesem Weibe gleich,
Erfüllt, was ich erfüllen sollte
In meinen Grenzen und Bereich;
Ich wollt, ich hätte so gewußt
Am Kelch des Lebens mich zu laben,
Und könnt am Ende gleiche Lust
An meinem Sterbehemde haben.

## Der Soldat

Es geht bei gedämpfter Trommel Klang,
Wie weit noch die Stätte, der Weg wie lang!
O käm er zur Ruh und wär es vorbei!
Ich glaub', es bricht mir das Herz entzwei.

Ich hab' in der Welt nur ihn geliebt,
Nur ihn, dem jetzt man den Tod doch gibt.
Bei klingendem Spiele wird paradiert,
Dazu bin ich auch kommandiert.

She saved up and she thought,
And bought flax and stayed up nights,
She spun the flax into fine thread,
She brought the thread to the weaver;
He wove it into linen.
She used the shears and the needle,
And with her own hands sewed herself
A flawless shroud.

She values her garment, her shroud,
She keeps it in a chest in a place of honor;
It is her all in all,
Her jewel, her hoarded treasure.
She puts it on every Sunday morning
To stamp the word of the Lord on her mind;
Then she puts it away with pleasure,
Until they lay her to rest in it.

And I, in the evening of my days, wish
That, like this woman, I had
Fulfilled what I should have fulfilled
Within my limits and domain;
I wish I had been so well able
To refresh myself at the cup of life,
And at the end, could take equal pleasure
In my shroud.

## The Soldier

We march to the sound of muffled drums,
How far the halting-place still is, how long the road is!
Oh, if he could only find rest and it were all over!
I think my heart is breaking in two.

I loved only him in the whole world,
Only the man who is now to be put to death.
We are parading to the sound of instruments,
And I, too, have been assigned to the detail.

Da schaut er auf zum letzten Mal
In Gottes Sonne freudigen Strahl;
Nun binden sie ihm die Augen zu—
Dir schenke Gott die ewige Ruh!

Es haben die Neun wohl angelegt,
Acht Kugeln haben vorbeigefegt;
Sie zitterten alle vor Jammer und Schmerz,
Ich aber, ich traf ihn mitten in's Herz.

Now he looks up for the last time
Into the joyful beam of God's sun;
Now they are blindfolding him—
May God grant you eternal rest!

The nine men have taken good aim,
Eight bullets have whizzed by him;
They were all trembling with sorrow and pain,
But I, I hit him right in the heart.

# Ludwig Uhland

## Der gute Kamerad

Ich hatt einen Kameraden,
Einen bessern findst du nit.
Die Trommel schlug zum Streite,
Er ging an meiner Seite
In gleichem Schritt und Tritt.

Eine Kugel kam geflogen;
Gilt's mir oder gilt es dir?
Ihn hat es weggerissen,
Er liegt mir vor den Füßen,
Als wär's ein Stück von mir.

Will mir die Hand noch reichen,
Derweil ich eben lad:
Kann dir die Hand nicht geben;
Bleib du im ew'gen Leben,
Mein guter Kamerad!

## Frühlingsglaube

Die linden Lüfte sind erwacht,
Sie säuseln und weben Tag und Nacht,
Sie schaffen an allen Enden.
O frischer Duft, o neuer Klang!
Nun, armes Herze, sei nicht bang!
Nun muß sich alles, alles wenden.

Die Welt wird schöner mit jedem Tag,
Man weiß nicht, was noch werden mag,
Das Blühen will nicht enden.
Es blüht das fernste, tiefste Tal:
Nun, armes Herz, vergiß der Qual!
Nun muß sich alles, alles wenden.

# Ludwig Uhland

## *The Good Comrade*

I had a comrade,
You wouldn't find a better one.
The drum sounded for combat,
He walked by my side
At the same pace.

A bullet came flying;
Was it meant for me or for you?
It tore him away,
He lay at my feet
As if it were a part of me.

He still wanted to give his hand to me,
Just while I was loading:
I can't give you my hand;
May you enjoy eternal life,
My good comrade!


## *Faith in Springtime*

The gentle breezes have awakened,
They murmur and stir day and night,
They are busy in all quarters.
O fresh fragrance, O new sounds!
Now, my poor heart, do not be alarmed!
Now everything, everything must undergo a change.

The world grows more beautiful with each day,
You cannot tell what may still develop,
There is no end to the blossoming.
The farthest, deepest valley is in blossom:
Now, my poor heart, forget your torment!
Now everything, everything must undergo a change.

# Joseph von Eichendorff

## *Das zerbrochene Ringlein*

In einem kühlen Grunde
Da geht ein Mühlenrad,
Mein' Liebste ist verschwunden,
Die dort gewohnet hat.

Sie hat mir Treu versprochen,
Gab mir ein'n Ring dabei,
Sie hat die Treu gebrochen,
Mein Ringlein sprang entzwei.

Ich möcht als Spielmann reisen
Weit in die Welt hinaus
Und singen meine Weisen
Und gehn von Haus zu Haus.

Ich möcht als Reiter fliegen
Wohl in die blut'ge Schlacht,
Um stille Feuer liegen
Im Feld bei dunkler Nacht.

Hör ich das Mühlrad gehen:
Ich weiß nicht, was ich will—
Ich möcht am liebsten sterben,
Da wär's auf einmal still!

## *Frische Fahrt*

Laue Luft kommt blau geflossen,
Frühling, Frühling soll es sein!
Waldwärts Hörnerklang geschossen,
Mut'ger Augen lichter Schein;
Und das Wirren bunt und bunter

# Joseph von Eichendorff

## *The Broken Ring*

In a cool valley
A mill wheel turns;
My sweetheart, who lived there,
Has vanished.

She promised to be true to me,
Gave me a ring when she said so;
She broke her faith,
My ring split in two.

I'd like to travel as a minstrel
Far out into the world,
And sing my melodies,
And go from house to house.

I'd like to dash as a cavalryman
Into a bloody battle,
To lie around quiet campfires
In the field when the night is dark.

When I hear the mill wheel turning,
I don't know what I want to do—
Most of all I'd like to die,
Then the wheel would suddenly be quiet!

## *Brisk Journey*

Warm breezes come flowing in the blue;
It must be springtime, springtime!
Horn calls shooting into the forest,
The bright glow of courageous eyes;
And the confusion, more and more variegated,

Wird ein magisch wilder Fluß,
In die schöne Welt hinunter
Lockt dich dieses Stromes Gruß.

Und ich mag mich nicht bewahren!
Weit von euch treibt mich der Wind,
Auf dem Strome will ich fahren,
Von dem Glanze selig blind!
Tausend Stimmen lockend schlagen,
Hoch Aurora flammend weht,
Fahre zu! ich mag nicht fragen,
Wo die Fahrt zu Ende geht!

## Der frohe Wandersmann

Wem Gott will rechte Gunst erweisen,
Den schickt er in die weite Welt;
Dem will er seine Wunder weisen
In Berg und Wald und Strom und Feld.

Die Trägen, die zu Hause liegen,
Erquicket nicht das Morgenrot;
Sie wissen nur von Kinderwiegen,
Von Sorgen, Last und Not um Brot.

Die Bächlein von den Bergen springen,
Die Lerchen schwirren hoch vor Lust,
Was sollt ich nicht mit ihnen singen
Aus voller Kehl und frischer Brust?

Den lieben Gott laß ich nur walten;
Der Bächlein, Lerchen, Wald und Feld
Und Erd und Himmel will erhalten,
Hat auch mein Sach aufs best bestellt!

Becomes a magically impetuous river;
Down into the beautiful world
This stream's greeting lures you.

And I don't want to hold out against it!
The wind drives me far from you;
I want to journey down that stream,
Blissfully blinded by its gleaming!
A thousand voices call alluringly,
Aurora[27] wafts ablaze high in the sky;
Onward! I don't want to ask
Where the journey will end!

## The Happy Wanderer

The man to whom God wishes to show real favor
He sends out into the wide world;
He wishes to show him His wonders
In mountain and forest and stream and field.

The lazy men who lie about at home
Are not exhilarated by the sunrise;
They know only about cradles,
About worries, burdens and shortage of bread.

The little brooks leap down from the mountains,
The larks whir high up out of pleasure;
Why shouldn't I sing along with them
At the top of my voice, with the strength of my lungs?

I leave everything to God;
He, Who wishes to preserve brooks, larks,
Forest and field and earth and sky,
Has also arranged things in the best way for me!

---

[27]Dawn.

## Elfe

Bleib bei uns! wir haben den Tanzplan im Tal
  Bedeckt mit Mondesglanze,
Johanneswürmchen erleuchten den Saal,
  Die Heimchen spielen zum Tanze.

Die Freude, das schöne leichtgläubige Kind,
  Es wiegt sich in Abendwinden:
Wo Silber auf Zweigen und Büschen rinnt,
  Da wirst du die schönste finden!

## In der Fremde

Aus der Heimat hinter den Blitzen rot
Da kommen die Wolken her,
Aber Vater und Mutter sind lange tot,
Es kennt mich dort keiner mehr.

Wie bald, wie bald kommt die stille Zeit,
Da ruhe ich auch, und über mir
Rauschet die stille Waldeinsamkeit
Und keiner mehr kennt mich auch hier.

## Sehnsucht

Es schienen so golden die Sterne,
Am Fenster ich einsam stand
Und hörte aus weiter Ferne
Ein Posthorn im stillen Land.
Das Herz mir im Leib entbrennte,
Da hab ich mir heimlich gedacht:
Ach, wer da mitreisen könnte
In der prächtigen Sommernacht!

## Elf

Stay with us! We have covered the dancing place
In the valley with moonlight;
Fireflies illuminate the hall,
The crickets provide music for dancing.

Joy, the beautiful, credulous child,
Is rocking on the evening breezes:
Where silver is flowing on branches and bushes
You will find the most beautiful girl!

## In Foreign Parts

From my home behind the red lightning flashes,
That is where the clouds are coming from;
But Father and Mother have long been dead,
No one knows me there anymore.

How soon, how soon the quiet time will come,
When I, too, shall rest, and above me
The beautiful solitary forest will rustle
And no one will know me here, either.

## Longing

The stars shone with such a golden light;
I was standing alone at the window
And heard from a great distance
A post horn in the quiet countryside.
My heart flared up in my breast;
Then I thought secretly to myself:
"Ah, if only I could travel with them
In the glorious summer night!"

Zwei junge Gesellen gingen
Vorüber am Bergeshang,
Ich hörte im Wandern sie singen
Die stille Gegend entlang:
Von schwindelnden Felsenschlüften,
Wo die Wälder rauschen so sacht,
Von Quellen, die von den Klüften
Sich stürzen in die Waldesnacht.

Sie sangen von Marmorbildern,
Von Gärten, die überm Gestein
In dämmernden Lauben verwildern,
Palästen im Mondenschein,
Wo die Mädchen am Fenster lauschen,
Wann der Lauten Klang erwacht
Und die Brunnen verschlafen rauschen
In der prächtigen Sommernacht.—

## Der Einsiedler

Komm, Trost der Welt, du stille Nacht!
Wie steigst du von den Bergen sacht,
Die Lüfte alle schlafen,
Ein Schiffer nur noch, wandermüd,
Singt übers Meer sein Abendlied
Zu Gottes Lob im Hafen.

Die Jahre wie die Wolken gehn
Und lassen mich hier einsam stehn,
Die Welt hat mich vergessen,
Da tratst du wunderbar zu mir,
Wenn ich beim Waldesrauschen hier
Gedankenvoll gesessen.

O Trost der Welt, du stille Nacht!
Der Tag hat mich so müd gemacht,
Das weite Meer schon dunkelt,

Two young fellows[28] were walking
Past on the slope of the hill;
As they strolled I heard them singing
All through the quiet surroundings:
About dizzying mountain chasms
Where the forests rustle so softly,
About springs that plunge from the clefts
Into the night of the forest.

They sang about marble statues,
About gardens running to seed
On stony ground in dusky bowers,
Palaces in the moonlight
Where girls listen at the window
When the sound of lutes awakens
And the fountains murmur drowsily
In the glorious summer night.—


## The Hermit

Come, solace of the world, you quiet night!
How softly you arise from the mountains;
All the breezes are asleep;
Only a boatman, weary with traveling,
Is still sending his evening song over the sea
In praise of God, in port.

The years pass like the clouds
And leave me here alone;
The world has forgotten me;
Then you stepped toward me miraculously
When, to the rustling of the forest,
I sat here lost in thought.

O solace of world, you quiet night!
The day has made me so weary;
The wide sea is already growing dark;

---

[28]Or, possibly, artisan journeymen on their wanderings.

Laß ausruhn mich von Lust und Not,
Bis daß das ew'ge Morgenrot
Den stillen Wald durchfunkelt.

## Mondnacht

Es war, als hätt der Himmel
Die Erde still geküßt,
Daß sie im Blütenschimmer
Von ihm nun träumen müßt.

Die Luft ging durch die Felder,
Die Ähren wogten sacht,
Es rauschten leis die Wälder,
So sternklar war die Nacht.

Und meine Seele spannte
Weit ihre Flügel aus,
Flog durch die stillen Lande,
Als flöge sie nach Haus.

Let me rest from pleasure and distress
Until the eternal sunrise
Sparkles through the quiet forest.

## Moonlit Night

It was as if the Sky
Had silently kissed the Earth,
So that she, in the glimmer of blossoms,
Now had to dream of him.

The breeze passed through the fields,
The ears of grain waved gently,
The forests rustled softly,
So starry-clear was the night.

And my soul spread
Its wings out wide,
And flew through the silent regions
As if it were flying home.

# Friedrich Rückert

## *"Du meine Seele, du mein Herz"*

Du meine Seele, du mein Herz,
Du meine Wonn', o du mein Schmerz,
Du meine Welt, in der ich lebe,
Mein Himmel du, darin ich schwebe,
O du mein Grab, in das hinab
Ich ewig meinen Kummer gab!
Du bist die Ruh, du bist der Frieden,
Du bist der Himmel, mir beschieden.
Daß du mich liebst, macht mich mir wert,
Dein Blick hat mich vor mir verklärt,
Du hebst mich liebend über mich,
Mein guter Geist, mein bessres Ich!


## *Kehr ein bei mir!*

Du bist die Ruh,
Der Friede mild,
Die Sehnsucht du
Und was sie stillt.

Ich weihe dir
Voll Lust und Schmerz
Zur Wohnung hier
Mein Aug und Herz.

Kehr ein bei mir
Und schließe du
Still hinter dir
Die Pforten zu!

Treib andern Schmerz
Aus dieser Brust!

# Friedrich Rückert

## "*You, my soul, you, my heart*"

You, my soul, you, my heart,
You, my bliss, O you, my pain,
You, my world in which I live,
You, my sky in which I soar,
O you, my grave, down into which
I sent my grief forever!
You are repose, you are peace,
You are heaven destined for me.
The fact that you love me gives me value in my own eyes,
Your glance has transfigured me in my own judgment;
With your love you lift me above my limitations,
My guardian spirit, my better self!


## *Come Live with Me!*

You are repose,
Gentle peace,
You are longing
And that which assuages it.

Full of pleasure and pain,
I consecrate to you
As a dwelling here
My eyes and heart.

Come live with me
And close
The portals
Quietly behind you!

Drive other pain
Out of my breast!

Voll sei dies Herz
Von deiner Lust.

Dies Augenzelt,
Von deinem Glanz
Allein erhellt,
O, füll es ganz!

## "In diesem Wetter, in diesem Braus"

In diesem Wetter, in diesem Braus,
Nie hätt' ich gesendet die Kinder hinaus;
Man hat sie hinausgetragen,
Ich durfte dazu nichts sagen.

In diesem Wetter, in diesem Saus,
Nie hätt' ich gelassen die Kinder hinaus,
Ich fürchtete, sie erkranken;
Das sind nun eitle Gedanken.

In diesem Wetter, in diesem Graus,
Hätt' ich gelassen die Kinder hinaus,
Ich sorgte, sie stürben morgen,
Das ist nun nicht zu besorgen.

In diesem Wetter, in diesem Braus,
Sie ruhn als wie in der Mutter Haus,
Von keinem Sturm erschrecket,
Von Gottes Hand bedecket.

## Mit vierzig Jahren

Mit vierzig Jahren ist der Berg erstiegen,
Wir stehen still und schaun zurück,
Dort sehen wir der Kindheit stilles liegen
Und dort der Jugend lautes Glück.

Let my heart be full
Of your pleasure.

This sky of my eyes,
Illuminated solely
By your shining light,
Oh, fill it completely!


## "In this storm, in this roar"

In this storm, in this roar,
I would never have sent the children out;
They were carried out,
I was not allowed any say in the matter.

In this storm, in this hubbub,
I would never have let the children out.
I would have been afraid of their getting sick;
Now those are idle thoughts.

In this weather, in this horror,
If I had let the children out,
I would have worried that they might die the next day;
Now that is nothing to worry over.

In this storm, in this roar,
They are resting as if in their mother's house,
Not frightened by any storm,
Covered by God's hand.


## At Forty

At forty the mountain has been climbed;
We stand still and look back;
There we see lying the quiet happiness of childhood
And there the boisterous happiness of youth.

Noch einmal schau, und dann gekräftigt weiter
Erhebe deinen Wanderstab!
Hindehnt ein Bergesrücken sich, ein breiter,
Und hier nicht, drüben gehts hinab.

Nicht atmend aufwärts brauchst du mehr zu steigen,
Die Ebne zieht von selbst dich fort;
Dann wird sie sich mit dir unmerklich neigen,
Und eh dus denkst, bist du im Port.


## "Ich bin müde, sterbensmüde"

Ich bin müde, sterbensmüde;
Ich bin müde, lebensmüde;
Dieses Bangens und Verlangens,
Dieses Hoffens, Bebens müde;
Dieses zwischen Erd und Himmel
Auf- und Niederschwebens müde;
Dieses spinnengleichen Wesens
Hirngespinste-Webens müde;
Müde dieser Torenweisheit,
Stolzen Überhebens müde.
Auf, o Geist, in diesen Fesseln
Ring dich nicht vergebens müde!
Schwing dich auf zu deinem Äther,
Des am Staube Klebens müde.

Look once again, and then with renewed strength once more
Lift your traveler's staff!
A mountain ridge extends before you, a broad one,
And the way down is not here but on the other side.

You no longer need to climb upward breathing heavily,
The plain draws you along of its own accord;
Then together with you it will imperceptibly incline,
And before you know it, you will be in port.

## *"I am weary, weary to death"*

I am weary, weary to death;
I am weary, weary of living;
Weary of this fear and desire,
Of this hoping and trembling;
Weary of this hovering up and down
Between earth and sky;
Weary of this spiderlike existence's
Weaving of fantasies;
Weary of this fool's wisdom,
Weary of proud arrogance.
Arise, my spirit, in these chains
No longer struggle in vain until weary!
Fly up to the heaven where you belong,
Weary of clinging to the dust.

# August von Platen

## Der Pilgrim vor St. Just

Nacht ist's, und Stürme sausen für und für,
Hispanische Mönche, schließt mir auf die Tür!

Laßt hier mich ruhn, bis Glockenton mich weckt,
Der zum Gebet euch in die Kirche schreckt!

Bereitet mir, was euer Haus vermag,
Ein Ordenskleid und einen Sarkophag!

Gönnt mir die kleine Zelle, weiht mich ein,
Mehr als die Hälfte dieser Welt war mein.

Das Haupt, das nun der Schere sich bequemt,
Mit mancher Krone ward's bediademt.

Die Schulter, die der Kutte nun sich bückt,
Hat kaiserlicher Hermelin geschmückt.

Nun bin ich vor dem Tod den Toten gleich
Und fall in Trümmer wie das alte Reich.

## Wie rafft ich mich auf

Wie rafft ich mich auf in der Nacht, in der Nacht
Und fühlte mich fürder gezogen,
Die Gassen verließ ich, vom Wächter bewacht,
Durchwandelte sacht
In der Nacht, in der Nacht
Das Tor mit dem gotischen Bogen.

# August von Platen

## The Pilgrim Outside the Yuste Monastery [29]

It is night and storms howl constantly;
"Spanish monks, open your door to me!

"Let me rest here until I am awakened by a tolling of bells
That will scare you into the church to pray!

"Prepare for me whatever your house can afford,
A monastic robe and a sarcophagus!

"Grant me a small cell, admit me to your order;
More than half this world was mine.

"The head that now submits to the shears
Was encircled by many a crown.

"The shoulders that now stoop to receive the cowl
Have been adorned with imperial ermine.

"Now in the face of death I am like the dead,
And I fall in ruins like the ancient empire."

## How I Roused Myself

How I roused myself in the night, in the night,
And felt myself drawn onward;
I left the narrow streets guarded by the night watchman,
And softly walked
In the night, in the night,
Through the gate with the Gothic arch.

---

[29]Literally, "outside San Yuste," but this is an error. In 1556 Holy Roman Emperor Charles V (King Charles I of Spain) abdicated and retired to the monastery of San Jerónimo at Yuste.

Der Mühlbach rauschte durch felsigen Schacht,
Ich lehnte mich über die Brücke,
Tief unter mir nahm ich der Wogen in acht,
Die wallten so sacht
In der Nacht, in der Nacht,
Doch wallte nicht eine zurücke.

Es drehte sich oben, unzählig entfacht,
Melodischer Wandel der Sterne,
Mit ihnen der Mond in beruhigter Pracht,
Sie funkelten sacht
In der Nacht, in der Nacht,
Durch täuschend entlegene Ferne.

Ich blickte hinauf in der Nacht, in der Nacht,
Ich blickte hinunter aufs neue:
O wehe, wie hast du die Tage verbracht,
Nun stille du sacht
In der Nacht, in der Nacht
Im pochenden Herzen die Reue!

## Tristan

Wer die Schönheit angeschaut mit Augen,
Ist dem Tode schon anheimgegeben,
Wird für keinen Dienst auf Erden taugen,
Und doch wird er vor dem Tode beben,
Wer die Schönheit angeschaut mit Augen!

Ewig währt für ihn der Schmerz der Liebe,
Denn ein Tor nur kann auf Erden hoffen,
Zu genügen einem solchen Triebe:
Wen der Pfeil des Schönen je getroffen,
Ewig währt für ihn der Schmerz der Liebe!

Ach, er möchte wie ein Quell versiechen,
Jedem Hauch der Luft ein Gift entsaugen
Und den Tod aus jeder Blume riechen:
Wer die Schönheit angeschaut mit Augen,
Ach, er möchte wie ein Quell versiechen!

The millstream babbled through a rocky gorge,
I leaned over the bridge;
Deep below me I perceived the waves,
Which were wandering so softly
In the night, in the night,
But not one of them wandered back.

Up above, glowing innumerably, the stars
Were rotating on their melodious course;
With them the moon in pacified splendor;
They twinkled softly
In the night, in the night,
Across the deceptively remote distance.

I looked upward in the night, in the night,
I looked downward again:
Alas, how have you spent your days!
Now softly
In the night, in the night,
Assuage the regret in your pounding heart!

## Tristan

The man who has looked upon beauty with his eyes
Is already handed over to death;
He will be no good for any earthly duties,
And yet he will tremble in the face of death,
The man who has looked upon beauty with his eyes!

The pain of love lasts eternally for him,
For only a fool can hope on earth
To satisfy such an urge:
Whoever has been smitten by the arrow of the beautiful,
The pain of love lasts eternally for him!

Ah, he would wish to sicken[30] like a fountain,
To such a poison from every breath of air,
And inhale death from every flower:
The man who has looked upon beauty with his eyes,
Ah, he would wish to sicken like a fountain!

---

[30]*Versiechen,* "sicken," a rare word and a bold variation on the more predictable *versiegen,* "dry up."

# Annette von Droste-Hülshoff

## Der Knabe im Moor

O schaurig ist's übers Moor zu gehn,
Wenn es wimmelt vom Heiderauche,
Sich wie Phantome die Dünste drehn
Und die Ranke häkelt am Strauche,
Under jedem Tritte ein Quellchen springt,
Wenn aus der Spalte es zischt und singt,
O schaurig ist's übers Moor zu gehn,
Wenn das Röhricht knistert im Hauche!

Fest hält die Fibel das zitternde Kind
Und rennt, als ob man es jage;
Hohl über die Fläche sauset der Wind—
Was raschelt drüben am Hage?
Das ist der gespenstische Gräberknecht,
Der dem Meister die besten Torfe verzecht;
Hu, hu, es bricht wie ein irres Rind!
Hinducket das Knäblein zage.

Vom Ufer starret Gestumpf hervor,
Unheimlich nicket die Föhre,
Der Knabe rennt, gespannt das Ohr,
Durch Riesenhalme wie Speere;
Und wie es rieselt und knittert darin!
Das ist die unselige Spinnerin,
Das ist die gebannte Spinnlenor',
Die den Haspel dreht im Geröhre!

Voran, voran! Nur immer im Lauf,
Voran, als woll es ihn holen!
Vor seinem Fuße brodelt es auf,
Es pfeift ihm unter den Sohlen
Wie eine gespenstige Melodei;
Das ist der Geigemann ungetreu,
Das ist der diebische Fiedler Knauf,
Der den Hochzeitheller gestohlen!

# Annette von Droste-Hülshoff

## *The Boy on the Moor*

Oh, it's frightening to walk across the moor
When it teems with heathy haze,
When the vapors twist like ghosts
And the tendrils knit themselves into the bushes,
When a little spring gushes under every footstep,
When there is hissing and singing from the crevices;
Oh, it's frightening to walk across the moor,
When the reeds clatter in the wind!

The trembling child holds his spelling-book tight
And runs as if he were being chased;
The wind roars dully over the flat land—
What is rustling over yonder at the boundary hedge?
It is the ghostly peat-digger's servant,
Who boozes away his master's best lumps of peat;
Hoo, hoo, it sounds like a stray steer breaking through!
The little boy cowers timorously.

From the bank, tree stumps stare out,
The pine tree nods eerily;
The boy runs, his ear tensely alert,
Through gigantic stalks like spears;
And the murmuring and the crackling that they make!
It is the luckless spinning woman,
It is the cursed Spinning Lenore
Who is turning her reel in the reeds!

Forward, forward, steadily at a run,
Forward, as if they were catching him;
In front of his feet, water bubbles up,
There is a whistling under his soles
Like a ghostly melody;
That is the unfaithful musician,
That is the thieving fiddler Knauf,
Who stole the wedding coin!

Da birst das Moor, ein Seufzer geht
Hervor aus der klaffenden Höhle;
Weh, weh, da ruft die verdammte Margret:
„Ho, ho, meine arme Seele!"
Der Knabe springt wie ein wundes Reh;
Wär nicht Schutzengel in seiner Näh,
Seine bleichenden Knöchelchen fände spät
Ein Gräber im Moorgeschwele.

Da mählich gründet der Boden sich,
Und drüben, neben der Weide,
Die Lampe flimmert so heimatlich,
Der Knabe steht an der Scheide.
Tief atmet er auf, zum Moor zurück
Noch immer wirft er den scheuen Blick:
Ja, im Geröhre war's fürchterlich,
O schaurig war's in der Heide!

## Am Turme

Ich steh auf hohem Balkone am Turm,
Umstrichen vom schreienden Stare,
Und laß gleich einer Mänade den Sturm
Mir wühlen im flatternden Haare;
O wilder Geselle, o toller Fant,
Ich möchte dich kräftig umschlingen,
Und, Sehne an Sehne, zwei Schritte vom Rand
Auf Tod und Leben dann ringen!

Und drunten seh ich am Strand, so frisch
Wie spielende Doggen, die Wellen
Sich tummeln rings mit Geklaff und Gezisch
Und glänzende Flocken schnellen.
O, springen möcht ich hinein alsbald,
Recht in die tobende Meute,
Und jagen durch den korallenen Wald
Das Walroß, die lustige Beute!

Now the moor bursts, a sigh emanates
From the gaping hollow:
Woe, woe, it is the doomed Margaret calling:
"Oh, oh, my poor soul!"
The boy leaps like a wounded deer;
If there were no guardian angel near him,
His bleaching little bones would be found long after
By some peat-digger in the moor's smoldering vapors.

Then gradually the ground becomes firm,
And over yonder, beside the willow,
The lamp is flickering with such a feeling of home;
The boy stands at the dividing line.
He draws a deep breath of relief, back to the moor
He still casts his timid glance;
Yes, it was terrifying in the reeds,
Oh, it was frightening on the heath!

## In the Tower

I stand on a high balcony in the tower,
Grazed by the screeching starlings,
And, like a Maenad,[31] I let the storm wind
Sweep through my streaming hair;
O wild fellow, crazy raw youth,
I'd like to wrap my arms around you tightly
And, sinew to sinew, two steps from the edge,
To wrestle there in a life-or-death match!

And down below I see on the shore, as lively
As playing mastiffs, the waves
Frisking all around with yelping and hissing,
And gleaming flakes of foam darting.
Oh, I'd like to leap in at once,
Right into the raging pack,
And through the coral forest to hunt
The walrus, the jolly quarry!

---

[31] In ancient Greece, a wild female devotee of the god Dionysos.

Und drüben seh ich ein Wimpel wehn
So keck wie eine Standarte,
Seh auf und nieder den Kiel sich drehn
Von meiner luftigen Warte;
O, sitzen möcht ich im kämpfenden Schiff,
Das Steuerruder ergreifen,
Und zischend über das brandende Riff
Wie eine Seemöve streifen.

Wär ich ein Jäger auf freier Flur,
Ein Stück nur von einem Soldaten,
Wär ich ein Mann doch mindestens nur,
So würde der Himmel mir raten;
Nun muß ich sitzen so fein und klar,
Gleich einem artigen Kinde,
Und darf nur heimlich lösen mein Haar
Und lassen es flattern im Winde!

## Im Moose

Als jüngst die Nacht dem sonnenmüden Land
Der Dämmrung leise Boten hat gesandt,
Da lag ich einsam noch in Waldes Moose.
Die dunklen Zweige nickten so vertraut,
An meiner Wange flüsterte das Kraut,
Unsichtbar duftete die Heiderose.

Und flimmern sah ich, durch der Linde Raum,
Ein mattes Licht, das im Gezweig der Baum
Gleich einem mächt'gen Glühwurm schien zu tragen.
Es sah so dämmernd wie ein Traumgesicht,
Doch wußte ich, es war der Heimat Licht,
In meiner eignen Kammer angeschlagen.

Ringsum so still, daß ich vernahm im Laub
Der Raupe Nagen, und wie grüner Staub
Mich leise wirbelnd Blätterflöckchen trafen.
Ich lag und dachte, ach so manchem nach,
Ich hörte meines eignen Herzens Schlag,
Fast war es mir als sei ich schon entschlafen.

And over yonder I see a pennant waving
As bold as a battle standard,
I see the keel bounding up and down
From my airy watchtower;
Oh, I'd like to be on that struggling ship,
To seize the steering wheel,
And, hissing over the breaker-washed shoals,
To glide like a seagull.

If I were a huntsman on an open stretch of country,
Or only the least bit of a soldier,
If only I were at least a man,
Heaven would advise me what to do;
As it is, I must sit so refinedly and purely,
Like a well-behaved child,
And only in secret may I undo my hair
And let it stream in the wind!

## In the Moss

Recently, when night sent the quiet messengers
Of twilight to the sun-weary land,
I was still lying all alone in the forest moss.
The dark boughs nodded so familiarly,
The grasses were whispering by my cheek,
The rock rose, though unseen, made its fragrance felt.

And, through the gaps in the lime tree, I saw glimmering
A dull light, which the tree seemed to carry
In its branches like a powerful firefly.
It looked as muted as a dream vision,
But I knew it was the light of home,
Placed in my own bedroom.

All about, it was so quiet that I heard the gnawing
Of caterpillars in the leaves, and, like green dust,
Particles of leaves struck me in a gentle flurry.
I lay and thought about ever so many things,
I heard the beating of my own heart;
I almost felt as if I had already fallen asleep.

Gedanken tauchten aus Gedanken auf,
Das Kinderspiel, der frischen Jahre Lauf,
Gesichter, die mir lange fremd geworden;
Vergeßne Töne summten um mein Ohr,
Und endlich trat die Gegenwart hervor,
Da stand die Welle, wie an Ufers Borden.

Dann, gleich dem Bronnen, der verrinnt im Schlund,
Und drüben wieder sprudelt aus dem Grund,
So stand ich plötzlich in der Zukunft Lande;
Ich sah mich selber, gar gebückt und klein,
Geschwächten Auges, am ererbten Schrein
Sorgfältig ordnen staub'ge Liebespfande.

Die Bilder meiner Lieben sah ich klar,
In einer Tracht, die jetzt veraltet war,
Mich sorgsam lösen aus verblichnen Hüllen,
Löckchen, vermorscht, zu Staub zerfallen schier,
Sah über die gefurchte Wange mir
Langsam herab die karge Träne quillen.

Und wieder an des Friedhofs Monument,
Dran Namen standen die mein Lieben kennt,
Da lag ich betend, mit gebrochnen Knieen,
Und—horch, die Wachtel schlug! Kühl strich der Hauch—
Und noch zuletzt sah ich, gleich einem Rauch,
Mich leise in der Erde Poren ziehen.

Ich fuhr empor, und schüttelte mich dann,
Wie einer, der dem Scheintod erst entrann,
Und taumelte entlang die dunklen Hage,
Noch immer zweifelnd, ob der Stern am Rain
Sei wirklich meiner Schlummerlampe Schein,
Oder das ew'ge Licht am Sarkophage.

One thought developed from another,
My childhood games, the course of my young years,
Faces that had long since become strange to me;
Forgotten sounds hummed around my ears,
And finally the present stepped forth;
There stood the waves, as if at the edge of the shore.

Then, like a spring that trickles away in a gully
And then gurgles out of the ground again some distance away,
I suddenly stood in the land of the future;
I saw myself, extremely stooped and small,
With weakened eyes, carefully arranging
Dusty love tokens beside my heirloom chest.

I clearly saw myself meticulously unwrapping
From faded coverings pictures of my loved ones
In clothing that was now long out of fashion,
Locks of hair, moldering, nearly crumbling into dust;
I saw a rare tear flowing slowly down
Over my furrowed cheek.

And again at the graveyard monument,
On which stood names familiar to my affections,
I lay in prayer, with aching knees,
And—listen, the quail called! A cool breeze blew—
And still at the last I saw myself passing quietly
Like smoke into the earth's pores.

I jumped up and shook myself then
Like someone who has just escaped a cataleptic fit,
And dashed along the dark boundary hedges,
Still in doubt whether the star by the ridge of the field
Was really the glow from my bedside lamp
Or the eternal light by the sarcophagus.

## Lebt wohl

Lebt wohl, es kann nicht anders sein!
Spannt flatternd eure Segel aus,
Laßt mich in meinem Schloß allein,
Im öden geisterhaften Haus.

Lebt wohl und nehmt mein Herz mit euch
Und meinen letzten Sonnenstrahl;
Er scheide, scheide nur sogleich,
Denn scheiden muß er doch einmal.

Laßt mich an meines Sees Bord,
Mich schaukelnd mit der Wellen Strich,
Allein mit meinem Zauberwort,
Dem Alpengeist und meinem Ich.

Verlassen, aber einsam nicht,
Erschüttert, aber nicht zerdrückt,
Solange noch das heil'ge Licht
Auf mich mit Liebesaugen blickt.

Solange mir der frische Wald
Aus jedem Blatt Gesänge rauscht,
Aus jeder Klippe, jedem Spalt
Befreundet mir der Elfe lauscht.

Solange noch der Arm sich frei
Und waltend mir zum Äther streckt
Und jedes wilden Geiers Schrei
In mir die wilde Muse weckt.

## Im Grase

Süße Ruh', süßer Taumel im Gras,
Von des Krautes Arom umhaucht,
Tiefe Flut, tief, tieftrunkne Flut,
Wenn die Wolk' am Azure verraucht,
Wenn aufs müde, schwimmende Haupt

## *Farewell*

Farewell, it cannot be otherwise!
Unfurl your sails and let them billow out,
Leave me alone in my castle,
In the barren, ghostlike house.

Farewell and take my heart with you
And my last ray of sunshine;
Let it depart, but let it depart at once,
For it must depart sometime.

Leave me by the edge of my lake,
Rocking myself with the passing of the waves,
Along with my words of magic,
The spirit of the Alps and my own self.

Forsaken but not alone,
Reeling but not crushed,
As long as the holy light still
Looks upon me with loving eyes.

As long as the fresh forest
Rustles songs to me from every leaf,
And the elf listens to me in friendship
From every crag and every cleft.

As long as my arms still freely
And masterfully stretch toward the heavens,
And the cry of every wild vulture
Awakens the wild Muse within me.

## *In the Grass*

Sweet rest, sweet ecstasy in the grass,
With the aroma of the herbs wafting around me,
Deep current, deep, deeply enraptured current,
When the cloud dissolves in the azure,
When onto my weary, dizzy head

Süßes Lachen gaukelt herab,
Liebe Stimme säuselt, und träuft
Wie die Lindeblüt' auf ein Grab.

Wenn im Busen die Toten dann,
Jede Leiche sich streckt und regt,
Leise, leise den Odem zieht,
Die geschlossne Wimper bewegt,
Tote Lieb', tote Lust, tote Zeit,
All die Schätze, im Schutt verwühlt,
Sich berühren mit schüchternem Klang
Gleich den Glöckchen, vom Winde umspielt.

Stunden, flüchtiger ihr als der Kuß
Eines Strahls auf den trauernden See,
Als des ziehenden Vogels Lied,
Das mir niederperlt aus der Höh',
Als des schillernden Käfers Blitz,
Wenn den Sonnenpfad er durcheilt,
Als der heiße Druck einer Hand,
Die zum letzten Male verweilt.

Dennoch, Himmel, immer mir nur,
Dieses eine nur: für das Lied
Jedes freien Vogels im Blau
Eine Seele, die mit ihm zieht,
Nur für jeden kärglichen Strahl
Meinen farbigschillernden Saum,
Jeder warmen Hand meinen Druck,
Und für jedes Glück meinen Traum.

Sweet laughter falls like an illusion,
When a lovely voice murmurs and drips down
Like the lime-tree blossoms onto a grave.

When in my heart the dead then,
Each corpse stretches and stirs,
Gently, gently draws a breath,
Moves its closed eyelashes;
When dead love, dead pleasure, dead time,
All the treasures, buried in the rubble,
Touch one another with a timid sound
Like that of little bells around which the wind is playing.

Hours, you are more fleeting than the kiss
Of a ray of light on the mourning lake,
Than the song of the migrating bird
That comes down to me like pearls from the heights,
Than the flash of the glittering beetle
When it hastens along the sunlit path,
Than the hot clasp of a hand
That lingers in yours for the last time.

And yet, heaven, just grant me this,
Just this one thing: for the song
Of every free bird in the blue,
A soul that migrates along with it;
For every scanty ray of light, only
My colorfully glittering margin of meadow;
For every warm hand, my clasp;
And for every happiness, my dream.

# Heinrich Heine

## "Aus alten Märchen winkt es"

Aus alten Märchen winkt es
Hervor mit weißer Hand,
Da singt es und da klingt es
Von einem Zauberland,

Wo große Blumen schmachten
Im goldnen Abendlicht,
Und zärtlich sich betrachten
Mit bräutlichem Gesicht;—

Wo alle Bäume sprechen,
Und singen wie ein Chor,
Und laute Quellen brechen
Wie Tanzmusik hervor;—

Und Liebesweisen tönen,
Wie du sie nie gehört,
Bis wundersüßes Sehnen
Dich wundersüß betört!

Ach, könnt' ich dorthin kommen
Und dort mein Herz erfreun,
Und aller Qual entnommen
Und frei und selig sein!

Ach! jenes Land der Wonne,
Das seh' ich oft im Traum;
Doch, kommt die Morgensonne,
Zerfließt's wie eitel Schaum.

# Heinrich Heine

## *"From old fairy tales"*

From old fairy tales
A white hand appears and beckons;
There is singing and playing of music
Concerning a magic land,

Where large flowers languish
In the golden evening light,
And delicately observe one another
With bridelike faces;—

Where all the trees speak
And sing like a choir,
And noisy springs gush forth
Like dance music;—

And songs of love resound
The like of which you never heard,
Until wondrous-sweet longing
Bemuses you wondrous-sweetly!

Ah, if I could get there
And rejoice my heart there,
And be released from all suffering,
And be free and blissful!

Ah, that land of rapture,
I see it often in dreams;
But when the morning sun arrives
It dissolves like mere foam.

## "Aus meinen großen Schmerzen"

Aus meinen großen Schmerzen
Mach' ich die kleinen Lieder;
Die heben ihr klingend Gefieder
Und flattern nach ihrem Herzen.

Sie fanden den Weg zur Trauten,
Doch kommen sie wieder und klagen,
Und klagen, und wollen nicht sagen,
Was sie im Herzen schauten.

## "Ich weiß nicht, was soll es bedeuten"

Ich weiß nicht, was soll es bedeuten,
Daß ich so traurig bin;
Ein Märchen aus alten Zeiten,
Das kommt mir nicht aus dem Sinn.

Die Luft ist kühl und es dunkelt,
Und ruhig fließt der Rhein;
Der Gipfel des Berges funkelt
Im Abendsonnenschein.

Die schönste Jungfrau sitzet
Dort oben wunderbar,
Ihr goldnes Geschmeide blitzet,
Sie kämmt ihr goldenes Haar.

Sie kämmt es mit goldenem Kamme,
Und singt ein Lied dabei;
Das hat eine wundersame,
Gewaltige Melodei.

Den Schiffer im kleinen Schiffe
Ergreift es mit wildem Weh;
Er schaut nicht die Felsenriffe,
Er schaut nur hinauf in die Höh.

## "*From my great sorrows*"

From my great sorrows
I make little songs;
They lift their musical wings
And flutter away wherever they wish.

They found their way to my sweetheart,
But they have come back and they lament,
And lament, and refuse to say
What they saw in her heart.

## "*I don't know what it may signify*"[32]

I don't know what it may signify
That I am so sad;
There's a tale from ancient times
That I can't get out of my mind.

The air is cool and it is growing dark,
And the Rhine is flowing calmly;
The peak of the mountain is sparkling
In the evening sunlight.

The loveliest maiden is sitting
Up there, wondrous to tell;
Her golden jewelry flashes,
She combs her golden hair.

She combs it with a golden comb,
And sings a song as she does so,
Which has a peculiar,
Powerful melody.

It seizes upon the boatman in his small boat
With unrestrained woe;
He does not look at the rocky shoals,
He only looks up at the heights.

---

[32]In some editions, this poem is given the title "Die Lorelei" (with various spellings).

Ich glaube, die Wellen verschlingen
Am Ende Schiffer und Kahn;
Und das hat mit ihrem Singen
Die Lore-Ley getan.

## "Leise zieht durch mein Gemüt"

Leise zieht durch mein Gemüt
Liebliches Geläute.
Klinge, kleines Frühlingslied,
Kling hinaus ins Weite.

Kling hinaus, bis an das Haus,
Wo die Blumen sprießen.
Wenn du eine Rose schaust,
Sag, ich laß sie grüßen.

## "Der Tod, das ist die kühle Nacht"

Der Tod, das ist die kühle Nacht,
Das Leben ist der schwüle Tag.
Es dunkelt schon, mich schläfert,
Der Tag hat mich müd gemacht.

Über mein Bett erhebt sich ein Baum,
Drin singt die junge Nachtigall;
Sie singt von lauter Liebe,
Ich hör es sogar im Traum.

## "Das ist ein schlechtes Wetter"

Das ist ein schlechtes Wetter,
Es regnet und stürmt und schneit;
Ich sitze am Fenster und schaue
Hinaus in die Dunkelheit.

If I'm not mistaken, the waters
Finally swallow both boatman and boat;
And with her singing
Lorelei did this.


## "Softly passing through my mind"

Softly passing through my mind
Is a lovely pealing sound.
Ring, little spring song,
Ring out into the distance.

Ring out till you reach the house
Where the flowers are sprouting.
If you see a rose,
Give her my regards.


## "Death is the cool night"

Death is the cool night,
Life is the sultry day.
It is already growing dark; I am drowsy;
The day has made me weary.

Over my bed there rises a tree,
In it the young nightingale is singing.
It is singing of nothing but love;
I hear it even in my dreams.


## "This is bad weather"

This is bad weather;
It's raining and storming and snowing;
I sit by my window and look
Out into the darkness.

Da schimmert ein einsames Lichtchen,
Das wandelt langsam fort;
Ein Mütterchen mit dem Laternchen
Wankt über die Straße dort.

Ich glaube Mehl und Eier
Und Butter kaufte sie ein;
Sie will einen Kuchen backen
Fürs große Töchterlein.

Die liegt zu Haus im Lehnstuhl,
Und blinzelt schläfrig ins Licht;
Die goldnen Locken wallen
Über das süße Gesicht.

## Die schlesischen Weber

Im düstern Auge keine Träne,
Sie sitzen am Webstuhl und fletschen die Zähne:
Deutschland, wir weben dein Leichentuch,
Wir weben hinein den dreifachen Fluch—
    Wir weben, wir weben!

Ein Fluch dem Gotte, zu dem wir gebeten
In Winterskälte und Hungersnöten;
Wir haben vergebens gehofft und geharrt,
Er hat uns geäfft und gefoppt und genarrt—
    Wir weben, wir weben!

Ein Fluch dem König, dem König der Reichen,
Den unser Elend nicht konnte erweichen,
Der den letzten Groschen von uns erpreßt
Und uns wie Hunde erschießen läßt—
    Wir weben, wir weben!

Ein Fluch dem falschen Vaterlande,
Wo nur gedeihen Schmach und Schande,
Wo jede Blume früh geknickt,
Wo Fäulnis und Moder den Wurm erquickt—
    Wir weben, wir weben!

There a solitary little light is glimmering,
Which moves ahead slowly;
A little old lady with her small lantern
Is tottering down the street there.

I think she has just purchased
Flour and eggs and butter;
She intends to bake a cake
For her grown-up daughter.

She is stretched out at home in the armchair,
Blinking drowsily at the light;
Her golden tresses tumble
Over her sweet face.

## The Silesian Weavers

No tears in their somber eyes,
They sit at the loom and show their teeth:
Germany, we are weaving your winding-sheet,
We are weaving into it the triple curse—
    We are weaving, we are weaving!

A curse on the God, to Whom we prayed
In winter's cold and in famines;
We hoped and waited in vain,
He mocked and cheated and fooled us—
    We are weaving, we are weaving!

A curse on the King, the King of the rich,
Whom our misery failed to soften,
Who squeezes the last pennies out of us
And lets us be shot down like dogs—
    We are weaving, we are weaving!

A curse on our false homeland,
Where only shame and disgrace flourish,
Where every flower is blighted too soon,
Where rot and mold nourish the worms—
    We are weaving, we are weaving!

Das Schiffchen fliegt, der Webstuhl kracht,
Wir weben emsig Tag und Nacht—
Altdeutschland, wir weben dein Leichentuch,
Wir weben hinein den dreifachen Fluch,
Wir weben, wir weben!

## Morphine

Groß ist die Ähnlichkeit der beiden schönen
Jünglingsgestalten, ob der eine gleich
Viel blässer als der andre, auch viel strenger,
Fast möcht ich sagen: viel vornehmer aussieht
Als jener andre, welcher mich vertraulich
In seine Arme schloß—Wie lieblich sanft
War dann sein Lächeln, und sein Blick wie selig!
Dann mocht es wohl geschehn, daß seines Hauptes
Mohnblumenkranz auch meine Stirn berührte
Und seltsam duftend allen Schmerz verscheuchte
Aus meiner Seel—Doch solche Linderung,
Sie dauert kurze Zeit; genesen gänzlich
Kann ich nur dann, wenn seine Fackel senkt
Der andre Bruder, der so ernst und bleich.—
Gut ist der Schlaf, der Tod ist besser—freilich
Das beste wäre, nie geboren sein.

## Gedächtnisfeier

Keine Messe wird man singen,
Keinen Kadosch wird man sagen,
Nichts gesagt und nichts gesungen
Wird an meinen Sterbetagen.

Doch vielleicht an solchem Tage,
Wenn das Wetter schön und milde,

The shuttle flies, the loom groans,
We weave busily day and night—
Old Germany, we are weaving your winding-sheet,
We are weaving into it the triple curse—
    We are weaving, we are weaving!


## *Morphine* [33]

Great is the resemblance between the two handsome
Images of youths,[34] although one of them
Looks much paler than the other, also much more severe,
I might almost say much more aristocratic,
Than that other one, who has intimately
Clasped me in his arms.—How sweetly gentle
His smile then was, and his gaze how blissful!
Then it may well have been true, that his head's
Garland of poppy flowers also touched my forehead
And with its strange fragrance dispelled all pain
From my soul.—But such relief
Lasts only a brief time; I can only
Recover completely when the other brother,
Who is so serious and pale, lowers his torch.—
Sleep is good, death is better.—Of course,
The best thing of all would be never to have been born.


## *Memorial Service*

No one will sing a Mass,
No one will say a kaddisch,
There will be nothing said and nothing sung
On the anniversaries of my death.

    But perhaps on such a day,
    If the weather is fair and mild,

---

[33]The title of the original is probably in French, since the German words for morphine
are *Morphium* or *Morphin*.

[34]Sleep and Death, as personified in Greco-Roman imagery.

Geht spazieren auf Montmartre
Mit Paulinen Frau Mathilde.

Mit dem Kranz von Immortellen
Kommt sie, mir das Grab zu schmücken
Und sie seufzet: "Pauvre homme!"
Feuchte Wehmut in den Blicken.

Leider wohn' ich viel zu hoch,
Und ich habe meiner Süßen
Keinen Stuhl hier anzubieten;
Ach! sie schwankt mit müden Füßen.

Süßes, dickes Kind, du darfst
Nicht zu Fuß nach Hause gehen;
An dem Barriere-Gitter
Siehst du die Fiaker stehen.


## "Ein Wetterstrahl, beleuchtend plötzlich"

Ein Wetterstrahl, beleuchtend plötzlich
Des Abgrunds Nacht, war mir dein Brief:
Er zeigte blendend hell, wie tief
Mein Unglück ist, wie tief entsetzlich.

Selbst dich ergreift ein Mitgefühl!
Dich, die in meines Lebens Wildnis
So schweigsam standest wie ein Bildnis,
Das marmorschön und marmorkühl.

O Gott, wie muß ich elend sein!
Denn sie sogar beginnt zu sprechen,
Aus ihrem Auge Tränen brechen,
Der Stein sogar erbarmt sich mein!

Erschüttert hat mich, was ich sah!
Auch du erbarm dich mein und spende
Die Ruhe mir, o Gott, und ende
Die schreckliche Tragödia.

Mrs. Mathilde[35] will take a walk
In Montmartre with Pauline.[36]

With a wreath of everlastings
She comes to decorate my grave,
And she sighs: "Pauvre homme!"[37]
With moist sorrow in her eyes.

Unfortunately I live far too high up,
And I have no chair here
To offer to my sweet one;
Alas! she staggers on tired feet.

Sweet, fat girl, you must not
Go home on foot;
At the customs barrier railing
You can see the fiacres waiting.

## "A flash of lightning, suddenly illuminating"

A flash of lightning, suddenly illuminating
The night of the abyss, your letter was to me:
It showed with blinding clarity how deep
My misfortune is, how deeply horrible.

Compassion touches even you!
You, who in the wilderness of my life
Stood as silently as a statue
Beautiful as marble and cold as marble.

O God, how utterly wretched I must be!
For even *she* begins to speak,
Tears gush from her eyes,
Even the stone takes pity on me!

I was shaken by what I saw!
You, too, God, take pity on me
And bestow rest upon me, and end
The fearful tragedy.

---

[35]The poet's wife.
[36]A family friend.
[37]"Poor man!" (in French).

# Nikolaus Lenau

## Die drei Zigeuner

Drei Zigeuner fand ich einmal
Liegen an einer Weide,
Als mein Fuhrwerk mit müder Qual
Schlich durch sandige Heide.

Hielt der eine für sich allein
In den Händen die Fiedel,
Spielte, umglüht vom Abendschein,
Sich ein feuriges Liedel.

Hielt der zweite die Pfeif im Mund,
Blickte nach seinem Rauche,
Froh, als ob er vom Erdenrund
Nichts zum Glücke mehr brauche.

Und der dritte behaglich schlief,
Und sein Zimbal am Baum hing,
Über die Saiten ein Windhauch lief,
Über sein Herz ein Traum ging.

An den Kleidern trugen die drei
Löcher und bunte Flicken;
Aber sie boten trotzig frei
Spott den Erdengeschicken.

Dreifach haben sie mir gezeigt,
Wenn das Leben uns nachtet,
Wie mans verraucht, verschläft, vergeigt
Und es dreimal verachtet.

Nach den Zigeunern lang noch schaun
Mußt ich im Weiterfahren,
Nach den Gesichtern dunkelbraun,
Den schwarzlockigen Haaren.

# Nikolaus Lenau

## *The Three Gypsies*

I once found three Gypsies
Lying by a willow,
As my carriage crawled with weary torment
Across a sandy heath.

One of them, for his own enjoyment, held
A fiddle in his hands,
And, with the glow of evening gleaming around him, played
Himself a fiery ditty.

The second had a pipe in his mouth,
And was watching his own smoke,
Merry as if he needed nothing more
From the world for his happiness.

And the third was sleeping comfortably,
And his cimbalom[38] was hanging on the tree.
A gust of wind swept over its strings,
And a dream passed over his heart.

On their clothes the three displayed
Holes and multicolored patches,
But, defiant and free, they showed
Scorn for earthly destinies.

In three ways they showed me,
When life grows dark for us,
How one can smoke, sleep and fiddle it away
And triply despise it.

I had to look back for a long time yet
At the Gypsies as we traveled on,
At their dark brown faces,
Their long, black hair.

---

[38]A Hungarian psaltery (or dulcimer); in this case, a small, portable one.

## Einsamkeit

### I

Hast du schon je dich ganz allein gefunden,
Lieblos und ohne Gott auf einer Heide,
Die Wunden schnöden Mißgeschicks verbunden
Mit stolzer Stille, zornig dumpfem Leide?

War jede frohe Hoffnung dir entschwunden,
Wie einem Jäger an der Bergesscheide
Stirbt das Gebell von den verlornen Hunden,
Wie's Vöglein zieht, daß es den Winter meide?

Warst du auf einer Heide so allein,
So weißt du auch, wie's einen dann bezwingt,
Daß er umarmend stürzt an einen Stein;

Daß er, von seiner Einsamkeit erschreckt,
Entsetzt empor vom starren Felsen springt
Und bang dem Winde nach die Arme streckt.

### II

Der Wind ist fremd, du kannst ihn nicht umfassen,
Der Stein ist tot, du wirst beim kalten, derben
Umsonst um eine Trosteskunde werben,
So fühlst du auch bei Rosen dich verlassen;

Bald siehst du sie, dein ungewahr, erblassen,
Beschäftigt nur mit ihrem eignen Sterben.
Geh weiter: überall grüßt dich Verderben
In der Geschöpfe langen, dunklen Gassen;

Siehst hier und dort sie aus den Hütten schauen,
Dann schlagen sie vor dir die Fenster zu,
Die Hütten stürzen, und du fühlst ein Grauen.

Lieblos und ohne Gott! der Weg ist schaurig,
Der Zugwind in den Gassen kalt; und du?—
Die ganze Welt ist zum Verzweifeln traurig.

## Loneliness

### I

Have you ever found yourself completely alone,
Loveless and without God upon a heath,
The wounds of disdainful misfortune bandaged
With proud taciturnity and angrily muted sorrow?

Had every hope of joy vanished for you,
As for a huntsman at a rift in the mountains
The barking of his lost dogs dies away,
As the songbird migrates to avoid the winter?

If you have been so alone on a heath,
Then you also know how a man is so overcome
That he dashes over to a stone and embraces it;

That, frightened by his loneliness,
He leaps up in horror from the rigid crag
And in his fear stretches out his arms to the wind.

### II

The wind is a stranger, you cannot embrace it;
The stone is dead; from that cold, rough thing
You will solicit a message of comfort in vain;
Even among roses you will feel neglected;

Soon you will see them fade, unaware of you,
Concerned solely with their own dying.
Pass onward: everywhere decay greets you
In the long, dark streets of God's creatures;

Here and there you see them looking out of their huts,
Then they slam their windows shut in your face,
The huts collapse and you feel a shudder of horror.

Loveless and without God! The way is frightful,
The gusty wind cold in the streets; and you?—
The whole world is so sad that you must give up hope.

## *Frage*

Bist du noch nie beim Morgenschein erwacht
Mit schwerem Herzen, traurig und beklommen,
Und wußtest nicht, wie du auch nachgedacht,
Woher ins Herz der Gram dir war gekommen?

Du fühltest nur: ein Traum wars in der Nacht;
Des Traumes Bilder waren dir verschwommen,
Doch hat nachwirkend ihre dunkle Macht
Dich, daß du weinen mußtest, übernommen.

Hast du dich einst der Erdennacht entschwungen,
Und werden, wie du meinst, am hellen Tage
Verloren sein des Traums Erinnerungen:

Wer weiß, ob nicht so deine Schuld hienieden
Nachwirken wird als eine dunkle Klage,
Und dort der Seele stören ihren Frieden?

## *"Rings ein Verstummen, ein Entfärben"*

Rings ein Verstummen, ein Entfärben;
Wie sanft den Wald die Lüfte streicheln,
Sein welkes Laub ihm abzuschmeicheln:
Ich liebe dieses milde Sterben.

Von hinne geht die stille Reise,
Die Zeit der Liebe ist verklungen,
Die Vögel haben ausgesungen,
Und dürre Blätter sinken leise.

Die Vögel zogen nach dem Süden,
Aus dem Verfall des Laubes tauchen
Die Nester, die nicht Schutz mehr brauchen,
Die Blätter fallen stets, die Müden.

In dieses Waldes leisem Rauschen
Ist mir, als hör' ich Kunde wehen,
Daß alles Sterben und Vergehen
Nur heimlichstill vergnügtes Tauschen.

## Question

Have you never yet awaked in the morning light
With a heavy heart, sad and oppressed,
And didn't know, no matter how much you thought about it,
From where the sorrow had come into your heart?

You only felt: it was a dream during the night;
The images of the dream had become blurred to you,
But their dark power had the aftereffect
Of taking possession of you until you had to weep.

When some day you have soared away from earthly night,
And, as you think, in the bright day
The recollections of the dream will be lost:

Who knows whether your guilt here below
Will not similarly later affect you like a dark lament,
And disturb your soul's peace there?

## *"All around, silence falls, color fades"*

All around, silence falls, color fades;
How softly the breezes caress the forest,
In order to coax it to give up its withered foliage:
I love this gentle dying.

The quiet journey takes its departure from here,
The time of love has died away,
The birds have sung their last song,
And dry leaves sink softly.

The birds have migrated south;
From the ruin of the foliage emerge
The nests, which no longer need protection;
The leaves, weary, keep falling.

In the gentle rustling of this forest
I seem to hear a message wafting,
That all dying and perishing
Is merely a secretly quiet, contented exchanging.

# Eduard Mörike

## *Gesang zu zweien in der Nacht*

SIE:
Wie süß der Nachtwind nun die Wiese streift
Und klingend jetzt den jungen Hain durchläuft!
Da noch der freche Tag verstummt,
Hört man der Erdenkräfte flüsterndes Gedränge,
Das aufwärts in die zärtlichen Gesänge
Der reingestimmten Lüfte summt.

ER:
Vernehm ich doch die wunderbarsten Stimmen,
Vom lauen Wind wollüstig hingeschleift,
Index, mit ungewissem Licht gestreift,
Der Himmel selber scheinet hinzuschwimmen.

SIE:
Wie ein Gewebe zuckt die Luft manchmal,
Durchsichtiger und heller aufzuwehen;
Dazwischen hört man weiche Töne gehen
Von sel'gen Feeen, die im blauen Saal
Zum Sphärenklang,
Und fleißig mit Gesang,
Silberne Spindeln hin und wider drehen.

ER:
O holde Nacht, du gehst mit leisem Tritt
Auf schwarzem Samt, der nur am Tage grünet,
Und luftig schwirrender Musik bedienet
Sich nun dein Fuß zum leichten Schritt,
Womit du Stund um Stunde missest,
Dich lieblich in dir selbst vergissest—
Du schwärmst, es schwärmt der Schöpfung Seele mit!

# Eduard Mörike

## *Duo in the Night*

SHE:
How sweetly the night wind now brushes the meadow,
And now resoundingly sweeps through the young grove!
While the impudent day is still mute,
One can hear the whispered pressure of the earth's forces,
Which hums upward into the delicate songs
Of the purely tuned breezes.

HE:
And yet I perceive the most wonderful voices,
Drawn forth voluptuously by the warm wind,
While, streaked with uncertain light,
The sky itself seems to be swimming away.

SHE:
The air quivers like a cloth from time to time,
In order to waft more transparently and brightly;
In between times, one can hear passing the soft tones
Of blissful fairies who, in their blue hall,
To the music of the spheres,
And diligently as they sing,
Are turning silver spindles back and forth.

HE:
O lovely night, you walk with gentle pace
On black velvet that only turns green in the daytime,
And your feet now make use
Of airily whirring music for their light steps,
With which you measure hour after hour,
Forgetting yourself sweetly in yourself—
You dream in rapture, and the soul of Creation dreams along with you!

## Um Mitternacht

Gelassen stieg die Nacht ans Land,
Lehnt träumend an der Berge Wand,
Ihr Auge sieht die goldne Waage nun
Der Zeit in gleichen Schalen stille ruhn;
    Und kecker rauschen die Quellen hervor,
    Sie singen der Mutter, der Nacht, ins Ohr
        Vom Tage,
    Vom heute gewesenen Tage.

Das uralt alte Schlummerlied,
Sie achtets nicht, sie ist es müd;
Ihr klingt des Himmels Bläue süßer noch,
Der flücht'gen Stunden gleichgeschwungnes Joch.
    Doch immer behalten die Quellen das Wort,
    Es singen die Wasser im Schlafe noch fort
        Vom Tage,
    Vom heute gewesenen Tage.


## Fußreise

Am frischgeschnittnen Wanderstab,
Wenn ich in der Frühe
So durch die Wälder ziehe,
Hügel auf und ab:
Dann, wie's Vögelein im Laube
Singet und sich rührt,
Oder wie die goldne Traube
Wonnegeister spürt
In der ersten Morgensonne:
So fühlt auch mein alter, lieber
Adam Herbst- und Frühlingsfieber,
Gottbeherzte,
Nie verscherzte
Erstlings-Paradieseswonne.

## At Midnight

Calmly Night has ascended the land;
She leans, dreaming, on the wall of the mountains;
Her eyes now see the golden balance
Of time reposing quietly with even scales;
  And the springs murmur forth more boldly;
  They sing into the ear of their mother, Night,
    About the day,
  About the day that has just ended.

The age-old, ancient slumber song,
She pays it no heed, she is weary of it;
The blue of the sky still sounds sweeter to her,
The evenly curved yoke of the fleeting hours.
  But the springs always have their way;
  In their sleep the waters still go on singing
    About the day,
  About the day that has just ended.

## Walking Tour

When, leaning on my freshly cut walking staff
In the morning
I pass through the forests like this,
Uphill and down:
Then, just as the songbird in the leaves
Sings and stirs,
Or as the golden grapes
Feel spirits of bliss
In the first morning sun:
Thus does my dear old Adam[39]
Feel autumn and spring fever,
The divinely inspirited,
Never-trifled-away
Pristine bliss of Paradise.

---

[39]That is, man's primal nature, unrectified by religion.

Also bist du nicht so schlimm, o alter
Adam, wie die strengen Lehrer sagen;
Liebst und lobst du immer doch,
Singst und preisest immer noch,
Wie an ewig neuen Schöpfungstagen,
Deinen lieben Schöpfer und Erhalter.

Möcht' es dieser geben,
Und mein ganzes Leben
Wär' im leichten Wanderschweiße
Eine solche Morgenreise!

## An eine Äolsharfe

Tu semper urges flebilibus modis
Mysten ademptum: nec tibi Vespero
Surgente decedunt amores,
Nec rapidum fugiente Solem.

*Horaz*

Angelehnt an die Efeuwand
Dieser alten Terrasse,
Du, einer luftgebornen Muse
Geheimnisvolles Saitenspiel,
Fang an,
Fange wieder an
Deine melodische Klage!

Ihr kommet, Winde, fern herüber
Ach! von des Knaben,
Der mir so lieb war,
Frisch grünendem Hügel.
Und Frühlingsblüten unterweges streifend,
Übersättigt mit Wohlgerüchen,
Wie süß bedrängt ihr dies Herz!

And so you are not as evil, O old
Adam, as the severe theologians say;
Just as on eternally new days of Creation,
You still love and praise,
You still sing and glorify
Your dear Creator and Sustainer.

If He grants it,
My whole life
Would be such a morning journey
In the light perspiration of travel!

## To an Aeolian Harp [40]

You constantly dwell on the death of Mystes[41]
With mournful melodies; neither when the evening star
    Rises does your love abate,
        Nor when it flees the rapid Sun.
                                    *Horace* [Odes II, 10].

Leaning against the ivy-covered wall
Of this old terrace,
You, the mysterious stringed instrument
Of an air-born muse,
Begin,
Begin once more
Your melodic lament!

You come here, winds, from afar,
Alas! from the newly green hill
Of the boy
Who was so dear to me.
And brushing against spring blossoms on your way,
Saturated with fragrances,
How sweetly you oppress this heart!

---

[40]A sweet-toned stringed box, placed outdoors or in a window, to be activated, or "played," by the wind.

[41]A beloved Greek boy slave (Horace is addressing a male Roman).

Und säuselt her in die Saiten,
Angezogen von wohllautender Wehmut,
Wachsend im Zug meiner Sehnsucht,
Und histerbend wieder.

Aber auf einmal,
Wie der Wind heftiger herstößt,
Ein holder Schrei der Harfe
Wiederholt, mir zu süßem Erschrecken,
Meiner Seele plötzliche Regung;
Und hier—die volle Rose streut, geschüttelt,
All ihre Blätter vor meine Füße!


## Schön-Rohtraut

Wie heißt König Ringangs Töchterlein?
Rohtraut, Schön-Rohtraut.
Was tut sie denn den ganzen Tag,
Da sie wohl nicht spinnen und nähen mag?
Tut fischen und jagen.
O daß ich doch ihr Jäger wär!
Fischen und Jagen freute mich sehr.
—Schweig stille, mein Herze!

Und über eine kleine Weil,
Rohtraut, Schön-Rohtraut,
So dient der Knab auf Ringangs Schloß
In Jägertracht und hat ein Roß,
Mit Rohtraut zu jagen.
O daß ich doch ein Königssohn wär!
Rohtraut, Schön-Rohtraut lieb ich so sehr.
—Schweig stille, mein Herze!

Einsmals sie ruhten am Eichenbaum,
Da lacht Schön-Rohtraut:
„Was siehst mich an so wunniglich?
Wenn du das Herz hast, küsse mich!"
Ach! erschrak der Knabe!
Doch denket er: „Mir ist's vergunnt",

And you murmur here into the strings,
Allured by euphonious melancholy,
Growing in the current of my longing,
And dying away again.

But all at once,
As the wind gusts this way more forcefully,
A lovely cry of the harp,
To my sweet alarm, repeats
The sudden stirring of my soul;
And here—the full-blown rose, shaken, scatters
All its petals at my feet!


## Fair Rohtraut

What is the name of King Ringang's young daughter?
    Rohtraut, fair Rohtraut,
What does she do, then, all day long,
Since she surely doesn't like spinning and sewing?
    She goes fishing and hunting.
Oh, if only I were her huntsman!
Fishing and hunting would greatly delight me.
    —Be silent, my heart!

And after a brief while—
    Rohtraut, fair Rohtraut—
The boy was serving in Ringang's castle
In huntsman's garb, and had a horse,
    To hunt with Rohtraut.
Oh, if only I were a prince!
I love Rohtraut, fair Rohtraut, so much
    —Be silent, my heart!

One day they were resting by the oak tree;
    Fair Rohtraut laughed:
"Why are you looking at me in such rapture?
If you have the courage, kiss me!"
    My! Was the boy frightened!
But he thought: "It is freely granted to me,"

Und küsset Schön-Rohtraut auf den Mund.
—Schweig stille, mein Herze!

Darauf sie ritten schweigend heim,
　Rohtraut, Schön-Rohtraut;
Es jauchzt der Knab in seinem Sinn:
„Und würdst du heute Kaiserin,
　Mich sollt's nicht kränken!
Ihr tausend Blätter im Walde wißt,
Ich hab Schön-Rohtrauts Mund geküßt!
—Schweig stille, mein Herze!"

## Der Feuerreiter

Sehet ihr am Fensterlein
Dort die rote Mütze wieder?
Nicht geheuer muß es sein,
Denn er geht schon auf und nieder.
Und auf einmal welch Gewühle
Bei der Brücke, nach dem Feld!
Horch! das Feuerglöcklein gellt:
　Hinterm Berg,
　Hinterm Berg
Brennt es in der Mühle!

Schaut! da sprengt er wütend schier
Durch das Tor, der Feuerreiter,
Auf dem rippendürren Tier,
Als auf einer Feuerleiter!
Querfeldein! Durch Qualm und Schwüle
Rennt er schon und ist am Ort!
Drüben schallt es fort und fort:
　Hinterm Berg,
　Hinterm Berg
Brennt es in der Mühle.

And kissed fair Rohtraut on the lips.
—Be silent, my heart.

After that they rode home without speaking—
Rohtraut, fair Rohtraut—
The boy was exulting in his mind:
"And even if you became empress today,
That wouldn't bother me!
You thousand leaves in the forest know
I have kissed fair Rohtraut's lips!
—Be silent, my heart!"

## The Fire Horseman[42]

Do you see at the small window
There the red cap again?
There must be something weird about it,
Because he is already going up and down.
And all at once what a hubbub
At the bridge, past the field!
Listen! The fire bell is shrieking;
  Behind the hill,
  Behind the hill
There's a fire in the mill!

Look! there he gallops nearly insane
Through the gate, the Fire Horseman,
On his thin beast with prominent ribs,
As if riding a fire ladder!
Across the fields! Through smoke and heat
He already races and is at the spot!
Yonder the clangor repeats again and again:
  Behind the hill,
  Behind the hill
There's a fire in the mill!

---

[42]Legendary figure who appears at fires and extinguishes them by riding around them.

Der so oft den roten Hahn
Meilenweit von fern gerochen,
Mit des heilgen Kreuzes Span
Freventlich die Glut besprochen—
Weh! dir grinst vom Dachgestühle
Dort der Feind im Höllenschein.
Gnade Gott der Seele dein!
   Hinterm Berg,
   Hinterm Berg
Rast er in der Mühle!

Keine Stunde hielt es an,
Bis die Mühle borst in Trümmer;
Doch den kecken Reitersmann
Sah man von der Stunde nimmer.
Volk und Wagen im Gewühle
Kehren heim von all dem Graus;
Auch das Glöcklein klinget aus:
   Hinterm Berg,
   Hinterm Berg
Brennts!—

Nach der Zeit ein Müller fand
Ein Gerippe samt der Mützen
Aufrecht an der Kellerwand
Auf der beinern Mähre sitzen:
Feuerreiter, wie so kühle
Reitest du in deinem Grab!
Husch! da fällts in Asche ab.
   Ruhe wohl,
   Ruhe wohl
Drunten in der Mühle!


## Auf einer Wanderung

In ein freundliches Städtchen tret' ich ein,
In den Straßen liegt roter Abendschein.
Aus einem offnen Fenster eben,
Über den reichsten Blumenflor
Hinweg, hört man Goldglockentöne schweben,

You who so often have smelled
The "red rooster" from miles away,
And with a splinter of the Holy Cross
Have shamelessly conjured away the blaze—
Alas! From the roof beams the Enemy
Is grinning at you there in the infernal glare.
God be merciful to your soul!
  Behind the hill,
  Behind the hill
He is raging in the mill!

It didn't take an hour
Before the mill burst into ruins;
But the brave rider
Was never seen from that time on.
People and carriages in a confused throng
Returned home from all that horror;
Even the bell died away:
  Behind the hill,
  Behind the hill
There's a fire!—

When time had passed, a miller found
A skeleton together with the cap
Sitting upright by the cellar wall
On the bony mare:
Fire Horseman, how coolly
You ride in your grave!
Suddenly it all crumbled to ash.
  Rest in peace,
  Rest in peace
Down in the mill!

## On a Jaunt

I enter a friendly little town;
In its streets lies the red glow of evening.
Just then out of an open window,
Past the most luxuriant display of flowers,
You can hear the sounds of golden bells floating,

Und *eine* Stimme scheint ein Nachtigallenchor,
Daß die Blüten beben,
Daß die Lüfte leben,
Daß in höherem Rot die Rosen leuchten vor.

Lang' hielt ich staunend, lustbeklommen.
Wie ich hinaus vors Tor gekommen,
Ich weiß es wahrlich selber nicht.
Ach hier, wie liegt die Welt so licht!
Der Himmel wogt in purpurnem Gewühle,
Rückwärts die Stadt in goldnem Rauch;
Wie rauscht der Erlenbach, wie rauscht im Grund die Mühle!
Ich bin wie trunken, irrgeführt—
O Muse, du hast mein Herz berührt
Mit einem Liebeshauch!


## Auf eine Lampe

Noch unverrückt, o schöne Lampe, schmückest du,
An leichten Ketten zierlich aufgehangen hier,
Die Decke des nun fast vergeßnen Lustgemachs.
Auf deiner weißen Marmorschale, deren Rand
Der Efeukranz von goldengrünem Erz umflicht,
Schlingt fröhlich eine Kinderschar den Ringelreihn.
Wie reizend alles! lachend, und ein sanfter Geist
Des Ernstes doch ergossen um die ganze Form—
Ein Kunstgebild der echten Art. Wer achtet sein?
Was aber schön ist, selig scheint es in ihm selbst.


## Denk es, o Seele!

Ein Tännlein grünet wo,
Wer weiß, im Walde,
Ein Rosenstrauch, wer sagt,
In welchem Garten?

And one voice seems like a chorus of nightingales,
So that the blossoms tremble,
So that the breezes come to life,
So that the roses shine forth with a heightened redness.

I halted for some time, amazed, oppressed with pleasure.
How I found myself outside the town gate
I really don't know myself.
Ah, here, how bright the world is!
The sky surges in purple confusion,
Behind me the city in a golden haze;
How the alder-lined brook murmurs, how the mill in the valley clatters!
I am as if intoxicated, mystified—
O Muse, you have touched my heart
With a breath of love!


## On a Lamp

Still unmoved, O beautiful lamp, gracefully hanging here
On light chains, you adorn
The ceiling of this now almost forgotten garden pavilion.
On your white marble bowl, whose rim
An ivy wreath of gold-green bronze surrounds,
A crowd of children merrily join hands in a round dance.
How charming it all is! Smiling, and a gentle spirit
Of gravity nevertheless diffused around the entire form—
An artwork of the true kind. Who pays attention to it?
But that which is beautiful seems to find bliss within itself.[43]


## Think of It, My Soul!

A little fir tree is in green leaf,
Who knows where, in the forest;
A rose bush, who can say
In which garden?

---

[43]There is a controversy about whether the *scheint* does mean "seems" or is to be translated "glows": "glows blissfully within itself." Why not both?

Sie sind erlesen schon,
Denk es, o Seele!
Auf deinem Grab zu wurzeln
Und zu wachsen.

Zwei schwarze Rößlein weiden
Auf der Wiese,
Sie kehren heim zur Stadt
In muntern Sprüngen.
Sie werden schrittweis gehn
Mit deiner Leiche;
Vielleicht, vielleicht noch eh
An ihren Hufen
Das Eisen los wird,
Das ich blitzen sehe!

They are already chosen,
Think of it, my soul!
To take root on your grave
And grow there.

Two black colts are grazing
In the meadow;
They return home to the city
In lively capers.
They will tread a slow pace
With your corpse,
Perhaps, perhaps even before
The iron that I see
Flashing on their hooves
Becomes loose!

# Friedrich Hebbel

## Nachtlied

Quellende, schwellende Nacht,
Voll von Lichtern und Sternen;
In den ewigen Fernen,
Sage, was ist da erwacht?

Herz in der Brust wird beengt;
Steigendes, neigendes Leben,
Riesenhaft fühle ichs weben,
Welches das meine verdrängt.

Schlaf, da nahst du dich leis
Wie dem Kinde die Amme,
Und um die dürftige Flamme
Ziehst du den schützenden Kreis.


## Sie seh'n sich nicht wieder

Von dunkelnden Wogen
Hinunter gezogen,
   Zwei schimmernde Schwäne, sie schiffen daher,
Die Winde, sie schwellen
Allmälig die Wellen,
   Die Nebel, sie senken sich finster und schwer.

Die Schwäne, sie meiden
Einander und leiden,
   Nun tun sie es nicht mehr, sie können die Glut
Nicht länger verschließen,
Sie wollen genießen,
   Verhüllt von den Nebeln, gewiegt von der Flut.

# Friedrich Hebbel

## Night Song

Flowing, swelling night,
Full of lights and stars;
In the eternal distances,
Tell me, what has awakened there?

My heart is tightened in my breast;
Rising, descending life,
I feel it stirring gigantically,
Suppressing my own.

Sleep, then you approach quietly
As a nurse comes to a child,
And around the feeble flame
You draw a protective circle.

## They Won't Meet Again

Carried downstream
By waves that are growing dark,
    Two gleaming swans sail this way;
The winds swell
The waves gradually;
    The mists descend, dark and heavy.

The swans avoid
Each other and suffer;
    Now they do so no more, they can no longer
Contain their passion;
They desire pleasure,
    Concealed by the mists, rocked by the current.

Sie schmeicheln, sie kosen,
Sie trotzen dem Tosen
    Der Wellen, die Zweie in Eines verschränkt,
Wie die sich auch bäumen,
Sie glühen und träumen,
    In Liebe und Wonne zum Sterben versenkt.

Nach innigem Gatten
Ein süßes Ermatten,
    Da trennt sie die Woge, bevor sie's gedacht.
Lasst ruh'n das Gefieder!
Ihr seht euch nicht wieder,
    Der Tag ist vorüber, es dämmert die Nacht.


## Ich und Du

Wir träumten voneinander
Und sind davon erwacht,
Wir leben, um uns zu lieben,
Und sinken zurück in die Nacht.

Du tratst aus meinem Traume,
Aus deinem trat ich hervor,
Wir sterben, wenn sich Eines
Im Andern ganz verlor.

Auf einer Lilie zittern
Zwei Tropfen, rein und rund,
Zerfließen in Eins und rollen
Hinab in des Kelches Grund.


## Sommerbild

Ich sah des Sommers letzte Rose stehn,
Sie war, als ob sie bluten könne, rot;
Da sprach ich schauernd im Vorübergehn:
So weit im Leben, ist zu nah am Tod!

They fondle and caress,
They defy the raging
    Of the waves, the two interlocked as one;
No matter how high the waves rear up,
They ardently dream,
    Plunged into love and rapture to the point of death.

After fervent mating,
Pleasant exhaustion;
    Then the waves separate them before they know it.
Let your plumage rest!
You won't meet again;
    The day is over, night is falling.

## I and You

We dreamed of each other
And awoke from that dream;
We live to love each other
And we sink back into the night.

You stepped out of my dream,
I stepped out of yours;
We shall die when one of us
Has become completely lost in the other.

On a lily there tremble
Two drops, pure and round,
They join into one and roll
Down to the bottom of the cup.

## Summer Picture

I saw the last rose of summer standing;
It was as red as if it could bleed;
Then I said, shuddering, as I walked by:
"So advanced in life is too close to death!"

Es regte sich kein Hauch am heißen Tag,
Nur leise strich ein weißer Schmetterling;
Doch, ob auch kaum die Luft sein Flügelschlag
Bewegte, sie empfand es und verging.

## Herbstbild

Dies ist ein Herbsttag, wie ich keinen sah!
　Die Luft ist still, als atmete man kaum,
Und dennoch fallen raschelnd, fern und nah,
　Die schönsten Früchte ab von jedem Baum.

O stört sie nicht, die Feier der Natur!
　Dies ist die Lese, die sie selber hält,
Denn heute löst sich von den Zweigen nur,
　Was vor dem milden Strahl der Sonne fällt.

Not a breeze stirred on that hot day,
Only a white butterfly gently passed;
But even though its wing beat barely moved
The air, the rose felt it and perished.


## Autumn Picture

This is an autumn day like none I've ever seen!
   The air is as still as if one were scarcely breathing,
And yet, far and near, the loveliest fruits
   Are falling from every tree with a rustle.

Oh, do not disturb it, this festival of Nature!
   This is the harvest that she garners herself,
For, today the only things detaching from the branches
   Are those the gentle sunbeams cause to fall.

# Theodor Storm

## Sommermittag

Nun ist es still um Hof und Scheuer,
Und in der Mühle ruht der Stein;
Der Birnenbaum mit blanken Blättern
Steht regungslos im Sonnenschein.

Die Bienen summen so verschlafen;
Und in der offnen Bodenluk,
Benebelt von dem Duft des Heues,
Im grauen Röcklein nickt der Puk.

Der Müller schnarcht und das Gesinde,
Und nur die Tochter wacht im Haus;
Die lachet still und zieht sich heimlich
Fürsichtig die Pantoffeln aus.

Sie geht und weckt den Müllerburschen,
Der kaum den schweren Augen traut:
„Nun küsse mich, verliebter Junge;
Doch sauber, sauber! nicht zu laut."

## Die Stadt

Am grauen Strand, am grauen Meer
Und seitab liegt die Stadt;
Der Nebel drückt die Dächer schwer,
Und durch die Stille braust das Meer
Eintönig um die Stadt.

Es rauscht kein Wald, es schlägt im Mai
Kein Vogel ohn' Unterlaß;
Die Wandergans mit hartem Schrei
Nur fliegt in Herbstesnacht vorbei,
Am Strande weht das Gras.

# Theodor Storm

## Summer Noon

Now it is quiet around the farmyard and the barn,
And in the mill the stone is in repose;
The pear tree with shiny leaves
Stands motionless in the sunshine.

The bees are buzzing in a drowsy way;
And in the open dormer window,
Tipsy with the fragrance of the hay,
Puck is nodding in his little gray coat.

The miller and his helpers are snoring,
And his daughter is the only one awake in the house;
She laughs softly, and in secrecy takes off
Her slippers carefully.

She goes and awakens the miller lad,
Who scarcely believes his heavy eyes:
"Now kiss me, you darling boy;
But easy, easy, not too loud."

## The City

By the gray shore, by the gray sea,
And out of the way, lies the city;
Fog presses hard on the roofs,
And through the silence the sea
Roars monotonously around the city.

No forest rustles, in May no bird
Sings uninterruptedly;
Only the migrating geese with a harsh call
Fly by on autumn nights;
By the shore the grass waves.

Doch hängt mein ganzes Herz an dir,
Du graue Stadt am Meer;
Der Jugend Zauber für und für
Ruht lächelnd doch auf dir, auf dir,
Du graue Stadt am Meer.

## Frauenhand

Ich weiß es wohl, kein klagend Wort
Wird über deine Lippen gehen;
Doch, was so sanft dein Mund verschweigt,
Muß deine blasse Hand gestehen.

Die Hand, an der mein Auge hängt,
Zeigt jenen feinen Zug der Schmerzen,
Und daß in schlummerloser Nacht
Sie lag auf einem kranken Herzen.

## Von Katzen

Vergangnen Maitag brachte meine Katze
Zur Welt sechs allerliebste kleine Kätzchen,
Maikätzchen, alle weiß mit schwarzen Schwänzchen.
Fürwahr, es war ein zierlich Wochenbettchen!
Die Köchin aber—Köchinnen sind grausam,
Und Menschlichkeit wächst nicht in einer Küche—
Die wollte von den sechsen fünf ertränken,
Fünf weiße, schwarzgeschwänzte Maienkätzchen
Ermorden wollte dies verruchte Weib.
Ich half ihr heim!—der Himmel segne
Mir meine Menschlichkeit! Die lieben Kätzchen,
Sie wuchsen auf und schritten binnen kurzem
Erhobnen Schwanzes über Hof und Herd;
Ja, wie die Köchin auch ingrimmig dreinsah,
Sie wuchsen auf, und nachts vor ihrem Fenster
Probierten sie die allerliebsten Stimmchen.
Ich aber, wie ich sie so wachsen sahe,
Ich pries mich selbst und meine Menschlichkeit.—
Ein Jahr ist um, und Katzen sind die Kätzchen,
Und Maitag ists!—Wie soll ich es beschreiben,
Das Schauspiel, das sich jetzt vor mir entfaltet!

But I am attached to you with all my heart,
You gray city by the sea;
The magic of youth, nevertheless,
Lies smiling perpetually upon you, upon you,
You gray city by the sea.

## A Woman's Hand

I know very well, no complaining word
Will pass your lips;
But that which your mouth so gently conceals in silence,
Your pale hand must confess.

The hand, from which I cannot take my eyes away,
Shows that delicate trace of sorrows,
And that during a sleepless night
It lay upon a sick heart.

## About Cats

On last May Day my cat brought
Into the world six darling little kittens,
May kittens, all of them white with little black tails.
Really, it was a charming little childbed!
But my cook—cooks are cruel,
And humanity doesn't thrive in a kitchen—
Wanted to drown five out of the six;
Five white, black-tailed May kittens
This evil woman wanted to murder.
I told her off!—May Heaven bless me
For my humanity! The dear cats
Grew up and before long were walking
With lifted tail around my house and home;
Yes, despite my cook's furious glances,
They grew up, and at night in front of her window
They tried out their darling little voices.
But I, seeing them grow up that way,
Praised myself and my humanity.—
A year has passed, and the kittens are now cats,
And it's May Day!—How shall I describe
The scene that unfolds itself before me now!

Mein ganzes Haus, vom Keller bis zum Giebel,
Ein jeder Winkel ist ein Wochenbettchen!
Hier liegt das eine, dort das andre Kätzchen,
In Schränken, Körben, unter Tisch und Treppen,
Die Alte gar—nein, es ist unaussprechlich,
Liegt in der Köchin jungfräulichem Bette!
Und jede, jede von den sieben Katzen
Hat sieben, denkt euch! sieben junge Kätzchen,
Maikätzchen, alle weiß mit schwarzen Schwänzchen!
Die Köchin rast, ich kann der blinden Wut
Nicht Schranken setzen dieses Frauenzimmers;
Ersäufen will sie alle neunundvierzig!
Mir selber, ach, mir läuft der Kopf davon—
O Menschlichkeit, wie soll ich dich bewahren!
Was fang ich an mit sechsundfünfzig Katzen!

## Juli

Klingt im Wind ein Wiegenlied,
Sonne warm herniedersieht,
Seine Ähren senkt das Korn,
Rote Beere schwillt am Dorn,
Schwer von Segen ist die Flur—
Junge Frau, was sinnst du nur?

## An Klaus Groth

Wenn't Abend ward,
Un still de Welt und still dat Hart;
Wenn möd upt Knee di liggt de Hand,
Un ut din Husklock an de Wand
Du hörst den Parpendikelslag,

My whole house, from the cellar to the gable,
Each and every corner is a little childbed!
Here lies one kitten, there lies another,
In closets, baskets, under tables and stairs;
The old cat even—no, it's unspeakable—
Is lying on my cook's virginal bed!
And every last one of the seven cats
Has seven, imagine! seven young kittens,
May kittens, all of them white with little black tails!
The cook is beside herself, I can't place any limits
On the blind rage of that female;
She wants to drown all forty-nine!
Even I, alas, I'm losing my head over it—
O humanity, how am I to preserve you!
What am I to do with fifty-six cats?—

## July

A lullaby is heard on the breeze;
The sun looks down, giving warmth;
The grainfield bows its ears;
Red berries swell on the thorn bushes;
Heavy with blessing[44] is the countryside—
Young woman, what are you thinking about?

## To Klaus Groth [45]

When evening comes,
And the world is quiet and the heart is quiet;
When your hands rest wearily on your knees,
And from your house clock on the wall
You hear the beating of the pendulum,

---

[44]The phrase connotes pregnancy.

[45]In High German (present editor's version): "Wenn es Abend wird/ Und still die Welt und still das Herz;/ Wenn müde auf dem Knie dir liegt die Hand,/ Und aus deiner Hausuhr an der Wand/ Du hörst den Perpendikelschlag,/ Der nicht zu Wort kam über Tag;/ Wenn das Schummern in den Ecken liegt,/ Und draußen all das Nachtgewölk fliegt;/ Wenn dann noch einmal guckt die Sonne/ Mit goldenem Schein zum Fenster herein,/ Und, ehe der Schlaf kommt und die Nacht,/ Noch einmal alles lebt und lacht,—/ Das ist so was für das Menschenherz,/ Wenn es Abend wird."

De nich to Woort keem över Dag;
Wenn't Schummern in de Ecken liggt,
Un buten all de Nachtswulk flüggt;
Wenn denn noch eenmal kiekt de Sünn
Mit golden Schiin to't Finster rin,
Un, ehr de Slap kümmt un de Nacht,
Noch eenmal allens lävt un lacht,—
Dat is so wat vör't Minschenhart,
       Wenn't Abend ward.

## Über die Heide

Über die Heide hallet mein Schritt;
Dumpf aus der Erde wandert es mit.

Herbst ist gekommen, Frühling ist weit—
Gab es denn einmal selige Zeit?

Brauende Nebel geisten umher;
Schwarz ist das Kraut und der Himmel so leer.

Wär ich hier nur nicht gegangen im Mai!
Leben und Liebe—wie flog es vorbei!

## In Bulemanns Haus

Es klippt auf den Gassen im Mondenschein;
Das ist die zierliche Kleine,
Die geht auf ihren Pantöffelein
Behend und mutterseelenallein
Durch die Gassen im Mondenscheine.

Sie geht in ein alt verfallenes Haus;
Im Flur ist die Tafel gedecket,
Da tanzt vor dem Monde die Maus mit der Maus,

Which didn't speak out to you during the day;
When dusk lies in the corners,
And outside all the night clouds are flying;
When then once more the sun peeps
Into your window with a golden glow,
And, before sleep and the night come,
Once more everything lives and laughs,—
That is really something for the human heart,
    When evening comes.

## Over the Heath

Over the heath my steps resound.
A muffled noise from inside the earth accompanies me.

Autumn has come, spring is far away—
Was there really ever a happy time?

Brewing mists spook all around;
Black is the grass and the sky so empty.

If only I hadn't walked here in May!
Life and love—how they flew by!

## In Bulemann's House [46]

There is a clipclop sound on the narrow streets in the moonlight;
It is the dainty little girl
Walking in her little slippers
Nimbly and all alone
Through the narrow streets in the moonlight.

She enters an old, dilapidated house;
In the vestibule the banqueting table is laid;
There, in front of the moon, mouse dances with mouse;

---

[46]A legendary abandoned town house overrun by mice, the subject of one of Storm's short stories (with a totally different plot).

Da setzt sich das Kind mit den Mäusen zu Schmaus,
Die Tellerlein werden gelecket.

Und leer sind die Schüsseln; die Mäuslein im Nu
Verrascheln im Mauer und Holze;
Nun läßt es dem Mägdlein auch länger nicht Ruh,
Sie schüttelt ihr Kleidchen, sie schnürt sich die Schuh,
Dann tritt sie einher mit Stolze.

Es leuchtet ein Spiegel aus goldnem Gestell,
Da schaut sie hinein mit Lachen;
Gleich schaut auch heraus ein Mägdelein hell,
Das ist ihr einziger Spielgesell;
Nun woll'n sie sich lustig machen.

Sie nickt voll Huld, ihr gehört ja das Reich;
Da neigt sich das Spiegelkindlein,
Da neigt sich das Kind vor dem Spiegel zugleich,
Da neigen sich beide gar anmutreich,
Da lächeln die rosigen Mündlein.

Und wie sie lächeln, so hebt sich der Fuß,
Es rauschen die seidenen Röcklein,
Die Händchen werfen sich Kuß um Kuß,
Das Kind mit dem Kinde nun tanzen muß,
Es tanzen im Nacken die Löcklein.

Der Mond scheint voller und voller herein,
Auf dem Estrich gaukeln die Flimmer:
Im Takte schweben die Mägdelein,
Bald tauchen sie tief in die Schatten hinein,
Bald stehn sie in bläulichem Schimmer.

Nun sinken die Glieder, nun halten sie an
Und atmen aus Herzensgrunde;
Sie nahen sich schüchtern, und beugen sich dann
Und knien voreinander, und rühren sich an
Mit dem zarten unschuldigen Munde.

Doch müde werden die beiden allein
Von all der heimlichen Wonne;
Sehnsüchtig flüstert das Mägdelein:

There the child sits down with the mice for a feast,
The little dishes are licked.

And the bowls are empty; in a twinkling, the little mice
Scramble away into the walls and woodwork;
Now the little girl can no longer contain herself;
She shakes out her little dress, she ties her shoelaces,
Then she walks about proudly.

A mirror is gleaming from its golden frame,
She looks into it laughlingly;
At once a little girl also looks out of it brightly,
That is her only playmate;
Now they want to enjoy themselves.

She nods full of graciousness—after all, the kingdom belongs to her—
Whereupon the child in the mirror bows.
Then the child bows to the mirror at the same time,
Then they both bow most charmingly,
Then their rosy little lips smile.

And as they smile, they raise their feet,
Their little silk skirts rustle;
With their little hands they blow kiss after kiss to each other;
Now the child must dance with the child,
On their necks the little tresses dance.

The moon shines in rounder and rounder,
On the shiny plastered floor the glimmers create illusions:
The little girls float to a musical measure;
Now they plunge deep into the shadows,
Now they stand in a faint bluish light.

Now their limbs sink, now they pause
And breathe as deeply as possible;
They approach each other timidly, and then stoop down
And kneel before each other, and touch each other
With their tender, innocent lips.

But the two of them merely grow weary
Of all this secret rapture;
Longingly the little girl whispers:

„Ich mag nicht mehr tanzen im Mondenschein,
Ach, käme doch endlich die Sonne!"

Sie klettert hinunter ein Trepplein schief
Und schleicht hinab in den Garten.
Die Sonne schlief, und die Grille schlief:
„Hier will ich sitzen im Grase tief,
Und der Sonne will ich warten."

Doch als nun morgens um Busch und Gestein
Verhuschet das Dämmergemunkel,
Da werden dem Kinde die Äuglein klein;
Sie tanzte zu lange beim Mondenschein,
Nun schläft sie bei Sonnengefunkel.

Nun liegt sie zwischen den Blumen dicht
Auf grünem, blitzendem Rasen;
Und es schauen ihr in das süße Gesicht
Die Nachtigall und das Sonnenlicht
Und die kleinen neugierigen Hasen.

"I don't want to dance in the moonlight any more,
Oh, if only the sun would finally come!"

She clambers down a crooked little staircase
And steals down into the garden.
The sun was sleeping, and the crickets were sleeping:
"Here I will sit in the deep grass,
And I will wait for the sun."

But when now, in the morning, around the bushes and stones
The muttering of the twilight scurries away,
The child's little eyes narrow,
She danced too long while the moon shone,
Now she sleeps while the sun sparkles.

Now she lies among the thickly growing flowers
On the green, flashing lawn;
And there look into her sweet face
The nightingale and the sunlight
And the little inquisitive hares.

# Klaus Groth

## *"Dein blaues Auge hält so still"*

Dein blaues Auge hält so still,
Ich blicke bis zum Grund.
Du fragst mich, was ich sehen will?
Ich sehe mich gesund.

Es brannte mich ein glühend Paar,
Noch schmerzt das Nachgefühl:
Das deine ist wie See so klar
Und wie ein See so kühl.

## *"O wüßt ich doch den Weg zurück"*

O wüßt ich doch den Weg zurück,
Den lieben Weg zum Kinderland!
O warum sucht ich nach dem Glück
Und ließ der Mutter Hand?

O wie mich sehnet auszuruhn,
Von keinem Streben aufgeweckt,
Die müden Augen zuzutun,
Von Liebe sanft bedeckt!

Und nichts zu forschen, nichts zu spähn
Und nur noch träumen leicht und lind;
Der Zeiten Wandel nicht zu sehn,
Zum zweiten Mal ein Kind!

O zeigt mir doch den Weg zurück,
Den lieben Weg zum Kinderland!
Vergebens such ich nach dem Glück,
Ringsum ist öder Strand.

# Klaus Groth

## *"Your blue eyes hold so still"*

Your blue eyes hold so still,
I can look all the way into them.
You ask me what I want to see.
I see my return to health.[47]

A blazing pair of eyes once burnt me,
The after-feeling still aches:
Yours are as clear as a lake
And as cool as a lake.

## *"Oh, if only I knew the way back"*

Oh, if only I knew the way back,
The charming way to the land of childhood!
Oh, why did I seek after happiness
And let go of my mother's hand?

Oh, how I long to get a thorough rest,
Awakened by no ambition,
To close my weary eyes,
Gently tucked in by love!

And to search for nothing, watch for nothing
And merely dream lightly and gently;
Not to see the changing of the times,
A child for the second time!

Oh, do show me the way back,
The charming way to the land of childhood!
In vain do I seek for happiness,
All around me is a barren coast.

---

[47]More literally, "I recover my health through looking (into your eyes)."

## Regenlied

Walle, Regen, walle nieder,
Wecke mir die Träume wieder,
Die ich in der Kindheit träumte,
Wenn das Naß im Sande schäumte!

Wenn die matte Sommerschwüle
Lässig stritt mit frischer Kühle
Und die blanken Blätter tauten
Und die Saaten dunkler blauten.

Welche Wonne, in dem Fließen
Dann zu stehn mit nackten Füßen!
An dem Grase hinzustreifen
Und den Schaum mit Händen greifen.

Oder mit den heißen Wangen
Kalte Tropfen aufzufangen
Und den neuerwachten Düften
Seine Kinderbrust zu lüften!

Wie die Kelche, die da troffen,
Stand die Seele atmend offen,
Wie die Blumen düftetrunken
In den Himmelstau versunken.

Schauernd kühlte jeder Tropfen
Tief bis an des Herzens Klopfen,
Und der Schöpfung heilig Weben
Drang bis ins verborgne Leben.

Walle, Regen, walle nieder,
Wecke meine alten Lieder,
Die wir in der Türe sangen,
Wenn die Tropfen draußen klangen!

Möchte ihnen wieder lauschen,
Ihrem süßen, feuchten Rauschen,
Meine Seele sanft betauen
Mit dem frommen Kindergrauen.

## Rain Song

Pour, rain, pour down,
Awaken my dreams again
That I dreamt in childhood
When the water foamed in the sand!

When the languid sultriness of summer
Struggled indolently with the fresh coolness
And there was dew on the bright leaves
And the grainfields turned a darker blue.

What bliss, to stand then
In the flow with bare feet!
To swish by the grass
And grab the foam with one's hands.

Or to catch cold drops
On one's hot cheeks
And to expose one's childish breast
To the newly awakened fragrances!

Like the flower cups that were dripping there,
One's soul was open and breathing,
Like the flowers drunk with fragrance,
Submerged in the heavenly dew.

Every drop, trembling, would cool you
Deep down to where your heart beat,
And the sacred stirring of Creation
Penetrated to the hidden wellsprings of life.

Pour, rain, pour down,
Awaken my old songs
That we sang in the doorway
When the drops pattered outside!

I would like to listen to them again,
To their sweet, damp murmur,
To bedew my soul softly
With the pious awe of childhood.

# Gottfried Keller

## An das Vaterland

O mein Heimatland! O mein Vaterland!
Wie so innig, feurig lieb' ich dich!
Schönste Ros', ob jede mir verblich,
Duftest noch an meinem öden Strand!

Als ich arm, doch froh, fremdes Land durchstrich,
Königsglanz mit deinen Bergen maß,
Thronenflitter bald ob dir vergaß,
Wie war da der Bettler stolz auf dich!

Als ich fern von dir war, o Helvetia!
Faßte manchmal mich ein tiefes Leid;
Doch wie kehrte schnell es sich in Freud',
Wenn ich einen deiner Söhne sah!

O mein Schweizerland, all mein Gut und Hab!
Wann dereinst die letzte Stunde kommt,
Ob ich Schwacher dir auch nichts gefrommt,
Nicht versage mir ein stilles Grab!

Werf' ich von mir einst dies mein Staubgewand,
Beten will ich dann zu Gott dem Herrn:
"Lasse strahlen deinen schönsten Stern
Nieder auf mein irdisch Vaterland!"

## Waldlied, 1

Arm in Arm und Kron an Krone steht der Eichenwald verschlungen,
Heut hat er bei guter Laune mir sein altes Lied gesungen.

Fern am Rande fing ein junges Bäumchen an sich sacht zu wiegen,
Und dann ging es immer weiter an ein Sausen, an ein Biegen;

# Gottfried Keller

## *To My Native Land*

O my homeland! O my native land!
How deeply, how ardently I love you!
Loveliest rose, though all of mine have faded,
You are still fragrant on my barren coast!

When, poor but happy, I wandered through foreign lands,
Measuring royal brilliance against your mountains,
Soon forgetting the tinsel of thrones in your favor,
How proud of you the beggarman then was!

When I was far from you, O Helvetia,
A deep sorrow sometimes gripped me;
But how quickly it turned into joy
Whenever I saw one of your sons!

O my Swiss land, all my property and possession!
When some day my last hour comes,
Even though, in my weakness, I was of no use to you,
Do not deny me a tranquil grave!

When some day I fling away this garment of dust,
I will then pray to the Lord God:
"Let your loveliest star shine
Down on my native land on earth!"

## *Forest Song, I*

Arm in arm and treetop to treetop the oak forest is entwined;
Today, in a good mood, it sang me its old song.

Far off at the edge a young sapling started swaying gently,
And then things went on and on till there was a roaring and a
    bending;

Kam es her in mächtgem Zuge, schwoll es an zu breiten Wogen,
Hoch sich durch die Wipfel wälzend kam die Sturmesflut gezogen.

Und nun sang und pfiff es graulich in den Kronen, in den Lüften,
Und dazwischen knarrt' und dröhnt' es unten in den Wurzelgrüften.

Manchmal schwang die höchste Eiche gellend ihren Schaft alleine,
Donnernder erscholl nur immer drauf der Chor vom ganzen Haine!

Einer wilden Meeresbrandung hat das schöne Spiel geglichen;
Alles Laub war weißlich schimmernd nach Nordosten hingestrichen.

Also streicht die alte Geige Pan der Alte laut und leise,
Unterrichtend seine Wälder in der alten Weltenweise.

In den sieben Tönen schweift er unerschöpflich auf und nieder,
In den sieben alten Tönen, die umfassen alle Lieder.

Und es lauschen still die jungen Dichter und die jungen Finken,
Kauernd in den dunklen Büschen sie die Melodien trinken.


## Winternacht

Nicht ein Flügelschlag ging durch die Welt,
Still und blendend lag der weiße Schnee.
Nicht ein Wölklein hing am Sternenzelt,
Keine Welle schlug im starren See.

Aus der Tiefe stieg der Seebaum auf,
Bis sein Wipfel in dem Eis gefror;
An den Ästen klomm die Nix herauf,
Schaute durch das grüne Eis empor.

It came this way in a mighty current, it swelled into broad waves;
Rolling high through the treetops the storm tide came along.

And now there was fearful singing and whistling in the tops, in the air,
And in between there was creaking and groaning down below in the
root hollows.

At times the loftiest oak swung its trunk alone, shrilly;
The choir of the entire grove always responded only with a more
thunderous roar!

The beautiful spectacle resembled the wild breakers of the ocean;
All the leaves, glimmering white, played[48] toward the northeast.

Thus does ancient Pan play his ancient fiddle loudly and softly,
Instructing his forests in the old melody of the worlds.

In the seven notes of the scale he tirelessly roves up and down,
In the seven ancient notes that comprise all songs.

And the young poets and the young finches listen quietly;
Cowering in the dark shrubbery, they drink in the melodies.


## Winter Night

Not a wing beat went through the world;
Silent and dazzling lay the white snow.
Not the slightest cloud hung from the starry canopy,
No wave beat in the rigid lake.

Out of the depths ascended the lake-tree
Until its top froze in the ice;
On its boughs the water nymph climbed up
And looked skyward through the green ice.

---

[48]The English translation here feebly reflects the pun in the German on the verb *streichen*
(rub, stroke, play a stringed instrument), used here for the movement of the leaves in the
wind and for Pan's performance on the fiddle.

Auf dem dünnen Glase stand ich da,
Das die schwarze Tiefe von mir schied;
Dicht ich unter meinen Füßen sah
Ihre weiße Schönheit Glied um Glied.

Mit ersticktem Jammer tastet' sie
An der harten Decke her und hin,
Ich vergeß das dunkle Antlitz nie,
Immer, immer liegt es mir im Sinn!

## Abendlied

Augen, meine lieben Fensterlein,
Gebt mir schon so lange holden Schein,
Lasset freundlich Bild um Bild herein:
Einmal werdet ihr verdunkelt sein!

Fallen einst die müden Lider zu,
Löscht ihr aus, dann hat die Seele Ruh;
Tastend streift sie ab die Wanderschuh,
Legt sich auch in ihre finstre Truh.

Noch zwei Fünklein sieht sie glimmend stehn
Wie zwei Sternlein, innerlich zu sehn,
Bis sie schwanken und dann auch vergehn,
Wie von eines Falters Flügelwehn.

Doch noch wandl ich auf dem Abendfeld,
Nur dem sinkenden Gestirn gesellt;
Trinkt, o Augen, was die Wimper hält,
Von dem goldnen Überfluß der Welt!

I stood there on the thin glassy surface
That separated me from the black depths;
Directly under my feet I saw
Her white beauty, limb after limb.

With suppressed sorrow she groped
Here and there along the hard covering;
I can never forget her gloomy face;
Always, always it preys on my mind!

## Evening Song

Eyes, my dear little windows,
You have already given me lovely light for so long,
You admit one image after another in a friendly way:
One day you will be darkened!

When once your weary lids fall,
You will be extinguished; then my soul will find rest;
Gropingly it will slip off its journeying shoes,
And will lay itself, too, in its dark box.

It will still see two little sparks faintly shining there,
Like two small stars, to be seen inwardly,
Until they waver, and then also go out,
As if fanned by a butterfly's wing beats.

But I am still walking in the fields at evening,
With only the setting sun for company;
Drink, O eyes, as much as your lashes hold,
Of the golden abundance of the world!

# Theodor Fontane

## Gorm Grymme

König Gorm herrscht über Dänemark,
Er herrscht' die dreißig Jahr,
Sein Sinn ist fest, seine Hand ist stark,
Weiß worden ist nur sein Haar,
Weiß worden sind nur seine buschigen Brau'n,
Die machten manchen stumm;
In Grimme liebt er dreinzuschaun,—
Gorm Grymme heißt er drum.

Und die Jarls kamen zum Feste des Jul,
Gorm Grymme sitzt im Saal,
Und neben ihm sitzt, auf beinernem Stuhl,
Thyra Danebod, sein Gemahl;
Sie reichen einander still die Hand
Und blicken sich an zugleich,
Ein Lächeln in beider Auge stand,—
Gorm Grymme, was macht dich so weich?

Den Saal hinunter, in offner Hall,
Da fliegt es wie Locken im Wind,
Jung-Harald spielt mit dem Federball,
Jung-Harald, ihr einziges Kind,
Sein Wuchs ist schlank, blond ist sein Haar,
Blau-golden ist sein Kleid,
Jung-Harald ist heut fünfzehn Jahr,
Und sie lieben ihn allbeid.

Sie lieben ihn beid; eine Ahnung bang
Kommt über die Königin,
Gorm Grymme aber, den Saal entlang
Auf Jung-Harald deutet er hin,
Und er hebt sich zum Sprechen,—sein Mantel rot
Gleitet nieder auf den Grund:
„Wer je mir spräche ‚er ist tot‘,
Der müßte sterben zur Stund."

# Theodor Fontane

## *Gorm the Grim*

King Gorm rules over Denmark,
He has ruled these thirty years;
His mind is firm, his hand is strong,
Only his hair has turned white;
Only his bushy brows, which have silenced
Many a man, have turned white.
He likes to cast furious glances,—
That's why he's called Gorm the Grim.

And the earls have come to the Yule feast;
Gorm the Grim sits in his hall
And beside him sits, on a chair carved from bone,
Thyra Danebod, his wife;
They silently give each other their hands
And at the same time they look at each other;
There was a smile in the eyes of both—
Gorm the Grim, what makes you so tender?

Down the room, in the open space,
Comes a stir as of hair flying in the wind;
Young Harald is playing with his shuttlecock,
Young Harald, their only child;
His form is slim, his hair is blond,
His robe is blue and gold;
Today Young Harald is fifteen,
And they both love him.

They both love him; a fearful foreboding
Steals over the Queen,
But Gorm the Grim points down the hall
At Young Harald,
And he rises to speak—his red mantle
Slips down to the ground:
"Whoever might one day say to me, 'He is dead,'
That person would have to die immediately!"

Und Monde gehn. Es schmolz der Schnee,
Der Sommer kam zu Gast,
Dreihundert Schiffe fahren in See,
Jung-Harald steht am Mast,
Er steht am Mast, er singt ein Lied,
Bis sich's im Winde brach,
Das letzte Segel, es schwand, es schied,—
Gorm Grymme schaut ihm nach.

Und wieder Monde. Grau-Herbstestag
Liegt über Sund und Meer,
Drei Schiffe mit mattem Ruderschlag
Rudern heimwärts drüber her.
Schwarz hängen die Wimpel; auf Brömsebro-Moor
Jung-Harald liegt im Blut,—
Wer bringt die Kunde vor Königs Ohr?
*Keiner* hat den Mut.

Thyra Danebod schreitet hinab an den Sund,
Sie hatte die Segel gesehn;
Sie spricht: „Und bangt sich euer Mund,
Ich meld ihm, was geschehn."
Ab legt sie ihr rotes Korallengeschmeid
Und die Gemme von Opal,
Sie kleidet sich in ein schwarzes Kleid
Und tritt in Hall und Saal.

In Hall und Saal. An Pfeiler und Wand
Goldteppiche ziehen sich hin,
Schwarze Teppiche nun mit eigener Hand
Hängt drüber die Königin,
Und sie zündet zwölf Kerzen, ihr flackernd Licht,
Es gab einen trüben Schein,
Und sie legt ein Gewebe, schwarz und dicht,
Auf den Stuhl von Elfenbein.

Ein tritt Gorm Grymme. Es zittert sein Gang,
Er schreitet wie im Traum,
Er starrt die schwarze Hall entlang,
Die Lichter, er sieht sie kaum,
Er spricht: „Es weht wie Schwüle hier,
Ich will an Meer und Strand,

And months pass. The snow melted,
The summer paid a visit;
Three hundred ships put out to sea;
Young Harald stands at the mast,
He stands at the mast, he sings a song
Until it was interrupted by the wind;
The last sail vanished, departed—
Gorm the Grim follows it with his eyes.

And again months. A gray-autumn day
Lies over bay and sea,
Three ships with weary oar strokes
Row homeward this way over the sea;
Black hang their pennants; on Brömsebro moor
Young Harald lies in his own blood—
Who is to bring the news to the King's ears?
No one has the courage.

Thyra Danebod strides down to the shore,
She had seen the sails;
She says: "And if your mouths are afraid,
I will report to him what has happened."
She takes off her red coral jewelry
And her opal gem,
She dresses in a black dress
And steps into hall and room.

Into hall and room. Over pillars and walls
Gold-worked tapestries extend;
Now the Queen with her own hands
Hangs black tapestries over them;
And she lights twelve tapers; their flickering shine
Gave a dismal glow,
And she lays a cloth, black and thick,
On the ivory chair.

Gorm the Grim enters. His steps are shaky,
He walks as if in a dream;
He stares down the black hall;
The candles, he hardly sees them;
He says: "There is a sultry air here,
I want to go down to the sea and shore;

Reich meinen rotgoldenen Mantel mir
Und reiche mir deine Hand."

Sie gab ihm um einen Mantel dicht,
Der war nicht golden, nicht rot,
Gorm Grymme sprach: „Was niemand spricht,
Ich sprech es: Er ist tot."
Er setzte sich nieder, wo er stand,
Ein Windstoß fuhr durchs Haus,
Die Königin hielt des Königs Hand,
Die Lichter loschen aus.

## Herr von Ribbeck auf Ribbeck im Havelland

Herr von Ribbeck auf Ribbeck im Havelland,
Ein Birnbaum in seinem Garten stand,
Und kam die goldene Herbsteszeit
Und die Birnen leuchteten weit und breit,
Da stopfte, wenn's Mittag vom Turme scholl,
Der von Ribbeck sich beide Taschen voll,
Und kam in Pantinen ein Junge daher,
So rief er: „Junge, wiste 'ne Beer?"
Und kam ein Mädel, so rief er: „Lütt Dirn,
Kumm man röwer, ick hebb 'ne Birn."

So ging es viel Jahre, bis lobesam
Der von Ribbeck auf Ribbeck zu sterben kam.
Er fühlte sein Ende. 's war Herbsteszeit,
Wieder lachten die Birnen weit und breit;
Da sagte von Ribbeck: „Ich scheide nun ab.
Legt mir eine Birne mit ins Grab."
Und drei Tage drauf, aus dem Doppeldachhaus,
Trugen von Ribbeck sie hinaus,
Alle Bauern und Büdner mit Feiergesicht

Hand me my red-gold mantle
And give me your hand."

She placed around him a thick mantle,
It was not gold, not red;
Gorm the Grim said: "That which no one will say,
I shall say it: He is dead."
He sat down, where he stood,
A gust of wind tore through the house;
The Queen held the King's hand,
The candles went out.

## Herr von Ribbeck auf Ribbeck in Havelland [49]

Herr von Ribbeck auf Ribbeck in Havelland,
A pear tree stood in his garden,
And when the golden autumn season came
And the pears glowed far and wide,
Then, when noon sounded from the tower,
The lord of Ribbeck stuffed both his pockets full,
And if a boy came along in peasant clogs,
He would call: "Boy, do you want a pear?"[50]
And if a girl came, he would call: "Little girl,
Come on over, I have a pear."[51]

And so it went for many years, until worthily
The time came for Herr von Ribbeck auf Ribbeck to die.
He felt his end drawing near; it was the autumn season,
Again the pears were laughing far and wide;
Then von Ribbeck said: "I am now departing.
Place a pear in my grave with me!"
And three days later, from the house with the double roof
They carried von Ribbeck out.
All the peasants and cottagers, with solemn faces,

---

[49]Herr von Ribbeck auf Ribbeck is a noble title, incorporating the name of the feudal domain; Havelland was a district in Brandenburg, Prussia.

[50]In High German, "willst du eine Beere [= Birne]?"

[51]"Kleine Dirne, komm mal herüber, ich habe eine Birne."

Sangen „Jesus meine Zuversicht",
Und die Kinder klagten, das Herze schwer:
„He is dod nu. Wer giwt uns nu 'ne Beer?"

So klagten die Kinder. Das war nicht recht,
Ach, sie kannten den alten Ribbeck schlecht;
Der neue freilich, der knausert und spart,
Hält Park und Birnbaum strenge verwahrt.
Aber der alte, vorahnend schon
Und voll Mißtraun gegen den eigenen Sohn,
Der wußte genau, was damals er tat,
Als um eine Birn ins Grab er bat,
Und im dritten Jahr aus dem stillen Haus
Ein Birnbaumsprößling sproßt heraus.

Und die Jahre gehen wohl auf und ab,
Längst wölbt sich ein Birnbaum über dem Grab,
Und in der goldenen Herbsteszeit
Leuchtet's wieder weit und breit.
Und kommt ein Jung übern Kirchhof her,
So flüstert's im Baume: „Wiste 'ne Beer?"
Und kommt ein Mädel, so flüstert's: „Lütt Dirn,
Kumm man röwer, ick gew di 'ne Birn."

So spendet Segen noch immer die Hand
Des von Ribbeck auf Ribbeck im Havelland.

Sang "Jesus, in Whom I Trust"
And the children lamented, with heavy heart:
"He is dead now. Who will give us a pear now?"[52]

Thus the children lamented. It was unfair—
Ah, they didn't really know old Ribbeck!
The new one, to be sure, is stingy and parsimonious,
He keeps the park and the pear tree strictly guarded.
But the old one, already prescient
And full of mistrust of his own son,
Knew exactly what he was doing at the time
When he requested that a pear be put in his grave;
And, in the third year, from that quiet abode
A pear-tree shoot emerged.

And the years certainly come and go;
For some time a pear tree has arched over the grave
And in the golden autumn season
They glow again far and wide.
And if a boy walks across the churchyard,
There is a whisper in the tree: "Want a pear?"
And if a girl comes, the whisper goes: "Little girl,
Come on over, I'll give you a pear."[53]

Thus bounty is still bestowed by the hand
Of von Ribbeck auf Ribbeck in Havelland.

---

[52]"Er ist tot nun. Wer gibt uns nun eine Beere?"
[53]"Ich gebe dir eine Birne."

# Conrad Ferdinand Meyer

## *Fülle*

Genug ist nicht genug! Gepriesen werde
Der Herbst! Kein Ast, der seiner Frucht entbehrte!
Tief beugt sich mancher allzureich beschwerte,
Der Apfel fällt mit dumpfem Laut zur Erde.

Genug ist nicht genug! Es lacht im Laube!
Die saftige Pfirsche winkt dem durstigen Munde!
Die trunknen Wespen summen in die Runde:
„Genug ist nicht genug!" um eine Traube.

Genug ist nicht genug! Mit vollen Zügen
Schlürft Dichtergeist am Borne des Genusses,
Das Herz, auch es bedarf des Überflusses,
Genug kann nie und nimmermehr genügen!

## *Eingelegte Ruder*

Meine eingelegten Ruder triefen,
Tropfen fallen langsam in die Tiefen.

Nichts, das mich verdroß! Nichts, das mich freute!
Niederrinnt ein schmerzenloses Heute!

Unter mir—ach, aus dem Licht verschwunden—
Träumen schon die schönern meiner Stunden.

Aus der blauen Tiefe ruft das Gestern:
Sind im Licht noch manche meiner Schwestern?

# Conrad Ferdinand Meyer

## Abundance

Enough is not enough! Praised be
The autumn! No bough that is lacking its fruit!
Many a one, all too richly burdened, is bending low;
The apple falls to the earth with a hollow sound.

Enough is not enough! There is laughter in the leaves!
The juicy peach beckons to the thirsty mouth!
The drunken wasps buzz all around,
"Enough is not enough!" as they circle a bunch of grapes.

Enough is not enough! In deep drafts
The poet's spirit drinks at the fountain of pleasure;
The heart, it too has need of profusion;
Enough can never, no, never be enough!

## Shipped Oars

My shipped oars are dripping,
Drops are falling slowly into the depths.

Nothing that vexed me! Nothing that delighted me!
A painless today trickles away!

Beneath me—ah, vanished from the light—
The more beautiful of my hours are already dreaming.

From the blue deep, yesterday calls:
"Are many of my sisters still in the light?"

## Säerspruch

Bemeßt den Schritt! Bemeßt den Schwung!
Die Erde bleibt noch lange jung!
Dort fällt ein Korn, das stirbt und ruht.
Die Ruh ist süß. Es hat es gut.
Hier eins, das durch die Scholle bricht.
Es hat es gut. Süß ist das Licht.
Und keines fällt aus dieser Welt
Und jedes fällt, wie's Gott gefällt.

## Ewig jung ist nur die Sonne

Heute fanden meine Schritte mein vergeßnes Jugendtal,
Seine Sohle lag verödet, seine Berge standen kahl.
Meine Bäume, meine Träume, meine buchendunkeln Höhn—
Ewig jung ist nur die Sonne, sie allein ist ewig schön.

Drüben dort in schilf'gem Grunde, wo die müde Lache liegt,
Hat zu meiner Jugendstunde sich lebend'ge Flut gewiegt,
Durch die Heiden, durch die Weiden ging ein wandernd Herd-
    getön—
Ewig jung ist nur die Sonne, sie allein ist ewig schön.

## Auf dem Canal grande

Auf dem Canal grande betten
Tief sich ein die Abendschatten,
Hundert dunkle Gondeln gleiten
Als ein flüsterndes Geheimnis.

Aber zwischen zwei Palästen
Glüht herein die Abendsonne,
Flammend wirft sie einen grellen
Breiten Streifen auf die Gondeln.

## Sower's Aphorism

Moderate your stride! Moderate your cast!
The earth will still remain young for a long time!
There falls a seed that dies and rests.
Rest is sweet. It is well-off.
Here is one that breaks through the sod.
It is well-off. Sweet is the light.
And none falls outside this world,
And each falls as it pleases God.

## Only the Sun Is Eternally Young

Today my steps found the forgotten valley of my youth;
Its bottom was laid waste, its mountains stood bare.
My trees, my dreams, my heights dark with beeches—
Only the sun is eternally young, it alone is eternally beautiful.

Over yonder in the sedgy hollow, where the weary pool lies,
In my youthful days a living stream pulsed;
Through the heaths, through the willows rang the bells of moving
        herds—
Only the sun is eternally young, it alone is eternally beautiful.

## On the Canal Grande

On the Canal Grande the evening shadows
Embed themselves deeply;
A hundred dark gondolas glide
Like a whispering secret.

But between two palaces
The evening sun glows red-hot;
Ablaze, it casts a broad,
Lurid stripe onto the gondolas.

In dem purpurroten Lichte
Laute Stimmen, hell Gelächter,
Überredende Gebärden
Und das frevle Spiel der Augen.

Eine kleine, kurze Strecke
Treibt das Leben leidenschaftlich
Und erlischt im Schatten drüben
Als ein unverständlich Murmeln.

## Stapfen

In jungen Jahren wars. Ich brachte dich
Zurück ins Nachbarhaus, wo du zu Gast,
Durch das Gehölz. Der Nebel rieselte,
Du zogst des Reisekleids Kapuze vor
Und blicktest traulich mit verhüllter Stirn.
Naß ward der Pfad. Die Sohlen prägten sich
Dem feuchten Waldesboden deutlich ein,
Die wandernden. Du schrittest auf dem Bord,
Von deiner Reise sprechend. Eine noch,
Die längre, folge drauf, so sagtest du.
Dann scherzten wir, der nahen Trennung klug
Das Angesicht verhüllend, und du schiedst,
Dort wo der First sich über Ulmen hebt.
Ich ging denselben Pfad gemach zurück,
Leis schwelgend noch in deiner Lieblichkeit,
In deiner wilden Scheu, und wohlgemut
Vertrauend auf ein baldig Wiedersehn.
Vergnüglich schlendernd, sah ich auf dem Rain
Den Umriß deiner Sohlen deutlich noch
Dem feuchten Waldesboden eingeprägt,
Die kleinste Spur von dir, die flüchtigste,
Und doch dein Wesen: wandernd, reisehaft,
Schlank, rein, walddunkel, aber o wie süß!
Die Stapfen schritten jetzt entgegen dem
Zurück dieselbe Strecke Wandernden:
Aus deinen Stapfen hobst du dich empor
Vor meinem innern Auge, Deinen Wuchs

In the purplish-red light
Are loud voices, bright laughter,
Seductive gestures
And a shameless interplay of glances.

For a small, brief while
Life is lived passionately
and is extinguished in the shadows yonder
Like an incomprehensible muttering.


## *Footprints*

It was in our youth. I brought you
Back to the neighbors' house, where you were visiting,
Through the small wood. The mist was trickling,
You pulled up the hood of your traveling dress
And looked at me intimately with your forehead covered.
The path was wet. Our soles stamped themselves
Distinctly onto the damp forest floor,
Our moving soles. You were walking on the rim,
Talking about your journey. Yet another one,
The longer one, would follow, you said.
Then we joked, cleverly covering the face
Of the impending separation, and you departed
At the spot where the roof ridge rises above the elms.
I walked comfortably back over the same path,
Still quietly reveling in your loveliness,
In your fierce shyness, and lightheartedly
Trusting that we would soon meet again.
Sauntering pleasantly, I saw on the field ridge
The outline of your soles still distinctly
Stamped into the damp forest floor,
The slightest trace of you, the most evanescent,
And yet your nature: wandering, traveling,
Slim, pure, forest-dark, but oh how sweet!
The footprints were now pointing in the direction opposite to mine
As I walked back over the same stretch:
Out of your footprints you arose
Before my inward eye. I caught sight of

Erblickt ich mit des Busens zartem Bug.
Vorüber gingst du, eine Traumgestalt.
Die Stapfen wurden jetzt undeutlicher,
Vom Regen halb gelöscht, der stärker fiel.
Da überschlich mich eine Traurigkeit:
Fast unter meinem Blick verwischten sich
Die Spuren deines letzten Gangs mit mir.

## In der Sistina

In der Sistine dämmerhohem Raum,
Das Bibelbuch in seiner nerv'gen Hand,
Sitzt Michelangelo in wachem Traum,
Umhellt von einer kleinen Ampel Brand.

Laut spricht hinein er in die Mitternacht,
Als lauscht ein Gast ihm gegenüber hier,
Bald wie mit einer allgewalt'gen Macht,
Bald wieder wie mit seinesgleichen schier:

„Umfaßt, umgrenzt hab ich dich, ewig Sein,
Mit meinen großen Linien fünfmal dort!
Ich hüllte dich in lichte Mäntel ein
Und gab dir Leib, wie dieses Bibelwort.

Mit wehnden Haaren stürmst du feurigwild
Von Sonnen immer neuen Sonnen zu,
Für deinen Menschen bist in meinen Bild
Entgegenschwebend und barmherzig du!

So schuf ich dich mit meiner nicht'gen Kraft:
Damit ich nicht der größre Künstler sei,
Schaff mich—ich bin ein Knecht der Leidenschaft—
Nach deinem Bilde schaff mich rein und frei!

Den ersten Menschen formtest du aus Ton,
Ich werde schon von härterm Stoffe sein,
Da, Meister, brauchst du deinen Hammer schon.
Bildhauer Gott, schlag zu! Ich bin der Stein.“

Your figure with the delicate curve of its bosom.
You walked past, a dream shape.
The footprints now became less distinct,
Half obliterated by the rain, which was falling harder.
Then a sadness crept over me:
Almost before my eyes there disappeared
The traces of your last walk with me.


## In the Sistine Chapel

In the high, dimly lit space of the Sistine,
The Bible in his sinewy hand,
Sits Michelangelo in a waking dream,
Illuminated by the flame of a small lamp.

He speaks aloud into the midnight hour,
As if a guest were opposite him here listening,
Now as if addressing an almighty power,
Now almost as if speaking to an equal:

"I have embraced and circumscribed You, Eternal Being,
With my strong contours five times there!
I have enveloped You in bright cloaks
And given You a body, like this Bible text.

With streaming hair You storm with fiery wildness
From suns to ever new suns;
In my picture You are accommodating[54]
And merciful to Your human being!

Thus I created You with my trivial strength:
In order that I may not be the greater artist of the two,
Create me—I am a slave to passion—
Create me pure and free in Your image!

You formed the first man out of clay,
I will surely be of a harder material;
For this, Master, you will now need Your hammer.
Sculptor God, strike! I am the stone."

---

[54]Literally, "hovering toward."

# Detlev von Liliencron

## *Wer weiß wo*

Auf Blut und Leichen, Schutt und Qualm,
Auf roßzerstampften Sommerhalm
Die Sonne schien.
Es sank die Nacht. Die Schlacht ist aus,
Und mancher kehrte nicht nach Haus
Einst von Kolin.

Ein Junker auch, ein Knabe noch,
Der heut das erste Pulver roch,
Er mußte dahin.
Wie hoch er auch die Fahne schwang,
Der Tod in seinen Arm ihn zwang,
Er mußte dahin.

Ihm nahe lag ein frommes Buch,
Das stets der Junker bei sich trug,
Am Degenknauf.
Ein Grenadier von Bevern fand
Den kleinen erdbeschmutzten Band
Und hob ihn auf.

Und brachte heim mit schnellem Fuß
Dem Vater diesen letzten Gruß,
Der klang nicht froh.
Dann schrieb hinein die Zitterhand:
„Kolin. Mein Sohn verscharrt im Sand.
Wer weiß wo.“

Und der gesungen dieses Lied,
Und der es liest, im Leben zieht
Noch frisch und froh.
Doch einst bin ich, und bist auch du
Verscharrt im Sand, zur ewigen Ruh,
Wer weiß wo.

# Detlev von Liliencron

## *Who Knows Where*

On blood and corpses, rubble and smoke,
On summer grass trampled down by horses,
The sun shone.
Night fell. The battle is over,
And many a man failed to return home
Once from Kolín.[55]

A nobleman, too, still a boy,
Who smelled his first powder today,
He had to die.
No matter how high he swung the flag,
Death forced him into its arms,
He had to die.

Near him lay a book of devotions,
Which the young nobleman always carried with him
Attached to the pommel of his sword-hilt.
A grenadier from Bevern[56] found
The small, earth-soiled volume
And picked it up and kept it.

And with speedy pace he brought home
To the father this last greeting,
Which had no happy ring.
Then the trembling hand wrote in it:
"Kolín. My son hastily buried in the sand.
Who knows where."

And the one who has sung this song,
And the one who is reading it, still goes
Through life healthy and happy.
But one day I too, and you too,
Will be buried in the sand, for eternal rest,
Who knows where.

---

[55]In Bohemia, site of an Austrian victory over the Prussians in 1757, during the Seven Years' War.

[56]A town near Hameln (Hamelin) in Lower Saxony.

## Four in hand

Vorne vier nickende Pferdeköpfe,
Neben mir zwei blonde Mädchenzöpfe,
Hinten der Groom mit wichtigen Mienen,
An den Rädern Gebell.

In den Dörfern windstillen Lebens Genüge,
Auf den Feldern fleißige Eggen und Pflüge,
Alles das von der Sonne beschienen
So hell, so hell.

## Einen Sommer lang

Zwischen Roggenfeld und Hecken
Führt ein schmaler Gang;
Süßes, seliges Verstecken
Einen Sommer lang.

Wenn wir uns von ferne sehen,
Zögert sie den Schritt,
Rupft ein Hälmchen sich im Gehen,
Nimmt ein Blättchen mit.

Hat mit Ähren sich das Mieder
Unschuldig geschmückt,
Sich den Hut verlegen nieder
In die Stirn gerückt.

Finster kommt sie langsam näher,
Färbt sich rot wie Mohn;
Doch ich bin ein feiner Späher,
Kenn die Schelmin schon.

Noch ein Blick in Weg und Weite,
Ruhig liegt die Welt,
Und es hat an ihre Seite
Mich der Sturm gesellt.

## Four in Hand

In front, four horses' nodding heads;
Beside me, a girl's two blonde braids;
Behind us, the groom, with self-important airs;
By the wheels, the sound of barking.

In the villages, the contentment of a becalmed life;
In the fields, busy harrows and plows;
All of this illuminated by the sun
So brightly, so brightly.

## One Entire Summer

Between the ryefield and the hedges
A narrow passage leads;
A sweet, blissful hiding place
One entire summer.

When we see each other from a distance,
She slows her pace,
Plucks a little blade of grass as she walks,
Takes along a little leaf.

She has innocently adorned
Her bodice with ears of grain,
She has self-consciously pulled
Her hat down over her brow.

Morosely she comes slowly closer,
Turns as red as a poppy;
But I am a shrewd scout,
I already know the little rogue.

One more glance into the distance,
The world is all at peace,
And a storm wind has carried
Me to her side.

Zwischen Roggenfeld und Hecken
Führt ein schmaler Gang;
Süßes, seliges Verstecken
Einen Sommer lang.

## Märztag

Wolkenschatten fliehen über Felder,
Blau umdunstet stehen ferne Wälder.

Kraniche, die hoch die Luft durchpflügen,
Kommen schreiend an in Wanderzügen.

Lerchen steigen schon in lauten Schwärmen,
Überall ein erstes Frühlingslärmen.

Lustig flattern, Mädchen, deine Bänder,
Kurzes Glück träumt durch die weiten Länder.

Kurzes Glück schwamm mit den Wolkenmassen,
Wollt' es halten, mußt' es schwimmen lassen.

Between the ryefield and the hedges
A narrow passage leads;
A sweet, blissful hiding place
One entire summer.


## March Day

Shadows of clouds fly over the fields,
Distant forests stand with a blue haze around them.

Cranes that are plowing the air up high
Arrive, calling, in migrating flights.

Larks are already rising in loud swarms,
Everywhere there is the first noise of springtime.

Merrily your ribbons stream, my girl,
Brief happiness is dreaming across the broad lands.

Brief happiness floated off with the masses of cloud,
I wanted to hold onto it, but had to let it float away.

# Friedrich Nietzsche

## *Ecce homo*

Ja, ich weiß, woher ich stamme!
Ungesättigt gleich der Flamme
Glühe und verzehr ich mich.
Licht wird alles, was ich fasse,
Kohle alles, was ich lasse:
Flamme bin ich sicherlich!

## *Das trunkene Lied*

O Mensch! Gib acht!
Was spricht die tiefe Mitternacht?
„Ich schlief, ich schlief—,
Aus tiefem Traum bin ich erwacht:—
Die Welt ist tief,
Und tiefer als der Tag gedacht.
Tief ist ihr Weh—,
Lust—tiefer noch als Herzeleid:
Weh spricht: Vergeh!
Doch alle Lust will Ewigkeit—,
Will tiefe, tiefe Ewigkeit!"

## *Parsifal-Musik*

—Ist Das noch deutsch?
Aus deutschem Herzen kam dies schwüle Kreischen?
Und deutschen Leibs ist dies Sich-selbst-Zerfleischen?
Deutsch ist dies Priester-Hände-Spreizen,
Dies weihrauchdüftelnde Sinne-Reizen?
Und deutsch dies Stürzen, Stocken, Taumeln,
Dies zuckersüße Bimbambaumeln?
Dies Nonnen-Äugeln, Ave-Glockenbimmeln,
Dies ganz falsch verzückte Himmel-Überhimmeln? . . .

# Friedrich Nietzsche

## *Ecce homo*

Yes, I know my origins!
Insatiable as a flame
I blaze and consume myself.
Everything I grasp turns to light;
Everything I release turns to coal:
I am surely flame!

## *The Drunken Song*

O man! Pay heed!
What does the deep midnight say?
"I slept, I slept—,
From a deep dream I have awakened:—
The world is deep,
And deeper than the day imagined.
Deep is its woe—,
Pleasure—deeper yet than heart's sorrow:
Woe says: 'Perish!,'
But every pleasure wants eternity,—
Wants deep, deep eternity!"

## *"Parsifal" Music*

—Is this still German?
Did this lascivious shrieking come from a German heart?
And is this self-laceration proper to a German body?
Is this spreading of priests' hands German,
This titillation of the senses accompanied by whiffs of incense?
And is this hurtling, stopping short and reeling German,
This saccharine dingdong-swinging?
This nunlike ogling, this tinkling of Angelus bells,
This altogether falsely ecstatic outheavening of heaven? . . .

—Ist Das noch deutsch?
Erwägt! Noch steht ihr an der Pforte . . .
Denn was ihr hört, ist *Rom,*—
*Roms Glaube ohne Worte!*


## Vereinsamt

Die Krähen schrein
Und ziehen schwirren Flugs zur Stadt:
Bald wird es schnein.—
Wohl dem, der jetzt noch—Heimat hat!

Nun stehst du starr,
Schaust rückwärts, ach! wie lange schon!
Was bist du Narr
Vor Winters in die Welt entflohn?

Die Welt—ein Tor
Zu tausend Wüsten stumm und kalt!
Wer das verlor,
Was du verlorst, macht nirgends halt.

Nun stehst du bleich,
Zur Winter-Wanderschaft verflucht,
Dem Rauche gleich,
Der stets nach kältern Himmeln sucht.

Flieg, Vogel, schnarr
Dein Lied im Wüstenvogel-Ton!—
Versteck, du Narr,
Dein blutend Herz in Eis und Hohn!

Die Krähen schrein
Und ziehen schwirren Flugs zur Stadt:
Bald wird es schnein,—
Weh dem, der keine Heimat hat!

—Is this still German?
Consider! You are still standing at the portal . . .
For what you are hearing is *Rome—*
*Rome's religion without the words!*

## Solitary

The crows call
And move on to the city with whirring wings.
Soon it will snow.—
Happy the man who now still—has a home![57]

Now you have been standing there stiff,
Looking backward, alas, for how long now!
Why, fool that you are, did you
Escape into the world as winter was coming?

The world—a gateway
To a thousand wildernesses mute and cold!
The man who has lost
What you have lost, never halts anywhere.

Now you are standing there pale,
Condemned by a curse to journey in winter,
Like the smoke
That constantly seeks colder skies.

Fly, bird, screech
Your song in the tones of a wilderness bird!—
Fool that you are, hide
Your bleeding heart in ice and scorn!

The crows call
And move to the city with whirring wings;
Soon it will snow,—
Woe is the man who has no home!

---

[57]*Heimat* refers not to a house, but a homeland, a native town, countryside, district, . . . .

## Venedig

An der Brücke stand
Jüngst ich in brauner Nacht.
Fernher kam Gesang:
Goldener Tropfen quoll's
Über die zitternde Fläche weg.
Gondeln, Lichter, Musik—
Trunken schwamm's in die Dämmrung hinaus ...

Meine Seele, ein Saitenspiel,
Sang sich, unsichtbar berührt,
Heimlich ein Gondellied dazu,
Zitternd vor bunter Seligkeit.
—Hörte jemand ihr zu? ...

## Das Feuerzeichen

Hier, wo zwischen Meeren die Insel wuchs,
Ein Opferstein jäh hinaufgetürmt,
Hier zündet sich unter schwarzem Himmel
Zarathustra seine Höhenfeuer an,
Feuerzeichen für verschlagne Schiffer,
Fragezeichen für Solche, die Antwort haben ...

Diese Flamme mit weißgrauem Bauche
—In kalte Fernen züngelt ihre Gier,
Nach immer reineren Höhn biegt sie den Hals—
Eine Schlange gerad aufgerichtet vor Ungeduld:
Dieses Zeichen stellte ich vor mich hin.

Meine Seele selber ist diese Flamme,
Unersättlich nach neuen Fernen
Lodert aufwärts, aufwärts ihre stille Glut.
Was floh Zarathustra vor Tier und Menschen?
Was entlief er jäh allem festen Lande?
Sechs Einsamkeiten kennt er schon—,
Aber das Meer selbst war nicht genug ihm einsam,
Die Insel ließ ihn steigen, auf dem Berg wurde er zur Flamme,

## Venice

At the bridge I stood
Recently in the brown night.
From far off came singing:
It was a flow of golden drops
Away over the trembling surface.
Gondolas, lights, music—
Intoxicated, it floated out into the twilight . . .

My soul, a stringed instrument,
Invisibly touched, secretly sang to itself
A gondolier's song as an accompaniment,
Trembling with confused blissfulness.
—Was anyone listening to it? . . .

## The Fire Signal

Here where the island grew between oceans,
A sacrificial stone precipitously thrust skyward,
Here beneath a black sky
Zarathustra lights his fires on the heights,
Fire signals for seamen blown off course,
Question marks for people who have an answer . . .

This flame with its gray-white belly
—Its voracity flickers into cold distances,
It bends its neck to reach purer and purer heights—
A snake that has reared upright out of impatience:
This signal I have placed before myself.

This flame is my very soul;
Insatiably craving new distances,
Its quiet blaze flares upward, upward.
Why did Zarathustra flee from animals and men?
Why did he suddenly escape from all dry land?
He is already familiar with *six* solitudes—,
But the ocean itself was not solitary enough for him,
The island let him ascend, and on the mountain he turned into flame;

Nach einer *siebenter* Einsamkeit
Wirft er suchend jetzt die Angel über sein Haupt.

Verschlagne Schiffer! Trümmer alter Sterne!
Ihr Meere der Zukunft! Unausgeforschte Himmel!
Nach allem Einsamen werfe ich jetzt die Angel:
Gebt Antwort auf die Ungeduld der Flamme,
Fangt mir, dem Fischer auf hohen Bergen,
Meine siebente *letzte* Einsamkeit! — —

In order to attain a *seventh* solitude
He now questingly casts out the fishing line over his head.

Seamen blown off course! Ruins of ancient stars!
You oceans of the future! Unexplored skies!
I am now casting my line for everything solitary:
Reply to the flame's impatience,
Catch for me, the fisherman on high mountains,
My seventh, *last* solitude! — —

# Alphabetical List of German Titles

Only distinct titles assigned by the poets are listed here; for poems identified by their first lines, see the Alphabetical List of German First Lines.

# Alphabetical List of German First Lines

# A CATALOG OF SELECTED
# DOVER BOOKS
## IN ALL FIELDS OF INTEREST

# A CATALOG OF SELECTED DOVER
# BOOKS IN ALL FIELDS OF INTEREST

CONCERNING THE SPIRITUAL IN ART, Wassily Kandinsky. Pioneering work by father of abstract art. Thoughts on color theory, nature of art. Analysis of earlier masters. 12 illustrations. 80pp. of text. 5⅜ × 8½.　　　23411-8 Pa. $3.95

ANIMALS: 1,419 Copyright-Free Illustrations of Mammals, Birds, Fish, Insects, etc., Jim Harter (ed.). Clear wood engravings present, in extremely lifelike poses, over 1,000 species of animals. One of the most extensive pictorial sourcebooks of its kind. Captions. Index. 284pp. 9 × 12.　　　23766-4 Pa. $11.95

CELTIC ART: The Methods of Construction, George Bain. Simple geometric techniques for making Celtic interlacements, spirals, Kells-type initials, animals, humans, etc. Over 500 illustrations. 160pp. 9 × 12. (USO)　　　22923-8 Pa. $8.95

AN ATLAS OF ANATOMY FOR ARTISTS, Fritz Schider. Most thorough reference work on art anatomy in the world. Hundreds of illustrations, including selections from works by Vesalius, Leonardo, Goya, Ingres, Michelangelo, others. 593 illustrations. 192pp. 7⅛ × 10¼.　　　20241-0 Pa. $8.95

CELTIC HAND STROKE-BY-STROKE (Irish Half-Uncial from "The Book of Kells"): An Arthur Baker Calligraphy Manual, Arthur Baker. Complete guide to creating each letter of the alphabet in distinctive Celtic manner. Covers hand position, strokes, pens, inks, paper, more. Illustrated. 48pp. 8¼ × 11.

24336-2 Pa. $3.95

EASY ORIGAMI, John Montroll. Charming collection of 32 projects (hat, cup, pelican, piano, swan, many more) specially designed for the novice origami hobbyist. Clearly illustrated easy-to-follow instructions insure that even beginning papercrafters will achieve successful results. 48pp. 8¼ × 11.　　　27298-2 Pa. $2.95

THE COMPLETE BOOK OF BIRDHOUSE CONSTRUCTION FOR WOOD-WORKERS, Scott D. Campbell. Detailed instructions, illustrations, tables. Also data on bird habitat and instinct patterns. Bibliography. 3 tables. 63 illustrations in 15 figures. 48pp. 5¼ × 8½.　　　24407-5 Pa. $1.95

BLOOMINGDALE'S ILLUSTRATED 1886 CATALOG: Fashions, Dry Goods and Housewares, Bloomingdale Brothers. Famed merchants' extremely rare catalog depicting about 1,700 products: clothing, housewares, firearms, dry goods, jewelry, more. Invaluable for dating, identifying vintage items. Also, copyright-free graphics for artists, designers. Co-published with Henry Ford Museum & Greenfield Village. 160pp. 8¼ × 11.　　　25780-0 Pa. $9.95

HISTORIC COSTUME IN PICTURES, Braun & Schneider. Over 1,450 costumed figures in clearly detailed engravings—from dawn of civilization to end of 19th century. Captions. Many folk costumes. 256pp. 8⅜ × 11¾.　　　23150-X Pa. $10.95

# CATALOG OF DOVER BOOKS

STICKLEY CRAFTSMAN FURNITURE CATALOGS, Gustav Stickley and L. & J. G. Stickley. Beautiful, functional furniture in two authentic catalogs from 1910. 594 illustrations, including 277 photos, show settles, rockers, armchairs, reclining chairs, bookcases, desks, tables. 183pp. 6½ × 9¼. 23838-5 Pa. $8.95

AMERICAN LOCOMOTIVES IN HISTORIC PHOTOGRAPHS: 1858 to 1949, Ron Ziel (ed.). A rare collection of 126 meticulously detailed official photographs, called "builder portraits," of American locomotives that majestically chronicle the rise of steam locomotive power in America. Introduction. Detailed captions. xi + 129pp. 9 × 12. 27393-8 Pa. $12.95

AMERICA'S LIGHTHOUSES: An Illustrated History, Francis Ross Holland, Jr. Delightfully written, profusely illustrated fact-filled survey of over 200 American lighthouses since 1716. History, anecdotes, technological advances, more. 240pp. 8 × 10¾. 25576-X Pa. $11.95

TOWARDS A NEW ARCHITECTURE, Le Corbusier. Pioneering manifesto by founder of "International School." Technical and aesthetic theories, views of industry, economics, relation of form to function, "mass-production split" and much more. Profusely illustrated. 320pp. 6⅛ × 9¼. (USO) 25023-7 Pa. $8.95

HOW THE OTHER HALF LIVES, Jacob Riis. Famous journalistic record, exposing poverty and degradation of New York slums around 1900, by major social reformer. 100 striking and influential photographs. 233pp. 10 × 7⅞. 22012-5 Pa $10.95

FRUIT KEY AND TWIG KEY TO TREES AND SHRUBS, William M. Harlow. One of the handiest and most widely used identification aids. Fruit key covers 120 deciduous and evergreen species; twig key 160 deciduous species. Easily used. Over 300 photographs. 126pp. 5⅜ × 8½. 20511-8 Pa. $3.95

COMMON BIRD SONGS, Dr. Donald J. Borror. Songs of 60 most common U.S. birds: robins, sparrows, cardinals, bluejays, finches, more—arranged in order of increasing complexity. Up to 9 variations of songs of each species. Cassette and manual 99911-4 $8.95

ORCHIDS AS HOUSE PLANTS, Rebecca Tyson Northen. Grow cattleyas and many other kinds of orchids—in a window, in a case, or under artificial light. 63 illustrations. 148pp. 5⅜ × 8½. 23261-1 Pa. $3.95

MONSTER MAZES, Dave Phillips. Masterful mazes at four levels of difficulty. Avoid deadly perils and evil creatures to find magical treasures. Solutions for all 32 exciting illustrated puzzles. 48pp. 8¼ × 11. 26005-4 Pa. $2.95

MOZART'S DON GIOVANNI (DOVER OPERA LIBRETTO SERIES), Wolfgang Amadeus Mozart. Introduced and translated by Ellen H. Bleiler. Standard Italian libretto, with complete English translation. Convenient and thoroughly portable—an ideal companion for reading along with a recording or the performance itself. Introduction. List of characters. Plot summary. 121pp. 5¼ × 8½. 24944-1 Pa. $2.95

TECHNICAL MANUAL AND DICTIONARY OF CLASSICAL BALLET, Gail Grant. Defines, explains, comments on steps, movements, poses and concepts. 15-page pictorial section. Basic book for student, viewer. 127pp. 5⅜ × 8½. 21843-0 Pa. $3.95

BRASS INSTRUMENTS: Their History and Development, Anthony Baines. Authoritative, updated survey of the evolution of trumpets, trombones, bugles, cornets, French horns, tubas and other brass wind instruments. Over 140 illustrations and 48 music examples. Corrected and updated by author. New preface. Bibliography. 320pp. 5⅜ × 8½.                                27574-4 Pa. $9.95

HOLLYWOOD GLAMOR PORTRAITS, John Kobal (ed.). 145 photos from 1926–49. Harlow, Gable, Bogart, Bacall; 94 stars in all. Full background on photographers, technical aspects. 160pp. 8⅜ × 11¼.                23352-9 Pa. $9.95

MAX AND MORITZ, Wilhelm Busch. Great humor classic in both German and English. Also 10 other works: "Cat and Mouse," "Plisch and Plumm," etc. 216pp. 5⅜ × 8½.                                                20181-3 Pa. $5.95

THE RAVEN AND OTHER FAVORITE POEMS, Edgar Allan Poe. Over 40 of the author's most memorable poems: "The Bells," "Ulalume," "Israfel," "To Helen," "The Conqueror Worm," "Eldorado," "Annabel Lee," many more. Alphabetical lists of titles and first lines. 64pp. 5³/₁₆ × 8¼.        26685-0 Pa. $1.00

SEVEN SCIENCE FICTION NOVELS, H. G. Wells. The standard collection of the great novels. Complete, unabridged. First Men in the Moon, Island of Dr. Moreau, War of the Worlds, Food of the Gods, Invisible Man, Time Machine, In the Days of the Comet. Total of 1,015pp. 5⅜ × 8½. (USO)    20264-X Clothbd. $29.95

AMULETS AND SUPERSTITIONS, E. A. Wallis Budge. Comprehensive discourse on origin, powers of amulets in many ancient cultures: Arab, Persian, Babylonian, Assyrian, Egyptian, Gnostic, Hebrew, Phoenician, Syriac, etc. Covers cross, swastika, crucifix, seals, rings, stones, etc. 584pp. 5⅜ × 8½. 23573-4 Pa. $12.95

RUSSIAN STORIES/PYCCKNE PACCKA3bl: A Dual-Language Book, edited by Gleb Struve. Twelve tales by such masters as Chekhov, Tolstoy, Dostoevsky, Pushkin, others. Excellent word-for-word English translations on facing pages, plus teaching and study aids, Russian/English vocabulary, biographical/critical introductions, more. 416pp. 5⅜ × 8½.                        26244-8 Pa. $8.95

PHILADELPHIA THEN AND NOW: 60 Sites Photographed in the Past and Present, Kenneth Finkel and Susan Oyama. Rare photographs of City Hall, Logan Square, Independence Hall, Betsy Ross House, other landmarks juxtaposed with contemporary views. Captures changing face of historic city. Introduction. Captions. 128pp. 8¼ × 11.                                25790-8 Pa. $9.95

AIA ARCHITECTURAL GUIDE TO NASSAU AND SUFFOLK COUNTIES, LONG ISLAND, The American Institute of Architects, Long Island Chapter, and the Society for the Preservation of Long Island Antiquities. Comprehensive, well-researched and generously illustrated volume brings to life over three centuries of Long Island's great architectural heritage. More than 240 photographs with authoritative, extensively detailed captions. 176pp. 8¼ × 11.   26946-9 Pa. $14.95

NORTH AMERICAN INDIAN LIFE: Customs and Traditions of 23 Tribes, Elsie Clews Parsons (ed.). 27 fictionalized essays by noted anthropologists examine religion, customs, government, additional facets of life among the Winnebago, Crow, Zuni, Eskimo, other tribes. 480pp. 6⅛ × 9¼.        27377-6 Pa. $10.95

FRANK LLOYD WRIGHT'S HOLLYHOCK HOUSE, Donald Hoffmann. Lavishly illustrated, carefully documented study of one of Wright's most controversial residential designs. Over 120 photographs, floor plans, elevations, etc. Detailed perceptive text by noted Wright scholar. Index. 128pp. 9¼ × 10¾.
27133-1 Pa. $11.95

THE MALE AND FEMALE FIGURE IN MOTION: 60 Classic Photographic Sequences, Eadweard Muybridge. 60 true-action photographs of men and women walking, running, climbing, bending, turning, etc., reproduced from rare 19th-century masterpiece. vi + 121pp. 9 × 12.
24745-7 Pa. $10.95

1001 QUESTIONS ANSWERED ABOUT THE SEASHORE, N. J. Berrill and Jacquelyn Berrill. Queries answered about dolphins, sea snails, sponges, starfish, fishes, shore birds, many others. Covers appearance, breeding, growth, feeding, much more. 305pp. 5¼ × 8¼.
23366-9 Pa. $7.95

GUIDE TO OWL WATCHING IN NORTH AMERICA, Donald S. Heintzelman. Superb guide offers complete data and descriptions of 19 species: barn owl, screech owl, snowy owl, many more. Expert coverage of owl-watching equipment, conservation, migrations and invasions, etc. Guide to observing sites. 84 illustrations. xiii + 193pp. 5⅜ × 8½.
27344-X Pa. $7.95

MEDICINAL AND OTHER USES OF NORTH AMERICAN PLANTS: A Historical Survey with Special Reference to the Eastern Indian Tribes, Charlotte Erichsen-Brown. Chronological historical citations document 500 years of usage of plants, trees, shrubs native to eastern Canada, northeastern U.S. Also complete identifying information. 343 illustrations. 544pp. 6½ × 9¼.
25951-X Pa. $12.95

STORYBOOK MAZES, Dave Phillips. 23 stories and mazes on two-page spreads: Wizard of Oz, Treasure Island, Robin Hood, etc. Solutions. 64pp. 8¼ × 11.
23628-5 Pa. $2.95

NEGRO FOLK MUSIC, U.S.A., Harold Courlander. Noted folklorist's scholarly yet readable analysis of rich and varied musical tradition. Includes authentic versions of over 40 folk songs. Valuable bibliography and discography. xi + 324pp. 5⅜ × 8½.
27350-4 Pa. $7.95

MOVIE-STAR PORTRAITS OF THE FORTIES, John Kobal (ed.). 163 glamor, studio photos of 106 stars of the 1940s: Rita Hayworth, Ava Gardner, Marlon Brando, Clark Gable, many more. 176pp. 8⅜ × 11¼.
23546-7 Pa. $10.95

BENCHLEY LOST AND FOUND, Robert Benchley. Finest humor from early 30s, about pet peeves, child psychologists, post office and others. Mostly unavailable elsewhere. 73 illustrations by Peter Arno and others. 183pp. 5⅜ × 8½.
22410-4 Pa. $5.95

YEKL and THE IMPORTED BRIDEGROOM AND OTHER STORIES OF YIDDISH NEW YORK, Abraham Cahan. Film Hester Street based on Yekl (1896). Novel, other stories among first about Jewish immigrants on N.Y.'s East Side. 240pp. 5⅜ × 8½.
22427-9 Pa. $5.95

SELECTED POEMS, Walt Whitman. Generous sampling from *Leaves of Grass*. Twenty-four poems include "I Hear America Singing," "Song of the Open Road," "I Sing the Body Electric," "When Lilacs Last in the Dooryard Bloom'd," "O Captain! My Captain!"—all reprinted from an authoritative edition. Lists of titles and first lines. 128pp. 5³⁄₁₆ × 8¼.
26878-0 Pa. $1.00

THE BEST TALES OF HOFFMANN, E. T. A. Hoffmann. 10 of Hoffmann's most important stories: "Nutcracker and the King of Mice," "The Golden Flowerpot," etc. 458pp. 5⅜ × 8½. 21793-0 Pa. $8.95

FROM FETISH TO GOD IN ANCIENT EGYPT, E. A. Wallis Budge. Rich detailed survey of Egyptian conception of "God" and gods, magic, cult of animals, Osiris, more. Also, superb English translations of hymns and legends. 240 illustrations. 545pp. 5⅜ × 8½. 25803-3 Pa. $11.95

FRENCH STORIES/CONTES FRANÇAIS: A Dual-Language Book, Wallace Fowlie. Ten stories by French masters, Voltaire to Camus: "Micromegas" by Voltaire; "The Atheist's Mass" by Balzac; "Minuet" by de Maupassant; "The Guest" by Camus, six more. Excellent English translations on facing pages. Also French-English vocabulary list, exercises, more. 352pp. 5⅜ × 8½. 26443-2 Pa. $8.95

CHICAGO AT THE TURN OF THE CENTURY IN PHOTOGRAPHS: 122 Historic Views from the Collections of the Chicago Historical Society, Larry A. Viskochil. Rare large-format prints offer detailed views of City Hall, State Street, the Loop, Hull House, Union Station, many other landmarks, circa 1904–1913. Introduction. Captions. Maps. 144pp. 9⅜ × 12¼. 24656-6 Pa. $12.95

OLD BROOKLYN IN EARLY PHOTOGRAPHS, 1865–1929, William Lee Younger. Luna Park, Gravesend race track, construction of Grand Army Plaza, moving of Hotel Brighton, etc. 157 previously unpublished photographs. 165pp. 8⅞ × 11¾. 23587-4 Pa. $12.95

THE MYTHS OF THE NORTH AMERICAN INDIANS, Lewis Spence. Rich anthology of the myths and legends of the Algonquins, Iroquois, Pawnees and Sioux, prefaced by an extensive historical and ethnological commentary. 36 illustrations. 480pp. 5⅜ × 8½. 25967-6 Pa. $8.95

AN ENCYCLOPEDIA OF BATTLES: Accounts of Over 1,560 Battles from 1479 B.C. to the Present, David Eggenberger. Essential details of every major battle in recorded history from the first battle of Megiddo in 1479 B.C. to Grenada in 1984. List of Battle Maps. New Appendix covering the years 1967–1984. Index. 99 illustrations. 544pp. 6½ × 9¼. 24913-1 Pa. $14.95

SAILING ALONE AROUND THE WORLD, Captain Joshua Slocum. First man to sail around the world, alone, in small boat. One of great feats of seamanship told in delightful manner. 67 illustrations. 294pp. 5⅜ × 8½. 20326-3 Pa. $5.95

ANARCHISM AND OTHER ESSAYS, Emma Goldman. Powerful, penetrating, prophetic essays on direct action, role of minorities, prison reform, puritan hypocrisy, violence, etc. 271pp. 5⅜ × 8½. 22484-8 Pa. $5.95

MYTHS OF THE HINDUS AND BUDDHISTS, Ananda K. Coomaraswamy and Sister Nivedita. Great stories of the epics; deeds of Krishna, Shiva, taken from puranas, Vedas, folk tales; etc. 32 illustrations. 400pp. 5⅜ × 8½. 21759-0 Pa. $9.95

BEYOND PSYCHOLOGY, Otto Rank. Fear of death, desire of immortality, nature of sexuality, social organization, creativity, according to Rankian system. 291pp. 5⅜ × 8½. 20485-5 Pa. $7.95

A THEOLOGICO-POLITICAL TREATISE, Benedict Spinoza. Also contains unfinished Political Treatise. Great classic on religious liberty, theory of government on common consent. R. Elwes translation. Total of 421pp. 5⅜ × 8½. 20249-6 Pa. $7.95

MY BONDAGE AND MY FREEDOM, Frederick Douglass. Born a slave, Douglass became outspoken force in antislavery movement. The best of Douglass' autobiographies. Graphic description of slave life. 464pp. 5⅜ × 8½.     22457-0 Pa. $8.95

FOLLOWING THE EQUATOR: A Journey Around the World, Mark Twain. Fascinating humorous account of 1897 voyage to Hawaii, Australia, India, New Zealand, etc. Ironic, bemused reports on peoples, customs, climate, flora and fauna, politics, much more. 197 illustrations. 720pp. 5⅜ × 8½.     26113-1 Pa. $15.95

THE PEOPLE CALLED SHAKERS, Edward D. Andrews. Definitive study of Shakers: origins, beliefs, practices, dances, social organization, furniture and crafts, etc. 33 illustrations. 351pp. 5⅜ × 8½.     21081-2 Pa. $7.95

THE MYTHS OF GREECE AND ROME, H. A. Guerber. A classic of mythology, generously illustrated, long prized for its simple, graphic, accurate retelling of the principal myths of Greece and Rome, and for its commentary on their origins and significance. With 64 illustrations by Michelangelo, Raphael, Titian, Rubens, Canova, Bernini and others. 480pp. 5⅜ × 8½.     27584-1 Pa. $9.95

PSYCHOLOGY OF MUSIC, Carl E. Seashore. Classic work discusses music as a medium from psychological viewpoint. Clear treatment of physical acoustics, auditory apparatus, sound perception, development of musical skills, nature of musical feeling, host of other topics. 88 figures. 408pp. 5⅜ × 8½. 21851-1 Pa. $9.95

THE PHILOSOPHY OF HISTORY, Georg W. Hegel. Great classic of Western thought develops concept that history is not chance but rational process, the evolution of freedom. 457pp. 5⅜ × 8½.     20112-0 Pa. $8.95

THE BOOK OF TEA, Kakuzo Okakura. Minor classic of the Orient: entertaining, charming explanation, interpretation of traditional Japanese culture in terms of tea ceremony. 94pp. 5⅜ × 8½.     20070-1 Pa. $2.95

LIFE IN ANCIENT EGYPT, Adolf Erman. Fullest, most thorough, detailed older account with much not in more recent books, domestic life, religion, magic, medicine, commerce, much more. Many illustrations reproduce tomb paintings, carvings, hieroglyphs, etc. 597pp. 5⅜ × 8½.     22632-8 Pa. $9.95

SUNDIALS, Their Theory and Construction, Albert Waugh. Far and away the best, most thorough coverage of ideas, mathematics concerned, types, construction, adjusting anywhere. Simple, nontechnical treatment allows even children to build several of these dials. Over 100 illustrations. 230pp. 5⅜ × 8½.     22947-5 Pa. $5.95

DYNAMICS OF FLUIDS IN POROUS MEDIA, Jacob Bear. For advanced students of ground water hydrology, soil mechanics and physics, drainage and irrigation engineering, and more. 335 illustrations. Exercises, with answers. 784pp. 6⅛ × 9¼.     65675-6 Pa. $19.95

SONGS OF EXPERIENCE: Facsimile Reproduction with 26 Plates in Full Color, William Blake. 26 full-color plates from a rare 1826 edition. Includes "The Tyger," "London," "Holy Thursday," and other poems. Printed text of poems. 48pp. 5¼ × 7.     24636-1 Pa. $3.95

OLD-TIME VIGNETTES IN FULL COLOR, Carol Belanger Grafton (ed.). Over 390 charming, often sentimental illustrations, selected from archives of Victorian graphics—pretty women posing, children playing, food, flowers, kittens and puppies, smiling cherubs, birds and butterflies, much more. All copyright-free. 48pp. 9¼ × 12¼.     27269-9 Pa. $5.95

PERSPECTIVE FOR ARTISTS, Rex Vicat Cole. Depth, perspective of sky and sea, shadows, much more, not usually covered. 391 diagrams, 81 reproductions of drawings and paintings. 279pp. 5⅜ × 8½. 22487-2 Pa. $6.95

DRAWING THE LIVING FIGURE, Joseph Sheppard. Innovative approach to artistic anatomy focuses on specifics of surface anatomy, rather than muscles and bones. Over 170 drawings of live models in front, back and side views, and in widely varying poses. Accompanying diagrams. 177 illustrations. Introduction. Index. 144pp. 8⅜ × 11¼. 26723-7 Pa. $7.95

GOTHIC AND OLD ENGLISH ALPHABETS: 100 Complete Fonts, Dan X. Solo. Add power, elegance to posters, signs, other graphics with 100 stunning copyright-free alphabets: Blackstone, Dolbey, Germania, 97 more—including many lower-case, numerals, punctuation marks. 104pp. 8⅛ × 11. 24695-7 Pa. $7.95

HOW TO DO BEADWORK, Mary White. Fundamental book on craft from simple projects to five-bead chains and woven works. 106 illustrations. 142pp. 5⅜ × 8. 20697-1 Pa. $4.95

THE BOOK OF WOOD CARVING, Charles Marshall Sayers. Finest book for beginners discusses fundamentals and offers 34 designs. "Absolutely first rate . . . well thought out and well executed."—E. J. Tangerman. 118pp. 7¾ × 10⅝. 23654-4 Pa. $5.95

ILLUSTRATED CATALOG OF CIVIL WAR MILITARY GOODS: Union Army Weapons, Insignia, Uniform Accessories, and Other Equipment, Schuyler, Hartley, and Graham. Rare, profusely illustrated 1846 catalog includes Union Army uniform and dress regulations, arms and ammunition, coats, insignia, flags, swords, rifles, etc. 226 illustrations. 160pp. 9 × 12. 24939-5 Pa. $10.95

WOMEN'S FASHIONS OF THE EARLY 1900s: An Unabridged Republication of "New York Fashions, 1909," National Cloak & Suit Co. Rare catalog of mail-order fashions documents women's and children's clothing styles shortly after the turn of the century. Captions offer full descriptions, prices. Invaluable resource for fashion, costume historians. Approximately 725 illustrations. 128pp. 8⅜ × 11¼. 27276-1 Pa. $10.95

THE 1912 AND 1915 GUSTAV STICKLEY FURNITURE CATALOGS, Gustav Stickley. With over 200 detailed illustrations and descriptions, these two catalogs are essential reading and reference materials and identification guides for Stickley furniture. Captions cite materials, dimensions and prices. 112pp. 6½ × 9¼. 26676-1 Pa. $9.95

EARLY AMERICAN LOCOMOTIVES, John H. White, Jr. Finest locomotive engravings from early 19th century: historical (1804–74), main-line (after 1870), special, foreign, etc. 147 plates. 142pp. 11⅜ × 8¼. 22772-3 Pa. $8.95

THE TALL SHIPS OF TODAY IN PHOTOGRAPHS, Frank O. Braynard. Lavishly illustrated tribute to nearly 100 majestic contemporary sailing vessels: Amerigo Vespucci, Clearwater, Constitution, Eagle, Mayflower, Sea Cloud, Victory, many more. Authoritative captions provide statistics, background on each ship. 190 black-and-white photographs and illustrations. Introduction. 128pp. 8⅞ × 11¾. 27163-3 Pa. $12.95

EARLY NINETEENTH-CENTURY CRAFTS AND TRADES, Peter Stockham (ed.). Extremely rare 1807 volume describes to youngsters the crafts and trades of the day: brickmaker, weaver, dressmaker, bookbinder, ropemaker, saddler, many more. Quaint prose, charming illustrations for each craft. 20 black-and-white line illustrations. 192pp. 4⅝ × 6.                                      27293-1 Pa. $4.95

VICTORIAN FASHIONS AND COSTUMES FROM HARPER'S BAZAR, 1867–1898, Stella Blum (ed.). Day costumes, evening wear, sports clothes, shoes, hats, other accessories in over 1,000 detailed engravings. 320pp. 9⅜ × 12¼.
22990-4 Pa. $13.95

GUSTAV STICKLEY, THE CRAFTSMAN, Mary Ann Smith. Superb study surveys broad scope of Stickley's achievement, especially in architecture. Design philosophy, rise and fall of the Craftsman empire, descriptions and floor plans for many Craftsman houses, more. 86 black-and-white halftones. 31 line illustrations. Introduction. 208pp. 6½ × 9¼.                               27210-9 Pa. $9.95

THE LONG ISLAND RAIL ROAD IN EARLY PHOTOGRAPHS, Ron Ziel. Over 220 rare photos, informative text document origin (1844) and development of rail service on Long Island. Vintage views of early trains, locomotives, stations, passengers, crews, much more. Captions. 8⅞ × 11¾.            26301-0 Pa. $13.95

THE BOOK OF OLD SHIPS: From Egyptian Galleys to Clipper Ships, Henry B. Culver. Superb, authoritative history of sailing vessels, with 80 magnificent line illustrations. Galley, bark, caravel, longship, whaler, many more. Detailed, informative text on each vessel by noted naval historian. Introduction. 256pp. 5⅜ × 8½.                                                         27332-6 Pa. $6.95

TEN BOOKS ON ARCHITECTURE, Vitruvius. The most important book ever written on architecture. Early Roman aesthetics, technology, classical orders, site selection, all other aspects. Morgan translation. 331pp. 5⅜ × 8½. 20645-9 Pa. $8.95

THE HUMAN FIGURE IN MOTION, Eadweard Muybridge. More than 4,500 stopped-action photos, in action series, showing undraped men, women, children jumping, lying down, throwing, sitting, wrestling, carrying, etc. 390pp. 7⅞ × 10⅝.
20204-6 Clothbd. $24.95

TREES OF THE EASTERN AND CENTRAL UNITED STATES AND CANADA, William M. Harlow. Best one-volume guide to 140 trees. Full descriptions, woodlore, range, etc. Over 600 illustrations. Handy size. 288pp. 4½ × 6⅜.
20395-6 Pa. $5.95

SONGS OF WESTERN BIRDS, Dr. Donald J. Borror. Complete song and call repertoire of 60 western species, including flycatchers, juncoes, cactus wrens, many more—includes fully illustrated booklet.            Cassette and manual 99913-0 $8.95

GROWING AND USING HERBS AND SPICES, Milo Miloradovich. Versatile handbook provides all the information needed for cultivation and use of all the herbs and spices available in North America. 4 illustrations. Index. Glossary. 236pp. 5⅜ × 8½.                                                      25058-X Pa. $5.95

BIG BOOK OF MAZES AND LABYRINTHS, Walter Shepherd. 50 mazes and labyrinths in all—classical, solid, ripple, and more—in one great volume. Perfect inexpensive puzzler for clever youngsters. Full solutions. 112pp. 8⅛ × 11.
22951-3 Pa. $3.95

PIANO TUNING, J. Cree Fischer. Clearest, best book for beginner, amateur. Simple repairs, raising dropped notes, tuning by easy method of flattened fifths. No previous skills needed. 4 illustrations. 201pp. 5⅜ × 8½. 23267-0 Pa. $5.95

A SOURCE BOOK IN THEATRICAL HISTORY, A. M. Nagler. Contemporary observers on acting, directing, make-up, costuming, stage props, machinery, scene design, from Ancient Greece to Chekhov. 611pp. 5⅜ × 8½. 20515-0 Pa. $11.95

THE COMPLETE NONSENSE OF EDWARD LEAR, Edward Lear. All nonsense limericks, zany alphabets, Owl and Pussycat, songs, nonsense botany, etc., illustrated by Lear. Total of 320pp. 5⅜ × 8½. (USO) 20167-8 Pa. $5.95

VICTORIAN PARLOUR POETRY: An Annotated Anthology, Michael R. Turner. 117 gems by Longfellow, Tennyson, Browning, many lesser-known poets. "The Village Blacksmith," "Curfew Must Not Ring Tonight," "Only a Baby Small," dozens more, often difficult to find elsewhere. Index of poets, titles, first lines. xxiii + 325pp. 5⅝ × 8¼. 27044-0 Pa. $8.95

DUBLINERS, James Joyce. Fifteen stories offer vivid, tightly focused observations of the lives of Dublin's poorer classes. At least one, "The Dead," is considered a masterpiece. Reprinted complete and unabridged from standard edition. 160pp. 5³⁄₁₆ × 8¼. 26870-5 Pa. $1.00

THE HAUNTED MONASTERY and THE CHINESE MAZE MURDERS, Robert van Gulik. Two full novels by van Gulik, set in 7th-century China, continue adventures of Judge Dee and his companions. An evil Taoist monastery, seemingly supernatural events; overgrown topiary maze hides strange crimes. 27 illustrations. 328pp. 5⅜ × 8½. 23502-5 Pa. $7.95

THE BOOK OF THE SACRED MAGIC OF ABRAMELIN THE MAGE, translated by S. MacGregor Mathers. Medieval manuscript of ceremonial magic. Basic document in Aleister Crowley, Golden Dawn groups. 268pp. 5⅜ × 8½. 23211-5 Pa. $7.95

NEW RUSSIAN-ENGLISH AND ENGLISH-RUSSIAN DICTIONARY, M. A. O'Brien. This is a remarkably handy Russian dictionary, containing a surprising amount of information, including over 70,000 entries. 366pp. 4½ × 6⅛. 20208-9 Pa. $8.95

HISTORIC HOMES OF THE AMERICAN PRESIDENTS, Second, Revised Edition, Irvin Haas. A traveler's guide to American Presidential homes, most open to the public, depicting and describing homes occupied by every American President from George Washington to George Bush. With visiting hours, admission charges, travel routes. 175 photographs. Index. 160pp. 8¼ × 11. 26751-2 Pa. $10.95

NEW YORK IN THE FORTIES, Andreas Feininger. 162 brilliant photographs by the well-known photographer, formerly with *Life* magazine. Commuters, shoppers, Times Square at night, much else from city at its peak. Captions by John von Hartz. 181pp. 9¼ × 10¾. 23585-8 Pa. $12.95

INDIAN SIGN LANGUAGE, William Tomkins. Over 525 signs developed by Sioux and other tribes. Written instructions and diagrams. Also 290 pictographs. 111pp. 6⅛ × 9¼. 22029-X Pa. $3.50

# CATALOG OF DOVER BOOKS

ANATOMY: A Complete Guide for Artists, Joseph Sheppard. A master of figure drawing shows artists how to render human anatomy convincingly. Over 460 illustrations. 224pp. 8⅜ × 11¼. 27279-6 Pa. $9.95

MEDIEVAL CALLIGRAPHY: Its History and Technique, Marc Drogin. Spirited history, comprehensive instruction manual covers 13 styles (ca. 4th century thru 15th). Excellent photographs; directions for duplicating medieval techniques with modern tools. 224pp. 8⅜ × 11¼. 26142-5 Pa. $11.95

DRIED FLOWERS: How to Prepare Them, Sarah Whitlock and Martha Rankin. Complete instructions on how to use silica gel, meal and borax, perlite aggregate, sand and borax, glycerine and water to create attractive permanent flower arrangements. 12 illustrations. 32pp. 5⅜ × 8½. 21802-3 Pa. $1.00

EASY-TO-MAKE BIRD FEEDERS FOR WOODWORKERS, Scott D. Campbell. Detailed, simple-to-use guide for designing, constructing, caring for and using feeders. Text, illustrations for 12 classic and contemporary designs. 96pp. 5⅜ × 8½. 25847-5 Pa. $2.95

OLD-TIME CRAFTS AND TRADES, Peter Stockham. An 1807 book created to teach children about crafts and trades open to them as future careers. It describes in detailed, nontechnical terms 24 different occupations, among them coachmaker, gardener, hairdresser, lacemaker, shoemaker, wheelwright, copper-plate printer, milliner, trunkmaker, merchant and brewer. Finely detailed engravings illustrate each occupation. 192pp. 4⅝ × 6. 27398-9 Pa. $4.95

THE HISTORY OF UNDERCLOTHES, C. Willett Cunnington and Phyllis Cunnington. Fascinating, well-documented survey covering six centuries of English undergarments, enhanced with over 100 illustrations: 12th-century laced-up bodice, footed long drawers (1795), 19th-century bustles, 19th-century corsets for men, Victorian "bust improvers," much more. 272pp. 5⅜ × 8¼. 27124-2 Pa. $9.95

ARTS AND CRAFTS FURNITURE: The Complete Brooks Catalog of 1912, Brooks Manufacturing Co. Photos and detailed descriptions of more than 150 now very collectible furniture designs from the Arts and Crafts movement depict davenports, settees, buffets, desks, tables, chairs, bedsteads, dressers and more, all built of solid, quarter-sawed oak. Invaluable for students and enthusiasts of antiques, Americana and the decorative arts. 80pp. 6½ × 9¼. 27471-3 Pa. $7.95

HOW WE INVENTED THE AIRPLANE: An Illustrated History, Orville Wright. Fascinating firsthand account covers early experiments, construction of planes and motors, first flights, much more. Introduction and commentary by Fred C. Kelly. 76 photographs. 96pp. 8¼ × 11. 25662-6 Pa. $7.95

THE ARTS OF THE SAILOR: Knotting, Splicing and Ropework, Hervey Garrett Smith. Indispensable shipboard reference covers tools, basic knots and useful hitches; handsewing and canvas work, more. Over 100 illustrations. Delightful reading for sea lovers. 256pp. 5⅜ × 8½. 26440-8 Pa. $7.95

FRANK LLOYD WRIGHT'S FALLINGWATER: The House and Its History, Second, Revised Edition, Donald Hoffmann. A total revision—both in text and illustrations—of the standard document on Fallingwater, the boldest, most personal architectural statement of Wright's mature years, updated with valuable new material from the recently opened Frank Lloyd Wright Archives. "Fascinating"—*The New York Times*. 116 illustrations. 128pp. 9¼ × 10¾.
27430-6 Pa. $10.95

**PHOTOGRAPHIC SKETCHBOOK OF THE CIVIL WAR,** Alexander Gardner. 100 photos taken on field during the Civil War. Famous shots of Manassas, Harper's Ferry, Lincoln, Richmond, slave pens, etc. 244pp. 10⅝ × 8¼.
22731-6 Pa. $9.95

**FIVE ACRES AND INDEPENDENCE,** Maurice G. Kains. Great back-to-the-land classic explains basics of self-sufficient farming. The one book to get. 95 illustrations. 397pp. 5⅜ × 8½.
20974-1 Pa. $6.95

**SONGS OF EASTERN BIRDS,** Dr. Donald J. Borror. Songs and calls of 60 species most common to eastern U.S.: warblers, woodpeckers, flycatchers, thrushes, larks, many more in high-quality recording.
Cassette and manual 99912-2 $8.95

**A MODERN HERBAL,** Margaret Grieve. Much the fullest, most exact, most useful compilation of herbal material. Gigantic alphabetical encyclopedia, from aconite to zedoary, gives botanical information, medical properties, folklore, economic uses, much else. Indispensable to serious reader. 161 illustrations. 888pp. 6½ × 9¼. 2-vol. set. (USO)
Vol. I: 22798-7 Pa. $9.95
Vol. II: 22799-5 Pa. $9.95

**HIDDEN TREASURE MAZE BOOK,** Dave Phillips. Solve 34 challenging mazes accompanied by heroic tales of adventure. Evil dragons, people-eating plants, bloodthirsty giants, many more dangerous adversaries lurk at every twist and turn. 34 mazes, stories, solutions. 48pp. 8¼ × 11.
24566-7 Pa. $2.95

**LETTERS OF W. A. MOZART,** Wolfgang A. Mozart. Remarkable letters show bawdy wit, humor, imagination, musical insights, contemporary musical world; includes some letters from Leopold Mozart. 276pp. 5⅜ × 8½.
22859-2 Pa. $6.95

**BASIC PRINCIPLES OF CLASSICAL BALLET,** Agrippina Vaganova. Great Russian theoretician, teacher explains methods for teaching classical ballet. 118 illustrations. 175pp. 5⅜ × 8½.
22036-2 Pa. $4.95

**THE JUMPING FROG,** Mark Twain. Revenge edition. The original story of The Celebrated Jumping Frog of Calaveras County, a hapless French translation, and Twain's hilarious "retranslation" from the French. 12 illustrations. 66pp. 5⅜ × 8½.
22686-7 Pa. $3.50

**BEST REMEMBERED POEMS,** Martin Gardner (ed.). The 126 poems in this superb collection of 19th- and 20th-century British and American verse range from Shelley's "To a Skylark" to the impassioned "Renascence" of Edna St. Vincent Millay and to Edward Lear's whimsical "The Owl and the Pussycat." 224pp. 5⅜ × 8½.
27165-X Pa. $4.95

**COMPLETE SONNETS,** William Shakespeare. Over 150 exquisite poems deal with love, friendship, the tyranny of time, beauty's evanescence, death and other themes in language of remarkable power, precision and beauty. Glossary of archaic terms. 80pp. 5³⁄₁₆ × 8¼.
26686-9 Pa. $1.00

**BODIES IN A BOOKSHOP,** R. T. Campbell. Challenging mystery of blackmail and murder with ingenious plot and superbly drawn characters. In the best tradition of British suspense fiction. 192pp. 5⅜ × 8½.
24720-1 Pa. $5.95

THE WIT AND HUMOR OF OSCAR WILDE, Alvin Redman (ed.). More than 1,000 ripostes, paradoxes, wisecracks: Work is the curse of the drinking classes; I can resist everything except temptation; etc. 258pp. 5⅜ × 8½. 20602-5 Pa. $4.95

SHAKESPEARE LEXICON AND QUOTATION DICTIONARY, Alexander Schmidt. Full definitions, locations, shades of meaning in every word in plays and poems. More than 50,000 exact quotations. 1,485pp. 6½ × 9¼. 2-vol. set.
Vol. 1: 22726-X Pa. $15.95
Vol. 2: 22727-8 Pa. $15.95

SELECTED POEMS, Emily Dickinson. Over 100 best-known, best-loved poems by one of America's foremost poets, reprinted from authoritative early editions. No comparable edition at this price. Index of first lines. 64pp. 5³⁄₁₆ × 8¼.
26466-1 Pa. $1.00

CELEBRATED CASES OF JUDGE DEE (DEE GOONG AN), translated by Robert van Gulik. Authentic 18th-century Chinese detective novel; Dee and associates solve three interlocked cases. Led to van Gulik's own stories with same characters. Extensive introduction. 9 illustrations. 237pp. 5⅜ × 8½.
23337-5 Pa. $5.95

THE MALLEUS MALEFICARUM OF KRAMER AND SPRENGER, translated by Montague Summers. Full text of most important witchhunter's "bible," used by both Catholics and Protestants. 278pp. 6⅝ × 10. 22802-9 Pa. $10.95

SPANISH STORIES/CUENTOS ESPAÑOLES: A Dual-Language Book, Angel Flores (ed.). Unique format offers 13 great stories in Spanish by Cervantes, Borges, others. Faithful English translations on facing pages. 352pp. 5⅜ × 8½.
25399-6 Pa. $8.95

THE CHICAGO WORLD'S FAIR OF 1893: A Photographic Record, Stanley Appelbaum (ed.). 128 rare photos show 200 buildings, Beaux-Arts architecture, Midway, original Ferris Wheel, Edison's kinetoscope, more. Architectural emphasis; full text. 116pp. 8¼ × 11. 23990-X Pa. $9.95

OLD QUEENS, N.Y., IN EARLY PHOTOGRAPHS, Vincent F. Seyfried and William Asadorian. Over 160 rare photographs of Maspeth, Jamaica, Jackson Heights, and other areas. Vintage views of DeWitt Clinton mansion, 1939 World's Fair and more. Captions. 192pp. 8⅞ × 11. 26358-4 Pa. $12.95

CAPTURED BY THE INDIANS: 15 Firsthand Accounts, 1750–1870, Frederick Drimmer. Astounding true historical accounts of grisly torture, bloody conflicts, relentless pursuits, miraculous escapes and more, by people who lived to tell the tale. 384pp. 5⅜ × 8½. 24901-8 Pa. $7.95

THE WORLD'S GREAT SPEECHES, Lewis Copeland and Lawrence W. Lamm (eds.). Vast collection of 278 speeches of Greeks to 1970. Powerful and effective models; unique look at history. 842pp. 5⅜ × 8½. 20468-5 Pa. $13.95

THE BOOK OF THE SWORD, Sir Richard F. Burton. Great Victorian scholar/adventurer's eloquent, erudite history of the "queen of weapons"—from prehistory to early Roman Empire. Evolution and development of early swords, variations (sabre, broadsword, cutlass, scimitar, etc.), much more. 336pp. 6⅛ × 9¼. 25434-8 Pa. $8.95

*CATALOG OF DOVER BOOKS*

AUTOBIOGRAPHY: The Story of My Experiments with Truth, Mohandas K. Gandhi. Boyhood, legal studies, purification, the growth of the Satyagraha (nonviolent protest) movement. Critical, inspiring work of the man responsible for the freedom of India. 480pp. 5⅜ × 8½. (USO) 24593-4 Pa. $7.95

CELTIC MYTHS AND LEGENDS, T. W. Rolleston. Masterful retelling of Irish and Welsh stories and tales. Cuchulain, King Arthur, Deirdre, the Grail, many more. First paperback edition. 58 full-page illustrations. 512pp. 5⅜ × 8½.
26507-2 Pa. $9.95

THE PRINCIPLES OF PSYCHOLOGY, William James. Famous long course complete, unabridged. Stream of thought, time perception, memory, experimental methods; great work decades ahead of its time. 94 figures. 1,391pp. 5⅜ × 8½. 2-vol. set.
Vol. I: 20381-6 Pa. $12.95
Vol. II: 20382-4 Pa. $12.95

THE WORLD AS WILL AND REPRESENTATION, Arthur Schopenhauer. Definitive English translation of Schopenhauer's life work, correcting more than 1,000 errors, omissions in earlier translations. Translated by E. F. J. Payne. Total of 1,269pp. 5⅜ × 8½. 2-vol. set. Vol. 1: 21761-2 Pa. $10.95
Vol. 2: 21762-0 Pa. $11.95

MAGIC AND MYSTERY IN TIBET, Madame Alexandra David-Neel. Experiences among lamas, magicians, sages, sorcerers, Bonpa wizards. A true psychic discovery. 32 illustrations. 321pp. 5⅜ × 8½. (USO) 22682-4 Pa. $8.95

THE EGYPTIAN BOOK OF THE DEAD, E. A. Wallis Budge. Complete reproduction of Ani's papyrus, finest ever found. Full hieroglyphic text, interlinear transliteration, word-for-word translation, smooth translation. 533pp. 6½ × 9¼.
21866-X Pa. $9.95

MATHEMATICS FOR THE NONMATHEMATICIAN, Morris Kline. Detailed, college-level treatment of mathematics in cultural and historical context, with numerous exercises. Recommended Reading Lists. Tables. Numerous figures. 641pp. 5⅜ × 8½. 24823-2 Pa. $11.95

THEORY OF WING SECTIONS: Including a Summary of Airfoil Data, Ira H. Abbott and A. E. von Doenhoff. Concise compilation of subsonic aerodynamic characteristics of NACA wing sections, plus description of theory. 350pp. of tables. 693pp. 5⅜ × 8½. 60586-8 Pa. $13.95

THE RIME OF THE ANCIENT MARINER, Gustave Doré, S. T. Coleridge. Doré's finest work; 34 plates capture moods, subtleties of poem. Flawless full-size reproductions printed on facing pages with authoritative text of poem. "Beautiful. Simply beautiful."—*Publisher's Weekly*. 77pp. 9¼ × 12. 22305-1 Pa. $5.95

NORTH AMERICAN INDIAN DESIGNS FOR ARTISTS AND CRAFTS-PEOPLE, Eva Wilson. Over 360 authentic copyright-free designs adapted from Navajo blankets, Hopi pottery, Sioux buffalo hides, more. Geometrics, symbolic figures, plant and animal motifs, etc. 128pp. 8⅜ × 11. (EUK) 25341-4 Pa. $7.95

SCULPTURE: Principles and Practice, Louis Slobodkin. Step-by-step approach to clay, plaster, metals, stone; classical and modern. 253 drawings, photos. 255pp. 8⅛ × 11. 22960-2 Pa. $9.95

THE INFLUENCE OF SEA POWER UPON HISTORY, 1660–1783, A. T. Mahan. Influential classic of naval history and tactics still used as text in war colleges. First paperback edition. 4 maps. 24 battle plans. 640pp. 5⅜ × 8½.
25509-3 Pa. $12.95

THE STORY OF THE TITANIC AS TOLD BY ITS SURVIVORS, Jack Winocour (ed.). What it was really like. Panic, despair, shocking inefficiency, and a little heroism. More thrilling than any fictional account. 26 illustrations. 320pp. 5⅜ × 8½. 20610-6 Pa. $7.95

FAIRY AND FOLK TALES OF THE IRISH PEASANTRY, William Butler Yeats (ed.). Treasury of 64 tales from the twilight world of Celtic myth and legend: "The Soul Cages," "The Kildare Pooka," "King O'Toole and his Goose," many more. Introduction and Notes by W. B. Yeats. 352pp. 5⅜ × 8½. 26941-8 Pa. $7.95

BUDDHIST MAHAYANA TEXTS, E. B. Cowell and Others (eds.). Superb, accurate translations of basic documents in Mahayana Buddhism, highly important in history of religions. The Buddha-karita of Asvaghosha, Larger Sukhavativyuha, more. 448pp. 5⅜ × 8½. , 25552-2 Pa. $9.95

ONE TWO THREE . . . INFINITY: Facts and Speculations of Science, George Gamow. Great physicist's fascinating, readable overview of contemporary science: number theory, relativity, fourth dimension, entropy, genes, atomic structure, much more. 128 illustrations. Index. 352pp. 5⅜ × 8½. 25664-2 Pa. $8.95

ENGINEERING IN HISTORY, Richard Shelton Kirby, et al. Broad, nontechnical survey of history's major technological advances: birth of Greek science, industrial revolution, electricity and applied science, 20th-century automation, much more. 181 illustrations. ". . . excellent . . ."—Isis. Bibliography. vii + 530pp. 5⅜ × 8¼.
26412-2 Pa. $14.95

*Prices subject to change without notice.*

Available at your book dealer or write for free catalog to Dept. GI, Dover Publications, Inc., 31 East 2nd St., Mineola, N.Y. 11501. Dover publishes more than 500 books each year on science, elementary and advanced mathematics, biology, music, art, literary history, social sciences and other areas.